With our Compliments

Standard
Chartered

# More Praise for *What the U.S. Can Learn from China*

"Ann Lee's *What the U.S. Can Learn from China* is a rare achievement in to-day's examinations of U.S.-China relations: it supplements an already sophis-ticated analysis with a deep cultural understanding that is richly valuable and laudably objective. Ann's ability to ask the tough questions helps Americans to understand China better and China to see itself clearer."
**—Nancy Yao Maasbach, Executive Director, Yale-China Association**

"This book sparkles on literally every page with surprising insights and cru-cial information that everybody in America—and China—simply must become acquainted with or be reminded of. Whether it be about education, culture, politics and economics, or business, Ms. Lee has much, much more to teach both Americans and Chinese than any of us knew that we had yet to learn."
**—Robert Hockett, Professor of Financial and International Economic Law, Cornell University**

"It is no secret that China has become a convenient scapegoat for America's troubles even as its success is envied. This book has a lofty goal: to reduce the potential for international conflict by increasing Westerners' understanding of that success. Ann Lee's well-written analysis shows that China's success is not merely based on a modern mercantilist policy but rather is due to adoption of best practices from the West—from building social safety nets to conducting business according to international standards. What is most interesting is Lee's main thesis: America needs to look to China to save itself by reimporting the lessons the West has forgotten. This is a serious book that should be read as an antidote to all the China-bashing myths circulating in America."
**—L. Randall Wray, Professor of Economics, University of Missouri–Kansas City, and Senior Scholar, Levy Economics Institute**

"There are so many insecurities we all share about China; this book brilliantly quantifies and identifies many of them. The author's perspective is one of the most interesting and unique. This makes the book an extremely compelling read. The message is loud and clear: Americans ignore China at their peril. This book answers so many questions we're unfortunately afraid to ask."
**—Lawrence G. McDonald, Senior Director, Credit Sales and Trading, Newedge USA, LLC**

# WHAT THE U.S. CAN LEARN FROM CHINA

## An Open-Minded Guide to Treating Our Greatest Competitor as Our Greatest Teacher

### ANN LEE

*with a foreword by*
**IAN BREMMER**

Berrett–Koehler Publishers, Inc.
San Francisco
*a BK Currents book*

Berrett-Koehler Publishers, Inc.
235 Montgomery Street, Suite 650
San Francisco, CA 94104-2916
Tel: (415) 288-0260   Fax: (415) 362-2512   www.bkconnection.com

**ORDERING INFORMATION**
**Quantity sales.** Special discounts are available on quantity purchases by corporations, associations, and others. For details, contact the "Special Sales Department" at the Berrett-Koehler address above.
**Individual sales.** Berrett-Koehler publications are available through most bookstores. They can also be ordered directly from Berrett-Koehler: Tel: (800) 929-2929; Fax: (802) 864-7626; www.bkconnection.com.
**Orders for college textbook/course adoption use.** Please contact Berrett-Koehler: Tel: (800) 929-2929; Fax: (802) 864-7626.
**Orders by U.S. trade bookstores and wholesalers.** Please contact Ingram Publisher Services: Tel: (800) 509-4887; Fax: (800) 838-1149; E-mail: customer.service@ ingrampublisherservices.com; or visit www.ingrampublisherservices.com/Ordering for details about electronic ordering.

Berrett-Koehler and the BK logo are registered trademarks of Berrett-Koehler Publishers, Inc.

PRINTED IN THE UNITED STATES OF AMERICA

Berrett-Koehler books are printed on long-lasting acid-free paper. When it is available, we choose paper that has been manufactured by environmentally responsible processes. These may include using trees grown in sustainable forests, incorporating recycled paper, minimizing chlorine in bleaching, or recycling the energy produced at the paper mill.

*Library of Congress Cataloging-in-Publication Data*

Lee, Ann.
    What the U.S. can learn from China : an open-minded guide to treating our greatest competitor as our greatest teacher / Ann Lee. — 1st ed.
        p.   cm.
    Includes bibliographical references and index.
    ISBN 978-1-60994-124-6 (hardcover : alk. paper)
    1. China—Politics and government—1949–  2. United States—Relations—China. 3. China—Relations—United States. I. Title. II. Title: What the United States can learn from China.
    JQ1510.L44 2011
    320.951—dc23                                                        2011036502

First Edition

15   14   13   12   11        9   8   7   6   5   4   3   2   1

Produced by BookMatters; edited by Tanya Grove, proofread by Janet Reed Blake, and indexed by Leonard Rosenbaum. Author photo by Suzanne Bernel. Cover designer: Irene Morris Design; cover image: White House: Sandra Henderson/Fotolia; cover image: Forbidden City: Ilya Terentyew/Vetta/GettyImages.

To my brother,
James Hsu Lee
1972–1999

The great aim of education is not knowledge but action.
—HERBERT SPENCER

# CONTENTS

# FOREWORD
**IAN BREMMER**

It's a provocative question for a turbulent time. The financial crisis of 2008–2009 accelerated an already inevitable shift in the world's balance of political and economic power from a U.S.-dominated global order toward one in which emerging powers have become indispensable for real solutions to a gathering storm of transnational problems. It's a transition from a global economy driven by the increasingly free flow across borders of ideas, information, people, money, goods, and services toward a system in which governments are using old tools in new ways to maintain political control in the face of rapid change. In Washington, it's a move from a world where policymakers debated how best to wield America's unmatchable power to one of self-doubt and second guessing, where politicians talk of American exceptionalism to ward off fears that it just ain't what it used to be. Assertions of hegemony have given way to whispers of default. This is a world in which the need to learn from the experience of others, particularly from the fastest-rising potential rival, leaves Americans angry and insecure. And it's a world where those lessons have never been more valuable.

That's why Ann Lee's serious question deserves a thoughtful answer, and who better to provide one than an author who knows both these countries so well? With a wary eye on the extraordinary changes gathering steam inside China, should Washington focus its planning on cooperation or competition? That's a false choice, Lee notes. Yes, the two governments have profoundly different political values and quite different takes on the role of capitalism in human development. No, the birth of a true middle class in China has not yet undermined the country's authoritarian political system. But the friction generated by this clash of first principles should not obscure the reality that both countries have profited from China's rise and that wise policies can ensure that the non-zero-sum game continues. If both sides play their cards right.

No one knows better than China's political leadership that the next stage of that country's development will prove even more complicated—and more dangerous—than the previous ones. China is on the verge of some of the largest-scale political engineering projects in human history as a new generation of leaders works to reorder a fast-growing economic system that Premier Wen Jiabao has acknowledged is "unstable, unbalanced, uncoordinated and unsustainable." It's no sure thing that they can pull this off, and fundamental changes to China's political system could be forced upon them. Talk of a "Chinese Century" is absurdly premature.

But China isn't going away, and as Americans work to restore vitality to their country's economy and balance to its democracy, they'll have to contend with a Chinese system grounded in fundamentally different principles. American companies will have to compete around the world (and sometimes partner) with Chinese state-owned rivals. Chinese and other emerging market-based companies won't simply bow to Western institutions or operate according to a decades-old playbook written in the West. America will resist the need to change, then struggle to adapt. But if we learn to compete and win in a new arena, Lee argues, China's rise, however it comes, need not imply the decline and fall of the American experiment.

A willingness to learn from China's triumphs and mistakes will further that goal, and Lee details some of China's strategies that are entirely compatible with a thriving democratic free market system. Americans must never renounce their faith in the political and economic principles that have helped them prosper, but the sometime excesses of our system remind us that short-term tactical thinking too often replaces sound long-term planning—both in Washington and on Wall Street.

What can the U.S. learn from China? Plenty.

**IAN BREMMER** is president of The Eurasia Group and author of the books *The End of the Free Market, The Fat Tail,* and *The J Curve.*

# PREFACE

I emigrated to the United States from Hong Kong with my parents in time to join the second grade. I learned English in addition to Cantonese and Mandarin, so I grew up with two cultures simultaneously, one related to my parents and their friends and one that I experienced with my peers at school and later at work. The process of assimilating in the United States while preserving Chinese values and traditions helped me master the important life skill of straddling cultures.

Being part of the U.S. melting pot makes me grateful to be an American. While my experiences in the United States are probably not so unusual, what distinguishes me from many Americans are my frequent trips to China for lengthy periods. I first returned in 1985, when I accompanied my mother, who was in search of her real mother after 36 years of separation. That year was when my mother learned from the man she'd always thought was her father that she was separated from her real parents during the Communist Revolution in the 1940s. Upon hearing news that the Communist soldiers were coming, the people I knew as my grandparents opted to buy safe passage out of the country and took along my mother—who was three years old at the time—without my grandmother's consent. The rest of my mother's family remained behind because they underestimated the length and severity of the civil war to come. Her father passed away during the revolution. In 1985, my biological grandmother was dying of cancer. My adopted grandfather had reconnected with her that same year, and he felt morally obligated to convey the news to my mother. Upon hearing the truth about her real parents, my mother bought the two of us tickets to China.

When my mother and I journeyed back to China, I didn't know what to expect. We traveled to Hangzhou where my grandmother awaited, and I was shocked by the level of poverty that she and all my relatives endured for decades. After walking down a narrow, curvy road filled with mud and cow dung, we arrived at Grandma's address. Her home had exactly two rooms with concrete floors, which was considered average living conditions by Chinese standards in those days. The kitchen was simply a single stove, and the bathroom was a shared community toilet without toilet paper or flushing. The majority of the homes in the town were dirty and dingy in varying degrees. Walls were uniformly black and brown with soot and other stains.

Back then, except for the occasional government vehicle, people either traveled by foot or bicycle, and everyone wore navy blue Mao suits. When I showed up wearing a white T-shirt, jeans, and sneakers, the townspeople stared at me as if I had come from Mars.

I later learned that because my relatives in China came from privileged backgrounds, they were treated especially cruelly by the Communists who came to power after the civil war ended in 1949. As wealthy intellectuals and business people, my aunts, uncles, and grandparents were forced out of their home, which was later converted into a hospital by the Communist government. All of their possessions were taken away or destroyed. Books were burned; eyeglasses were smashed; and art was desecrated. The widespread destruction during the Cultural Revolution was promoted in the name of social equality so that elites would appreciate manual labor. Against their will, my relatives were separated and sent to work in the fields as part of the Communists' effort to create a more egalitarian society. Grandmother didn't reconnect with any of her children until years later.

I was surprised to discover that despite the extreme poverty, the Chinese I met were notably sanguine. One of my uncles who traveled from Wuhan to come see my mother and me was an electrical engineer by training but was confined to farm work for most of his adult life. When he met me, he showed me designs he had sketched for various electronic equipment that had not yet been invented. He even shared with me his fantasies of working with an American company and asked me if I could assist him someday.

My cousin, Yao Qun, was optimistic about China's future. She was the only relative who spoke English and wanted to converse with me in English every opportunity she had so that she could practice. Over the course of the summer while I lived there, she asked me thousands of questions about what living in the United States was like. She continued to write me letters after I returned to the States, even though it was obvious from the torn envelopes that all our correspondence was opened and read by the government officials.

I saw Yao Qun again in 1995, but this time we met in Shanghai. We were naturally excited to see each other and talked a great deal about all the changes that were happening in China. It was clear to me that at this point Yao Qun no longer pined to be in the United States. Life in China, though still antiquated, was starting to show signs of improvement, both economic and civic. Government officials were no longer reading her mail and monitoring her every step. Women began to express themselves through fashion, makeup, and hairstyles. Such materialistic forms of expression didn't exist under Mao's rule, but they were among the first manifestations of the liberalization and modernization that was taking place in China.

I traveled to China for personal and business reasons numerous times on trips that usually lasted less than a month. But in 2008, I went back for an extended stay to teach graduate finance and economics as a visiting professor at Peking University in Beijing.

During the course of my stay, I met a number of high-level Chinese government officials who learned about my financial expertise on credit derivatives. Some heard about me from my students, while others I met through fellow professors. These officials consulted me privately about my predictions for the financial system and the global economy. Though some of them, notably from the Ministry of Finance, found my forecast of a global financial collapse unbelievable, they nonetheless listened with interest to observations and analyses in the beginning of 2008 before the market crashed.

I had predicted the credit crisis as early as 2005, and in 2006 I wrote a 30-page paper titled "Wall Street's House of Cards" that was sent to U.S. government officials such as former National Economic Council (NEC) director, Lawrence Lindsay, and former commissioner of the U.S. Securities and Exchange Commission (SEC), Annette Nazareth, who dismissed it. I also sent the piece to dozens of policy journals whose editors initially expressed interest. But upon reading its contents, they responded to me by saying either that the concept of regulating credit derivatives was too esoteric for general public consumption or that the idea of increased financial regulation was just flat out against the politics of the think tank publications connected to the financial institutions that were their large donors.

Suffice it to say, the Chinese officials with whom I had come into contact showed greater receptiveness to my warnings about the unsustainable financial system than their American counterparts. In return, these individuals such as Shi Zulin, Hu Xuanwen, Erh-Cheng Hwa, and dozens of others have given me perspective and insight into China's approach to governance that I thought was worth sharing with the broader public.

As a former stock research analyst for an investment bank, I fashioned a career out of making predictions. Though I was more certain about the coming credit crisis back in 2005 than I ever was about short-term stock price movements, I've come to appreciate how difficult it is to report a story that the politically powerful do not want released, even in a country such as the United States that is known for investigative journalism and free speech. It is deeply unfortunate for the citizens of the world that it took the domino collapse of Fannie and Freddie, Lehman Brothers, AIG, and dozens of other American financial institutions before the U.S. government and the media would admit to the general public that the modern financial system and the U.S. economy were sick patients that required intensive care. The few souls who read my paper anticipating the credit crisis back in 2006, such as Charles Kolb, who heads the Committee for Economic Development, have asked on various occasions for my next predictions.

One prediction I hope I never have to make is a world war between nations; I do worry that conflict will become more likely unless we make room for a more civilized way to oversee international relations and cooperate more effectively to solve global problems. Though such a disastrous outcome may be remote, the accumulation of small stresses may be likened to a "death by a thousand cuts." If we fail to take seriously even the smallest of problems and we make no effort to repair them, they can escalate out of hand. We live in precarious times, which will require extraordinary international leadership. While the United States has a leading role to play, some of the leadership is already coming from China. By offering a perspective about China's development and governance that is not widely shared in the West, I hope that Americans and people around the world will find more inspiration to work through our growing tensions over economic fortunes and political relations and find the will to drive a quiet but productive revolution in human enlightenment.

# A New Year's Resolution

Never doubt that a small group of thoughtful,
committed citizens can change the world, indeed
it is the only thing that ever has.  —MARGARET MEAD

**AS INDIVIDUALS, WE ARE NOT QUITE SATISFIED** with ourselves most of the time. We are keenly aware of our shortcomings and try to make resolutions to correct them. Whether it is to lose weight, quit smoking, or address some other personal issue, we know we will fail unless we work hard to achieve our goals, stay focused, and remain committed to success for however long it takes to materialize.

As a nation, we have had a similar process. Throughout history, various constituencies that were not content with the status quo have coalesced to create political movements to change national policy. When the United States had to resolve an internal contradiction between the Constitutional rights of life, liberty, and the pursuit of happiness and the institution of slavery, abolitionists in the 19th century were prepared to fight to their death for what they believed. Similarly, the women's suffrage movement in the early 20th century lasted almost two decades before the right to vote was granted to women.

Today, the United States faces another moment of discontent. What some labeled *malaise* under the Carter years—the slow erosion

1

of the American Dream for most citizens—culminated into a financial crisis of global proportions in 2008.[1]

This crisis in turn has morphed not only into a domestic economic crisis with government adding trillions of dollars to its debt and persistent high unemployment, but also into crises of governance and of confidence.[2] Americans are frustrated by the state of current political dysfunction and have palpable anxiety that it cannot be fixed. The clear mandate Obama had with his 2008 election landslide was challenged two years into his presidency after the Congressional elections when Republicans took over majority leadership in the House. Americans have begun to suspect that neither party can deliver on their promises to represent their interests and have made their displeasure known through Gallup polls, Tea Parties, and even renouncements of U.S. citizenship.[3]

While a great polarization of interests does divide the country, I believe it is less about Republicans versus Democrats and more about the haves versus the have-nots.[4] The haves want to continue outsourcing labor to developing countries and see booming financial markets through continued lax financial regulation while the have-nots want a job with a decent wage and a future where their children have a fair chance at improving their lives. How these disparate priorities get resolved will have profound implications for growth and movement in the American domestic economy. Feelings of apprehension and uncertainty over these outcomes underscore the common worry that the nation may not maintain its competitive edge.[5]

These worries couldn't come at a worse time; America has been suffering from the worst economic situation since the Great Depression while elsewhere around the globe, more people are demanding a share of the economic prosperity that America has enjoyed for decades.[6] Understandably, many Americans feel threatened by all this new competition from the developing world. On one side, China, boasting a population of over a billion low-wage workers, has absorbed most of the dirty manufacturing jobs that have long left

America. India also has absorbed many American jobs, but mostly in the service sector like customer-service call centers, computer software programming, and even legal work where Indians can perform the same services as skilled Americans but at a fraction of the cost. Job insecurity has gripped most working Americans, and their fear has spawned anti-China rhetoric and anti-immigration legislation.[7]

China has become a convenient scapegoat for American economic problems. American ethnic prejudice, as documented in Iris Chang's book, *The Chinese in America: A Narrative History,* combined with envy for China's recent successes—such as the resumption of strong economic growth shortly after the 2008 financial crisis—and a perceived lack of democracy make China an easy target. I use *perceived* because I explain in chapter 3 that the current set of Chinese leaders formulate policies with the greater public interest in mind. China bashing has become almost a contact sport on television with both left- and right-wing commentators trying to outbash each other with China aspersions. Even Michael Lewis, author of *The Big Short,* satirically noted this phenomenon in his opinion piece titled "All You Need to Know about Why Things Fell Apart."[8] Such negative rhetoric fuels more complaining and misunderstanding rather than productive problem solving.

Unlike foreign channels such as the British Broadcasting Corporation (BBC), American mainstream media mostly air American-centric views without devoting equal time to thoughtful discussions from foreign perspectives, perspectives that might shed light on subjects less familiar to Americans. But Americans are capable of inspired action that rises above media tirades. Throughout history, Americans have consistently united to meet challenges at the darkest hours—working collectively on the war effort during World War II and turning out in droves to volunteer aid after 9/11. More recently, the television show *60 Minutes* reported that in 2011 American families welcomed newly homeless neighbors into their homes, while foreclosures swept the country.

Today, Americans may face one of the most challenging tests of will. The challenge is not as simple and straightforward as facing an enemy like the Soviet Union during the Cold War. Rather, the challenge to America is how our nation will coexist in a world of rising powers and diminishing natural resources, both of which may threaten our chosen way of life. As developing nations around the world continue their unrelenting drive to improve their economic fortunes, can the United States blaze a trail that will lead to peaceful and sustainable outcomes? Some, myself included, worry that the West, particularly America, will fall behind in an increasingly competitive and unpredictable future. President Obama has called China's economic and technological rise the new Sputnik moment, and former Speaker of the House Newt Gingrich articulated that technological supremacy by China would amount to a "potentially catastrophic threat" to Americans.[9] These worries have begun to generate some innovative policy proposals such as those announced by the Department of Energy to invest in clean energy research, but action has not been as forthcoming, and much more needs to be done. The problems will require practical solutions, metaphysical reflections on America's evolving identity, and national resolve for meeting these challenges.

At a minimum, America must become more competitive than in the recent past across the board. With more challengers, supremacy will be a more difficult position to defend. Though America's military is second to none, it would be unwise to unduly rely on it to maintain America's superpower status. Rather, America must strengthen its diverse portfolio of capabilities, because even with its military force, it is impossible to control everything everywhere all the time; nor should it try.

America is arguably at an inflection point in its role as a global empire.[10] The financial crisis has uncovered weaknesses in our financial system and regulatory oversight that were formerly thought of as strengths, and its reputation internationally as a land of opportunity is being questioned more aggressively. At the same time, the consensus for a march forward is hard to find. Although America remains the most powerful nation in the world, as of the start of the 21st century, America also risks losing its position through arrogance and inertia. It is in America's interest to be open and eager about learning new ways of doing things, if these new policies, methodologies, and frameworks can help our democracy function better in a world that is vastly different from the one when the Founding Fathers were alive. By borrowing ideas from the Chinese, America has the greatest chance of fulfilling its resolution to be the best it can be and of remaining a powerful and noble nation.

An enduring maxim throughout history is the wisdom of learning from the competition. The best U.S. corporations evolve and survive when competition forces them to win in a new environment. Similarly, governments also rise to prominence or fall from legitimacy depending on how leaders respond to the winds of change. The logical place to start then is to understand the strategies of the strongest competitor and then to customize those ideas to fit one's unique makeup and situation.

Like Olympians who must train long and hard for the gold medal, America must work on improving itself in the following ways:

- rebuild trust
- regain lost credibility
- restore integrity
- revive education
- rewrite poor legislation
- reinvest in infrastructure
- remove negativity
- remain focused on competitiveness
- realize the unlocked potential within many Americans

In short, America should be compelled to reinvent itself within the context of a quickly changing, globally competitive landscape. Such advice may be difficult to hear, but the longer Americans remain complacent about their position in the world, their extravagant spending habits, and even their moral authority, the greater the chance that America will be caught by surprise in the defensive position.

If there is a parallel in history for today's relationship between America and the rest of the world, it is found in the fate of the 15th-century Spaniards whose wealth and power were bankrolled by the Italian Medici bankers. Spain began building its empire with the New World and expanded to almost every continent through conquest. Unprecedented in its reach and power during its time, the Spanish Empire was known as "the empire on which the sun never set" hundreds of years before England made such a claim. However the empire met an untimely end due to inflation from debasing its currency, dependency on foreign sources for manufactured goods, and stretched military resources from multiple wars. During the 17th century, Spain became stagnant while other countries reformed their governments and ascended to power. By the 19th century, anticolonial uprisings put an end to Spanish territories. The similarities to the current U.S. empire are uncanny.

Though the United States does not engage in colonialism per se, the practice of foreign "aid" and arms sales to unpopular dictatorships that oppress the local population in the name of U.S. interests resembles colonialism in substance if not in form. U.S. inflation from currency debasement has been steady since the 1970s. A home that cost $25,000 in 1970 now easily costs $250,000 or more. The same is true of most commodities, ranging from gasoline to food. While official reports of inflation appear subdued, it is well known among many in the financial community that actual inflation rates are much higher. The items that make up the Consumer Price Index (CPI) are continuously modified with substitutions and alterations to calculations. These changes reduce the reported level of inflation in the economy. Had the items that make up the CPI remained the same, official inflation rates would actually be higher and perhaps more reflective of the declining standard of living experienced by many Americans. If the United States fails to resolutely deal with its shortcomings, the world may watch us repeat Spain's history.

In this book, I hope to show that an answer to America's challenge may come from understanding the Chinese and borrowing some of their ideas for governance that can be reformulated to fit American democracy and culture. Obviously China has its own deficiencies, particularly in the area of human rights, which are almost inconceivable to condone. China will never become great if it also doesn't continually evolve its policies and improve its government regulations. But setting aside common Western concerns for a moment, since this book is not about human rights or China's other inadequacies, I believe that sharing some of China's best practices and principles could prove beneficial for sustainable economic growth and development around the world. Often, nations in the West have overlooked these practices because they assume that China stands for values that are polar opposites from their own. However, in many cases, that is not true.

Implementing some of the ideas presented in this book will largely depend on politicians and policymakers. But the way to reach those people running the country is through grassroots campaigns that spread awareness and get them to take these ideas seriously. Public pressure is predominantly the impetus for progressive change in everything from social justice and economic opportunity to environmental protection. It is a phenomenon that has happened throughout history and throughout the world. The end of slavery and the end of apartheid are testaments to the power of minority activists who raise the conscience of societies.

The bottom line is that the world needs global leadership to cooperate on the most serious worldwide issues now more than ever in recent history. That will be difficult to accomplish unless the world's powerful countries can see eye to eye and honor their commitments equally.

Throughout the book, I use the terms the *United States* and *America* interchangeably. When I use these terms, I am referring to the citizen-based style of government that I know my audience and nation want. Some progressives may argue that the current U.S. government is no longer the citizen-based style it was designed to be and that the current political system is a different animal. That distinction is not made here, but it's also not lost on me.

My book is certainly not a cure-all for the contemporary ills of America since there is far too much information to cover between these two large civilizations. But it will highlight some crucial points that the West ought to consider when discussing how we shape our collective future. My assertions about the United States are not meant as a comprehensive historical account but are based more on my contemporary observations that our country's original principles seem to have changed or gotten lost. America is undoubtedly still a great nation, but it needs to return to an older version of itself in some ways. In recent years, China has demonstrated things such as economic dynamism and a reform orientation that America once demonstrated in spades as an emerging nation. If Americans can critically appraise ourselves while objectively evaluating other nations, we can once again remind ourselves of what we once were and rediscover the course of where we must go.

# 1

# The China Miracle

Success usually comes to those who are too busy
to be looking for it.   —HENRY DAVID THOREAU

**CHINA'S STEADY AND SPECTACULAR RISE** in the last twenty years has
perplexed many experts in Western circles. It has generated much
intellectual debate as well as a wide range of emotions among Western academics, policymakers, politicians, and the public at large as
people struggle to understand the manifold causes for the shift in
international, economic, and political power.

Once isolated from the world and threatened by the West, China
learned to change its fortunes dramatically in these last three decades.
China burst onto the world stage a little while after the diplomatic
breakthrough between it and the United States in 1972. Particularly in
the last decade, since its accession to the World Trade Organization,
China astounded observers around the world with its speed of urbanization, its modernization, its reduction of the number of people in
poverty, and the sheer volume of foreign-exchange reserves it holds.
China has accomplished much just in the last 15 years including the
following:

- 118 megacities with over 1 million people each[1]
- Over 6 million college students graduating per year[2]

- Over 420 million Internet users[3]
- Over 800 million cell phone users[4]
- 271 billionaires[5]
- High-tech exports reaching 20 percent of the total global market[6]
- Auto sales reaching 18 million units a year, making China the world's largest auto market[7]
- Largest number of Initial Public Offering (IPO) issuers in the world, making up 46 percent of global IPO value[8]

Though China is still considered an emerging market economy (EME), most experts would put it in a separate category from developed and developing nations because of its unique set of features. It can be described as simultaneously rich and poor, advanced and backward. With 56 ethnic groups and an even greater number of dialects, most experts agree that China is so vast, complex, and dynamic that discussing it as one entity gets tricky.

Nonetheless, I intend to select and explain a few key concepts about China's development that I believe have broader applications for the benefit of the United States and the world. By highlighting these specific practices and principles used by the Chinese that contributed much to their recent successes, I hope to export their model for economic accomplishment and gradual civil society reforms so that other countries can modify their systems of governance to match China's effectiveness. This is not to say that China's model is perfect or that it should be duplicated in every way. The suggestion, rather, is to set aside societal conditioning that could blind us from learning from a worthy competitor.

While certain personalities and other singular factors have no doubt influenced history, the overriding reasons for China's success lie in institutionalized values and methods that have worked for generations. Their way of governance has elicited the willing participation of over a billion people even post–Tiananmen Square,

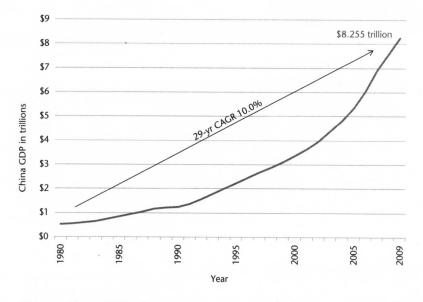

**FIGURE 1**  China GDP 1980–2009

Source: World Bank. Note: GDP is in 2005 purchasing power parity; CAGR = compound annual growth rate

despite what some Western media would have us believe. The Communists, though not seen as infallible by the Chinese, at least have been credited with freeing China from a century of foreign imperialism, a period in their history that they view as dark, shameful, and never to be repeated. To the extent that the Chinese can feel proud of their nation's accomplishments and confident that the government can steer their progress, they prefer the current government to alternatives.

Surely, some of the ways China competes now in global trade are not dissimilar to the mercantilist tendencies of the United States before World War I. The United States also used to compete with the Europeans by undercutting Europe's prices. Like the Chinese today, the United States collected a large current account surplus in the process.

America's once-polluted cities and poor labor conditions, as evidenced by the Triangle Shirtwaist Factory Fire of 1911, also have contemporary parallels in China. The poor working conditions in some of China's big cities have lead some to believe—particularly Americans who currently live in China—that China is simply following America's trajectory in history. China's modern development undeniably will exhibit some of the same characteristics of early 20th-century America. China, for instance, has even started to redistribute income with minimum wage laws and transfer payments through higher taxes.[9] But misunderstanding or overlooking some of the differences between U.S. development and China's development can cause Americans to miss opportunities to learn from the Chinese. Historical study can offer only a partial guide for developing future policy initiatives. Understanding China's strategies and appreciating the implications of those differences, on the other hand, can lay the groundwork for potentially more advanced civilizations than what exists today.

While I have no doubt that some will disagree with sections of my analyses and/or conclusions for how they might be applicable to the United States, their very disagreements will hopefully propagate more reasonable opinions and ideas because in-depth discussions can beget real progress. There will always be critics who will remain unconvinced no matter what facts, figures, or reasons are presented. One such critic is my own father, who has admitted to me that he will be biased against China's leadership no matter what evidence I cite because the Chinese Communist Party (CCP) ruined his family, stole their wealth, and condemned them to a life of hardship and misery when it came to power under Mao Tse Tung. However, my intention in writing this book is not to stir emotional outbursts but to arouse reasonable debate and out-of-the-box thinking. The book, I hope, will promote more deliberative discussion about the appropriate role of governments, the extent of their powers, the conditions and circumstances of when those powers should be granted, and which elements are worth keeping and which ones should be tossed. Worlds are beginning to collide, so we will be forced to think about these issues sooner or later.

Global problems will require new global leadership to address with courage the serious issues of unsustainable natural-resource depletion and pollution that have been allowed to fester for decades. Business as usual could eventually lead to a worldwide crisis that surpasses everyone's worst fears. The fundamental thesis of this book is that all nations can and need to work together to avoid an eventual Malthusian crisis, a catastrophe in which the planet can no longer support the human population, as predicted by Thomas Malthus. The key to cooperating may be found in some examples of China's governance. China is not a totalitarian regime like Russia during the Cold War. Unlike those in most authoritarian regimes, China's leaders have earned their authority through a lifetime of meritocratic service that is far from arbitrary. Their system of earned authority actually resonates strongly with Western values, is surprisingly popular with its population, and may even be used to strengthen today's democratic institutions.

A country must choose its allies and enemies carefully. Like the Roman Empire whose seeds of its own destruction resulted from its miscalculated relationship with the Germanic world due to its perceived Persian threats, the United States risks destroying itself if it attempts to fight imagined enemies like China and bestows misplaced trust in dubious allies such as the Pakistan government or Afghanistan's president Hamid Karzai who are arguably more corrupt, bigger violators of human rights, and potentially more dangerous than China. By diverting precious time, energy, and talent toward fighting endless wars rather than funneling them for more constructive uses, the United States may unwittingly create its own downfall. Overextended military aggression abroad and unrestrained military buildup at the expense of other investments can ultimately backfire. Fighting for a larger share of a shrinking pie could yield far less than working cooperatively with nations like China to grow the pie so that all parties can enjoy bigger pieces. The United States needs the wisdom not to let hubris get in the way and the courage to root out its own corrupting elements. Both of these will be discussed in detail in the following chapters. Borrowing some of China's best practices may help the United States close the gap between our current reality and our professed democratic ideal.

## Another Japan?

Skeptics simply say that Americans should ignore China because they've heard the same hysteria before when Japan was on the rise in the 1980s. The fear that the Japanese were going to take over the world was laid to rest after the Plaza Accord. In this agreement, the developed nations requested that Japan more than double the value of its currency in relation to the U.S. dollar between 1985 and 1987. When the Japanese exports all doubled in price in a timeframe spanning less than two years, naturally the country was unable to export the same volume to the world. Japanese companies suffered severe financial losses. Layoffs and massive reductions in labor wages followed for the next two decades, now referred to as Japan's Lost Decades. Even if some argue that Japan's problems were homegrown, the timing of this agreement no doubt precipitated and exacerbated the subsequent fall. Foreign exchange plays an integral role in all cross-border commerce. In the case of Japan, where the lion's share of its economy was dependent on exports, the forced appreciation of its exchange rate caused many of its businesses to become less profitable. When loans to these less profitable businesses soured, Japan's banking sector was thus harmed, causing a dramatic fall in its stock market as a domino effect.

Certainly it is within the realm of possibility that the United States will attempt to do the same thing to China to neutralize it as a potential economic threat. The *Financial Times* reported on February 8, 2011, that the United States had attempted to enlist Brazil in a united front against China's pegged currency policy ahead of a G-20 meeting. This move is just one of the ways that the United States attempted to hobble China's economic growth. It follows years of Western media and policymakers calling China a manipulator of currency in attempts to pressure China to appreciate its currency, the yuan, faster or to loosen its peg so that the yuan would free float. "Deregulation of China's currency" is merely another way of saying "Let the foreign exchange traders have the power to manipulate the value of the currency to their ends."

Many differences between Japan and China, however, lessen the likelihood the United States will pursue this route, starting with the fact that China has welcomed significant direct investment from the United States and other countries while Japan was a more closed society. Japan's exports were largely high-end electronic products, designed and produced entirely by Japanese companies. Japan did not experience a flood of foreign direct investment. Its success came as Dr. W. Edwards Deming helped Japanese companies become the most competitive in the world with his theories of Total Quality Management (later modified and elaborated upon by other management experts so that now these ideas are collectively referred to as *Six Sigma* by manufacturing concerns). Dr. Deming had first approached American manufacturing companies with his theories of benchmarking and other ideas for improving production quality, but he was rejected by all of them because he was considered too radical by top American executives back in the 1940s and 50s. As it turned out, Dr. Deming discovered that the Japanese openly embraced his ideas, so he worked with them instead and helped them rebuild their manufacturing capabilities after World War II to become the best in the world.

Fast-forward to China, and we see a different story. Unlike Japan, China threw open its doors to the world and received significant foreign investment from every corner of the earth. China offered the dual allure of a giant consumer market and a seemingly infinite supply of cheap labor, attractions that foreign companies found irresistible despite the innumerable risks of doing business in a Communist country. Additionally, the explosion of Internet services, which didn't exist during Japan's rise, made it possible to coordinate offshoring and outsourcing with greater ease and at lower cost. With costs of communication and shipping coming down, multinational companies and entrepreneurs from around the world were able to rely on the Chinese to turn their ideas and dreams into reality.

So unlike Japan, exports out of China are not Chinese exports per se but instead belong to American companies, German companies, Dutch companies, and a long list of others who have vertically integrated China into their supply-chain processes. The goods leaving China and arriving in the United States mostly originated from American businesses and are sold to American consumers; the Chinese merely assisted in putting the products together and account for no more than a quarter of the value added. In 2009 Behzad Kianian and Kei-Mu Yi at the Federal Reserve Bank of Philadelphia reported that of the $644 billion the U.S. consumer spent on goods made in China in 2007, roughly $322 billion was attributed to wholesale markup, retail markup, domestic shipping, and profit margin for U.S. companies. Of the remaining balance, an estimated $161 billion was attributed to imported inputs, and only $161 billion went to the Chinese for assembly or other labor intensive work.

The evidence is clear; the aisles of a typical store in America are filled with U.S. branded products made in China but virtually no Chinese brands. These American brands range from well-known companies like Nike and Apple to the millions of small, unknown business owners running businesses out of their own homes. Just because the goods crossed national borders doesn't mean that the Chinese owned them or made the lion's share of profits. Rather, when foreign companies chose to assemble their widgets in China rather than in their home markets, they were making a decision on what would make their business operations most profitable.

Perception rather than reality is dictating U.S. policy when it comes to jobs. It's not necessarily the case that China took jobs away from American workers. Those jobs may have never existed in the first place if China hadn't provided the inexpensive labor. The wages in developed countries are much higher, a factor that could have deterred entrepreneurs from even launching a business. But with China in the picture, more companies were willing to take the risk because the profit potential was more attractive. China's cheap labor and manufacturing capabilities enticed Western entrepreneurs to pursue projects that in turn required support at home in other areas, for example, sales, marketing, branding, retailing, accounting, legal services, and finance. Thus China indirectly contributed to the United States moving up the food chain toward what is now referred to as a *knowledge economy.* In contrast to an industrial economy, the critical drivers of job creation and economic growth in a knowledge economy are entrepreneurial ideas, intellectual property, and the reliance on expertise such as research and development (R&D) professionals.[10]

Since the profitability and even viability of many U.S. companies both large and small are directly tied to the cost of their operations in China, it is not in their interest to see the Chinese currency appreciate rapidly. A rapid rise would immediately impact the profits of U.S. companies since they cannot quickly move their operations to Vietnam or India where production costs are low, but the physical infrastructures are significantly poorer than in China. In addition, a rise in the value of Chinese currency would decrease the relative value of the dollar, reducing American consumer spending power and resulting in a loss of sales for American businesses.

A rapidly rising yuan would also be bad for the United States because the Chinese could use its stronger currency to buy up even more natural resources around the world or snap up U.S. assets at fire-sale prices. Moreover, an American company with overseas profits will not want to repatriate its profits back home if it will be more profitable to keep the money in a rapidly appreciating currency. If American companies were to keep their money in China, then they would invest less at home, spelling even higher unemployment in the United States.

Finally, if the yuan were to appreciate too rapidly, precipitating a Japanese-style Lost Decade, most Chinese export companies that operate on razor-thin margins would go bankrupt and lay off millions of Chinese workers; this happened during the financial crisis of 2008.[11] Without a growing middle class in China, the world will have no immediate replacement market to sell its wares, given that citizens of developed economies are still hamstrung with enormous debt loads and many developing nations rely overwhelmingly on China to continue their economic growth.[12] Global trade would again come to a screeching halt, and the United States would probably be blamed for crafting such an agreement. So for all the above reasons, it is unlikely that the United States would push for another deal like the Plaza Accord, despite the vituperative threats from Senator Charles Schumer or other American politicians who regularly engage in bashing China because they think the yuan should be artificially appreciated.

## Another Bubble?

Others, such as hedge fund manager Jim Chanos, believe that China will eventually implode due to its inefficient allocation of resources to infrastructure investment. They believe that China's high growth rate due to its building frenzy is unsustainable. Some see this as Russia redux in which too much central planning from a powerful government will ultimately bankrupt its economy.

While the Chinese investment in infrastructure is indeed high compared to other nations, it is actually not so out of line when compared to the United States during its Industrial Revolution over a century ago. For example, the United States had four times the number of railroad miles during that time period than exist today, but such "overinvestment" did not derail the young nation. Similarly, China will undoubtedly create wasteful infrastructure from less-than-optimal allocation of resources. Stories of empty office and apartment buildings abound. But a closer look reveals that most infrastructure investment since the 2008 crisis has gone to retail housing where demand shows no sign of relenting. Construction and real estate have stayed steady at roughly 10 percent of the gross domestic product (GDP) since the mid 1990s. Total property investment as a share of total fixed asset investment was roughly 20 percent in 2008, and residential property made up approximately half of that number.[13]

The migrant workers that flow into China's coastal cities from Western China are akin to the waves of immigrants in the tens of millions that arrived on American shores throughout the Industrial Revolution. The share of the urban population in China went from less than 30 percent in 1990 to almost 50 percent by 2009, while the share of agricultural employment has dropped from 60 percent to 40 percent during the same time period.[14] We can expect China's urban population to rise another 20 percent if it is to reach comparable urbanization rates of other developed countries like Japan and Korea.

Furthermore, the risk of China imploding from overinvestment seems highly unlikely because credit expansion is small compared to the West even after the financial crisis of 2008. According to Fitch Ratings, China's government debt-to-GDP ratio is 21.5 percent. The U.S. federal debt-to-GDP ratio, on the other hand, was just shy of 100 percent in 2010. American household debt-to-GDP reached 100 percent in 2007, while the Chinese household debt-to-GDP was a mere 12 percent in 2008. Union Bank of Switzerland (UBS) and Goldman Sachs estimated that in China, household debt as a share of disposable income was under 60 percent in 2009 and will likely remain so for some time to come given the government's proactive tightening of credit. Household debt in the United States, by contrast, is estimated at over 120 percent of disposable income in 2009. Excess leverage that defaults or causes fear of defaults is usually the trigger of financial crises. Based on conventional measures of debt levels compared to the amount of equity and bank reserves borrowed against them, that condition is far from reaching a tipping point in China. Besides, housing is the only financial asset for many Chinese. Excess housing units that sit empty won't get abandoned because they were secured with substantial down payments of 50 percent or more and so function as a store of wealth. Some have been paid for in full in the same way some investors hold gold bullion in vaults as a hedge against inflation.[15]

Finally, Westerners must also not overlook that private market forces can be enormously inefficient and won't necessarily do a better job than government-induced investments. After all, private markets were responsible for the speculative manias that funded everything from Dutch tulips to profitless Internet companies. By now, volumes of research, coming from such organizations as the Bank for International Settlements (BIS), indicates that market failures happen regularly, so China's political economy should be no more likely to suffer an economic setback than more self-proclaimed market-oriented economies.

Economic bumps on the road in China obviously cannot be ruled out as property prices and stock market prices fluctuate. However, I would argue that fluctuations in valuation must not be confused with the bigger fundamental picture of steadily growing development needs. But regardless of what China's fate will be in the coming decade, the Chinese leaders have already proven in the last few decades that they have created a compelling recipe for running a country with a population more than four times the size of the population in the United States. Francis Fukuyama, the author best known for writing the book *The End of History,* stated in the *Financial Times* on January 18th, 2011, that "its [China's] specific mode of governance is difficult to describe, much less emulate, which is why it is not up for export." I have to politely disagree. Even if China and the West seem worlds apart in history, culture, and governance, it is possible that the United States can learn from China just as China has learned and continues to learn from the West. Let me just cite a few examples of what China has already learned from the West:

- China has learned to adopt capitalist market principles (within a Communist framework).

- China has learned to manufacture many types of products it never used to have, from laptops to high-speed trains.
- China has learned to conduct business according to international rules created by Western countries, like the United States.
- China has learned to incorporate religion in a way that doesn't pose a threat to the State.
- China has learned to appreciate Western fashion, fast food, rock music, and reality shows that were completely foreign to their culture.
- China has learned to create social safety nets like pension plans and health insurance for its population.

No doubt there is still plenty for China to learn from the West. The last chapter of this book highlights some of the things that the United States does particularly well that China should adopt. There are obviously many areas that China needs to address or improve, but the main thrust of this book is to talk about what works in China, so that Americans can seize an opportunity to learn and improve in areas that the United States has been lacking in our recent past. Some of our weaknesses are some of China's strengths. No country, including China and the United States, has a monopoly on superior morality or knowledge, but the nations who understand their weaknesses and strengths, and can evolve accordingly, will have time on their side.

China's leaders still face significant problems in the years ahead, and the governance of the Peoples Republic of China (PRC) is not guaranteed to succeed in the coming decades. Among some of the serious challenges facing Chinese leaders are their ability to continue growing without inflation getting out of control, their ability to manage the large wealth inequalities, and their ability to smoothly transition from a heavy industrial economy to a more service-oriented economy while cleaning up the vast environmental pollution.

However, China's principles for governance provide a powerfully viable framework for economic progress that has thus far enabled it to dodge the bullets that would have taken down a weaker government. Instead of wallowing in negativity and despair over their misfortunes, the Chinese turned perceived threats—such as the global financial crisis of 2008—into opportunities and advantages around the world. When a government appears credible by maintaining stability and benign conditions for people to thrive, people are motivated to work and achieve because their faith in the institutions and its leaders makes them believe they have a future. They endure significant hardships through the belief that the fruits of their labor will someday be rewarded even if the rewards are not immediate. So as long as the Chinese believe in their government's ability to lead, it is reasonable to expect that the citizens of China will continue to find ways to prosper despite the multitude of obstacles.

This is good news for America and the world. For decades, America and Washington DC–based institutions such as the World Bank and the International Monetary Fund (IMF) dictated their market-friendly, economic reform policies known as the Washington Consensus to weaker developing countries.[16] There is now overwhelming evidence that this set of policies contributed to the downfall of those economies.[17] After the financial crisis, the World Bank and IMF began rethinking those policy recommendations when the Seoul Development Consensus was endorsed by the G-20 in 2010.[18] Had China listened to Western policymakers, it is highly probable that its continuous growth in the last two decades would not have been achieved. China might have looked more like Argentina or many other countries that adopted the Washington Consensus to modernize their economies after suffering from a colonial past. But China has been one of the few countries wise enough to resist Washington's economic demands to open its financial markets prematurely, choosing instead to pursue its own policies, which have served it well thus far.[19] It is one of the few industrialized nations of the world that has not allowed its economy to be crippled by *financialization*, a phenomenon that I explain in chapter 6. Without China's growth,

America and the rest of the world most likely would have hit bottom almost a decade earlier when the Internet bubble burst. But because of China's steady and rapid development, U.S. corporations were able to continue achieving record profits. These corporations grew their profits by increasingly selling to overseas markets, lowering their labor costs through outsourcing and offshoring jobs, and accessing low borrowing costs as an indirect result of China's reinvestment in U.S. Treasuries.[20] China's large purchases of U.S. Treasuries (over $1 trillion) helped keep interest rates low in the United States. By providing a steady demand for U.S. bonds, bond prices did not fall and thus interest rates remained low.[21] In other words, China's well-managed political economy gave the rest of the world a new lease on life the same way America was a powerful economic growth engine for the world during the 20th century.

## Game Changer

In the following chapters, I explain in greater detail the institutional as well as cultural elements that I believe have catapulted China from a backward agrarian nation into a leading economic power. The significance of China is not that it may overtake the United States in traditional measures of power, but that it will take on an important role in changing the game being played. With the benefit of hindsight, historians can look back and see how the Industrial Revolution in Britain changed the world. Had someone recognized the economic, technological, and political trends back then, one might have predicted the extensive reach and duration of the British Empire. More importantly, I discuss how China turns its aspirations into reality, and I point out how these methods could apply to Western democracies. China can play an integral part of the solution in the coming decades with its rapidly modernizing economy and incipient innovations in process manufacturing and product development. Americans ought to resist the temptation to fight the inevitable rise of China's importance and its contributions to the world economy. By treating China as a critical partner in solving global problems, America and the rest of the world may avert the frictions that could lead to Armageddon and instead pave the way for the next Renaissance.

As part of my discussion about why China succeeded, I also provide context as to how China has interacted with the nations of the world based on their institutions, their thought processes, their values, and their history. I also cover how China will likely address the major long-term issues facing the world today. Make no mistake, this is not a book about China, but rather about the enduring principles China has reliably followed for approaching global problems, the way America brought Western democratic capitalism to the world. In order to unleash much pent-up talent and increase the natural rate of innovation, a new ideology must replace old belief systems and ways of doing things. Integrating China's methodologies into Western practices could be a promising way of getting there.

Research for this book comes from years of discussions and interviews with countless individuals in both the private and public sectors in the United States and China. My work as a professor at both Peking University and at New York University as well as my position as a senior fellow at Demos, a nonpartisan think tank, give me the benefit of exchanging ideas and information with people around the world, who include CEOs, academics, investors, ambassadors, journalists, students, inventors, entrepreneurs, media executives, policymakers, lawyers, engineers, and bankers. Sifting through all this information for my classes, speeches, and other engagements, certain trends became increasingly obvious to me. By describing these trends and providing a framework through this book, I seek to introduce a distinct perspective for interpreting today's world and offer solutions that have rarely been discussed in mainstream media.

# 尊師重道

## 2
# Confucian Philosophy

Riches and power are but gifts of blind fate, whereas
goodness is the result of one's own merits.  —HELOISE

**DESPITE BEING KNOWN** as the melting pot of the world, the modern
U.S. culture has largely been shaped by Judeo-Christian religions
and Western ideas passed down through the Enlightenment and
dominated by the influences of Modernity. The democratic political
system, the official holidays like Christmas, and the assumed importance of the notions of Freedom and Reason largely define modern
Western civilization. Comparatively speaking, modern Americans
know relatively little about Eastern religions and philosophies. While
many factors define a nation's identity, few would dispute that underlying cultural and religious beliefs shape and influence a nation's
character. One of the most visual examples of how cultural differences manifest themselves is the disparity between the way Americans and the Japanese conducted themselves in the aftermath of two
devastating storms. The widespread looting after Hurricane Katrina
stands in stark contrast to the stoic temperaments of the Japanese
who stood in line for emergency help soon after the 2011 tsunami
that destroyed Fukushima.

Perhaps surprisingly, American culture and Chinese culture do share a common heritage. When Ben Franklin re-edited his book, *Poor Richard's Almanac,* he advocated Confucian values as the universal principle. Today, the United States and China still share some of the same characteristics, including the national knack for entrepreneurialism and a future-oriented focus. America's immigrant population that continually keeps America in the forefront of innovation and technology has a counterpart in China that is just as curious and eager to make breakthroughs. These similarities have only been reinforced by the close economic ties between the two countries and their mutual recognition that they cannot become closed societies like Japan even if some domestic factions advocate protectionism.

There are, however, stark contrasts as well. Despite the thousands of protests in small towns across China, Chinese citizens have largely been very pacific and nonviolent. Police in the big cities, for example, do not carry guns. Violent crime is much lower per capita in China than in the United States despite China being a much poorer nation on a per capita basis as well as its overall GDP. According to data from the Federal Bureau of Investigation (FBI) reported in 2009, homicide rates for the United States registered 5 per 100,000 people. From 2003 to 2008 China's homicide rate was 1.2 per 100,000, according to statistics from the UNODC. Compared to other major developing countries, China stands out further. Russia's homicide rate is 14.9 per 100,000 and Brazil's is 22 per 100,000.

China also churns out the most engineers in the world and has been leading the way among developing countries in catching up with the West from a post-colonial past. The question many ask is why Asians, and particularly the Chinese, are so hard working and productive. While it is extremely difficult or impossible to calibrate how much culture (as opposed to government policies) has played a role in China's development, culture has undeniably been an influence in motivating over a billion people toward shared national goals. Obviously policies and other factors are also important, but culture does shape our unconscious behavior. David Brooks argues in his book *The Social Animal* that pervasive social influences that affect the unconscious processes in the mind will always trump conscious reasoning or rationality. So any meaningful change in society will require a complete cultural shift. After thousands of years of Confucian education and upbringing, it is safe to assume that China's cultural fabric is heavily steeped in Confucian philosophy. Although Confucianism has come under critical attack multiple times throughout China's history—including during Mao's rise and rule because Confucius was blamed for anti-egalitarian ideas—Confucianism had already become embedded in the DNA of most Chinese and perhaps most Asians for that matter. As Amy Chua's book, *The Battle Hymn of a Tiger Mom,* appears to confirm, these values and virtues have been transferred from generation to generation over centuries. No parental handbook, no state laws, and no media propaganda were required to indoctrinate over a billion people in these values. Just like an unspoken agreement, the Chinese citizens intuitively understand this social contract they have with their ancestors and with each other.

What is Confucian philosophy? Confucianism summarizes the philosophical teachings of a Chinese philosopher, Confucius, who lived in the 5th century BC. It refers to a set of beliefs that encompass ethical, social, political, and philosophical realms, and it has heavily influenced East Asian cultures and history for thousands of years. A central theme that runs through the Confucian message is that individuals should place as their highest priority the cultivation of a strong moral compass and a lifetime of self-improvement for the benefit of society. At its heart, Confucianism emphasizes that humaneness must be developed through the acts of everyday life and can be summarized by the Golden Rule of "Do unto others what you would have them do unto you." Similar to ancient Greek philosophies, Confucianism urges everyone to strive to become a perfect person, defined as someone who is saintly, scholarly, and benevolent. This in turn has translated into the modern virtues of integrity, diligence, frugality, modesty, comity, honesty, generosity, trustworthiness, respectfulness, and studiousness.

## We Are the World

One of the strongest tenets of Confucian philosophy is the need to create harmony in society because only when harmony exists can individuals shine. Without this collective determination to serve the greater good of the community, societies will fall apart. Community Confucianism in action can be seen through informal group cooperation such as credit communes in China that are similar to credit unions in the United States. In these credit communes, members in the community regularly contribute a set amount to a community fund. Then whoever needs the pot of cash for a specific purpose, like sending a son to college, can take the entire sum of cash without returning it if they are the winning bidder for the cash in that period. The only requirement is that the receiver of the cash continues to contribute to the community fund uninterrupted so that another person can benefit next time. There is no interest payment involved, no other strings attached. It is operated completely by the community members based solely on trust. This version of Chinese financing is most similar to venture capital by friends and family. In its purest sense, its Confucian roots are similar to the Christian philosophy of love thy neighbor as thyself. With this mindset of everyone pitching in to help for the long haul, it has spawned one of the largest entrepreneurial streaks in history.

The United States with its well-developed financial system will unlikely replicate China's commune credit. However, the lesson here the United States can learn is that individual success can never be possible without the supporting infrastructure of the society. The Chinese recognize unquestioningly that one's success is never individual but is the direct result of societal support and of existing institutions that enable individuals the opportunity to flourish.

The equivalent mindset in America would compel us to give generously back to the community in the form of philanthropy, volunteering, and other unselfish activities, recognizing that the wealth which comes from individual success is only possible through the help from others who may not have reaped direct benefits or the direct attribution, since many who play small roles often go unrecognized. But such a mindset may be in short supply. The percentage of individuals who donate charitably is difficult to measure, but total charitable donations recorded a decline across different types of recipients since the start of the 2008 recession, according to Giving USA Foundation.[1] Rather than coming together in hardship, individuals and communities have pulled back from each other. An even more disappointing indicator of altruism in the United States is the way donations often come with strings attached so that the donation merely serves as another form of public relations. Steve Schwarzman, a multibillionaire cofounder of the Blackstone Group, donated millions to the New York Public Library on the condition that his name would appear on the building. Thus the renamed Stephen A. Schwarzman building is a perfect example of bastardized philanthropy.

Even though China's Confucian culture comes from the ground up, it also spreads from the top down. Confucius-style harmony has been articulated in the CCP's now official Twelfth Five-Year Plan, in which the government has made it a priority to rebalance the Chinese economy away from an export-driven model so that wealth inequality will become less pronounced. Specific measures such as creating more service industry jobs, raising labor wages, building larger social safety nets, and investing in newer industries like biotechnology signify the government's carefully considered commitment to address social issues with a Confucian compass.

Wealth inequality has become as much a problem in the United States in recent years as it has been for China, but our government has not yet devised a long-term plan to address this. Instead, when a Republican majority was elected into Congress during the 2010 mid-term elections, none of the political rhetoric offered concrete plans for addressing wealth inequality, not even the most subversive kinds associated with corruption. Wealth that results in productive activity from exceptional talent and hard work is generally more palatable to society than wealth that arises from unfair advantages. The usual platitudes about reinstating Bush-era tax cuts for the rich and cutting spending for a variety of domestic programs characterized the debates between the two parties. Though addressing inequality in the United States would require different measures than the Chinese, since the inequality stems from different sources, there doesn't appear to be an overriding national moral imperative to make it a priority. Rather, the political tenor emanating from Washington reflects a general disregard for others in society and a single-minded desire to maximize one's own fortunes regardless of the long-term consequences. In his *New York Times* op-ed piece, "The Modesty Manifesto," on March 10, 2011, David Brooks eloquently touches upon this national problem by writing, "I wonder if Americans are unwilling to support the sacrifices that will be required to avert fiscal catastrophe in part because they are less conscious of themselves as components of a national project."

## Education, Education, Education

One of the most prominent manifestations of Confucianism in Chinese culture is an obsession with education. Both primary and secondary school education demonstrate the power of Confucianism actively at work. In 2010, Chinese students outperformed the entire world while U.S. students continued to drop in K–12 educational rankings. As was widely reported, the Programme for International Student Assessment (PISA) test scores administered by the Paris-based Organisation for Economic Co-operation and Development (OECD) were highest among students in Shanghai while the United States turned in results for math that were below 30 other countries.

The Chinese have long attached great importance to study and have regarded that the true foundation for conducting oneself in society is through genuine knowledge or competence. As to be expected, numerous Confucius proverbs that emphasize learning have been passed down throughout China's long history, such as "To be fond of learning is to be near to wisdom," "Real knowledge is to know the extent of one's ignorance," and "Learning without thought is useless, but thought without learning is perilous." Going back over 3000 years to the Zhou Dynasty, the Chinese government had already pioneered the idea that the state should offer education by having officials act as part-time teachers. But it was Confucius who put forth the idea that any person regardless of social status and wealth had the right to receive an education, an idea that he brought to life by opening a school in his hometown. Today, the Chinese government funds all primary and secondary school education, and student enrollment has reached 85 percent even in the poorest areas.[2]

As a result of the high regard placed on education, educators in China are quite uniformly held in high esteem. The Chinese often call teachers Honorable Masters and accord them respect and priority in life. China even designated September 10 as Teachers Day in order to honor the profession. Additionally, the government raised teachers' pay and made Teachers' Colleges free of tuition in an effort to attract more people to the teaching profession. Finally, continuing education for teachers has been established throughout the country in order to upgrade the quality of teaching continually to meet the needs of the rapidly changing economy.

But the Chinese officials know that unless they have world-class professors and teachers, the population will not receive a first-class education. So in an effort to ensure the best education for future generations, the CCP has created government programs that cover the major costs for Chinese students to study abroad and receive PhDs from other countries. The Institute of International Education reported in a study that nearly 128,000 Chinese students enrolled in United States universities during the 2009–2010 academic year.[3]

Chinese leaders believe that these students will return home one day to teach another generation. They hope that their investment will pay off.

Although the Chinese leadership encourages studies abroad, the formal education system within China is nonetheless very demanding. Most of the students engage in studies from morning until night seven days a week. Many students attend high school even throughout the summer, starting classes at 7 AM and ending the day around 11 PM. Almost all of the students aspire to go to college because of the high prestige it bestows on the family, and given the shortage of slots available for higher education, competition among students is fierce.

To encourage competition among students, teachers announce student rankings publicly and seat the highest-ranking students at the front of the classroom. Students who cannot keep up with the school curricula are forced to drop out simply because there are too many students for the educational resources available. Finally, parents cannot interfere in this highly structured environment. Teachers have total control over their classrooms.

The curriculum required much memorization in the past, but because of criticisms that the schools did not encourage enough creativity and dialogue, many schools have since revamped their teaching methods. Today, grade schools now incorporate more field trips, and high schools encourage more dialogue and essay writing. The universities also now promote a more multidisciplinary approach, where studies used to be more compartmentalized.

Reports suggest that the United States is losing its lead in science and technology because more engineers are graduating from Chinese universities than from American universities. Of course the quality of higher education is not necessarily comparable. As of this writing, the most sophisticated scientific research still comes from the United States and developed countries in Europe, and some Western scientists estimate that the lead is roughly twenty years. But China is catching up quickly.

Valuable research is being conducted in China. At Beijing Daxue (also known as Peking University or Beida) a professor shared with me her research on the shrinking fish population. She explained that male fish are becoming females due to the elevated estrogen levels caused by toxins in the environment. However, more basic research could be conducted if professors didn't feel the need to make extra money on the side to keep up with the rapidly rising costs of inflation in China, a phenomenon often associated with high economic growth. Even this environmental professor had considered a proposal by a venture capital (VC) firm to commercialize her studies.

Finally, while most Chinese are literate, since the schools provide a basic classical education, the overall population does not have a wide variety of skills. For instance, classes for graphic arts, art conservation, or any number of courses that students can take here in the United States are often not available in China. As a result of this narrow knowledge, most Western companies looking to hire skilled Chinese workers will find that they must invest a lot in training for even the most rudimentary tasks.

But despite the shortcomings, the Chinese universities are headed in the right direction. While teaching at Peking University, I lived in the on-campus guesthouse, which was designed to facilitate an easy exchange of ideas among visiting faculty. The building was like a Holiday Inn with a formal restaurant downstairs where all the tenants were free to mix and mingle over meals. The number of visiting professors invited to stay there must have been in the hundreds, and the diversity of backgrounds and opinions that the Chinese welcomed was impressive to say the least. Providing access to top talent throughout the world certainly contributes to the richness of the educational environment. So perhaps it's not surprising that Chinese universities have been ascending the list of top academic institutions in the world.

Most of the students at Peking University speak English as well as comprehend it. The exceptions are the older graduate students who didn't have an opportunity to learn English growing up during more tumultuous times. While students at Peking may not be representative of all Chinese college graduates, many Chinese in the younger generation have become quite fluent since they started learning English in grade school. The lucky ones had teachers whose native language was English. The Chinese school system has had a formal national program to attract young foreigners who wish to teach English while learning Mandarin. The Chinese government pays for room, board, salary, and round-trip plane tickets for Americans who want such jobs. Through this program, the Chinese youths not only learn fluent English, but also hear about America and Europe firsthand.

Not only is the government making education a priority, but so are the parents. Xinran, the author of *Chinese Witness,* has documented some Chinese mothers who worked tirelessly behind the scenes in previous generations to create the workforce that now embodies China's economic and political power. One of the stories she tells is about a woman who toiled for 28 years in backbreaking work in order to send her son to get a PhD and her daughter to Peking University. Neither child received government assistance. They were just one of millions of Chinese families who lived homeless in utter poverty and used public bathrooms to provide water for drinking and cooking every day.

The youths, likewise, understand the importance of education from an early age. Ma Yan, a 14-year-old girl who lived in western China, documented in her diary that it was like a death sentence not to be able to study in school because her parents were too poor to afford that luxury for her. Her mother in desperation handed Ma Yan's diary to a French journalist, Pierre Hasky, begging him to help. Hasky was so moved by the diary that he arranged for excerpts of it to be printed in French newspapers. Those excerpts were subsequently reproduced in 19 languages and published as a book, *The Diary of Ma Yan: The Struggles and Hopes of a Chinese Schoolgirl.* Eventually Ma Yan was granted her dream of schooling through a fund that was raised in 2002 known as the Children of Ningxia.

Their work ethic is second to none. As a visiting professor at Beida, my responsibilities included lecturing to a class with over a hundred students that met twice a week, four hours a day for an entire semester. While it was grueling for me to prepare all the material to be covered in these lectures, I quickly realized that the students there had an even more intense academic load. The campus classrooms were occupied day and night, seven days a week by lectures. Both undergraduate and graduate students worked around the clock. Study breaks usually consisted of jogging around campus with a date or fellow classmates late at night. I never heard of a single frat party taking place anywhere on campus.

Not only are they hard working, the Chinese students are also incredibly curious. I was always doubly impressed with how much they already knew about U.S. history and current affairs, often surpassing the knowledge of most American students I have taught. Dozens of my graduate students often took me out to dinner simply because they wanted to continue to learn from me even after listening to one my lectures for four straight hours. (They also didn't seem to understand the idea of taking a break whenever I gave them ten-minute breaks during these marathon lectures.) During these dinners, they came armed with so many questions that the dinners also became multi-hour affairs. I often wondered when they found time to sleep.

In *Fault Lines,* Professor Raghuram Rajan argues that the single most important cause of wealth inequality boils down to education. Most economists would agree with that statement, as would political and social scientists. The Chinese meanwhile have known this pearl of wisdom for almost their entire civilization. Except for the brief moment in history during the Cultural Revolution when Mao encouraged the Red Army to destroy all things intellectual and cultural in the country, the Chinese have long revered academic studies and have pursued intellectual activities with zeal. As documented by Joseph Needham, some of the world's most important inventions unquestionably originated in China, such as the compass, paper, and gunpowder.

However, after a century of decline, the Chinese realized that they had a lot of catching up to do if they wanted to enjoy the developed world's standard of living. This involved learning at every opportunity, including on the job from foreigners who had set up joint ventures with Chinese companies. By working together, the Chinese learned about new technologies and processes. Some less ethical Chinese companies stole the intellectual property from foreigners while others reverse-engineered components and machinery to duplicate what Westerners had invented. But in most cases, the Chinese saw the inpouring of foreign direct investment as an opportunity for apprenticeships. All the Chinese could offer at the time were people who were willing to work long and hard. The tradeoff, they believe, has been worth it. Their Confucian obsession with learning and improving themselves has in no small part enabled China to gain a competitive advantage globally across multiple disciplines in fairly short order.

Incredible love and sacrifice describe much of how human capital was built in China. The countless stories of overcoming great odds such as the ones I mentioned cannot be explained solely by economic or political policies. Though government rules and mandates are important in channeling productive energy, the Chinese understand that the root cause of their modern economic and political power was built by the blood, tears, and sweat of their parents who go unrecognized but who supplied the foundation for China's current success. Because these parents held tightly to the Confucian notion that education for their children would be the surest route for them to escape a life of poverty, they sacrificed their own lives for that end and produced a generation of young Chinese with incredible motivation to learn and improve the world. Thus, to most Chinese, the Confucian precept to respect their elders becomes inextricably tied to the maxim to make education a priority. When seen in this context, it is easy for most Chinese who have grown up poor to respect a person based on scholarship and character rather than wealth.

## Two Americas

The modern U.S. experience differs greatly from China's in many regards. For one, the United States luckily never had to solve the conundrum of over a billion people living on less than two dollars a day. As the only major country to emerge from World War II unscathed, America became the undisputed superpower by default and has had the good fortune of enjoying great wealth for decades. Furthermore, thanks to the liberal attitudes that once shaped the creation of the New Deal and other domestic programs that followed World War II, the United States not only enjoyed phenomenal prosperity, it also was able to spread the wealth throughout its population. The great Western leaders, such as Franklin Delano Roosevelt (FDR), embodied noblesse oblige and demonstrated foresight and humaneness by crafting U.S. policies that decreased wealth inequality and created a middle class that was the envy of the world.

But in the last thirty-plus years, beginning around the 1970s, our great system has started showing signs of atrophying. The span of wealth inequality is the widest it's been in our nation's post-war history.[4] While an increasing number of Americans become impoverished, the desires of Americans in the top 5 percent grow increasingly frivolous.[5] When American adults buy Wii systems to play air guitar for hours and spend hundreds of dollars on American Girl doll clothes, one can safely argue that either these people have too much time and money on their hands or have skewed priorities. When it was reported that 67-year-old Gail Posner bequeathed millions of dollars to her dogs, the news underscored the fact that today's level of inequality is not so different from previous periods like the one just before the French Revolution.

Everywhere we look, the American middle class has steadily lost ground. Economics professors and analysts have documented that the middle class in America has been shrinking for several decades and that wealth inequality has shown no signs of stabilizing or reversing its trajectory. According to the Internal Revenue Service in 2005, the top 1 percent of income earners saw an increase of 14 percent or $139,000, and average incomes of the bottom 90 percent dropped 0.6 percent or $172 over the previous year.[6] The share of total income that went to the top 1 percent was 8.9 percent in 1976, but increased to 23.5 percent by 2007 while the average inflation-adjusted hourly wage went down by more than 7 percent over the same time period.[7] Jack Rasmus, author of *The War at Home* and *The Trillion Dollar Income Shift*, estimates that "well over $1 trillion in income is transferred annually from the roughly 90 million working-class families in America to corporations and the wealthiest non-working class households. While a hundred new billionaires were created since 2001, real weekly earnings for 100 million workers are less in 2007 than in 1980 when Ronald Reagan took office." As the inequality in wealth distribution becomes more extreme, studies have suggested that it could be a precursor to political instability.[8]

At the same time, America's postwar liberalism has substantially morphed into a postmodern value system that no longer extols the traditions of morality and social responsibility to the degree it did historically. For one, the notion of sacrifice doesn't seem to have a place in our lexicon anymore. Certainly not all Americans share this view of the world, but the nation as a whole has largely viewed unemployment checks, social security, and home ownership as rights they deserve.[9] Even many large corporations have come to view government subsidies as something to be counted upon.[10] With an entitlement mentality, even the politicians recognize the electorate's lack of willingness to shoulder greater responsibilities and to see beyond one's immediate needs. This is apparent in their rhetoric, which no longer makes appeals to notions of shared sacrifice.

Rather, in this postmodern value system, many Americans have become conditioned to believe that being rich and powerful is all that matters. The movie, *The Social Network,* which documents Facebook founder Mark Zuckerberg's unethical ascent to wealth and stardom, epitomizes America's cultural proclivity to tolerate business behavior that may be deemed immoral even if it is not technically illegal. The unfairness of America's justice system allows Wall Street executives who have defrauded millions of people around the world to walk free while one in nine black men between the ages of 20 and 34 are incarcerated for minor infractions.[11] Such hypocrisy further underscores America's indiscriminate worship of people with money regardless of how it was earned.

How did these values come about? America's postmodern values have been cultivated in part through the iconic images of Hollywood stars, sports celebrities, and Wall Street financiers who dominate American pop culture. Many American youths find school irrelevant and boring because they don't see a connection between education and success. A record 8.9 million Americans watch the reality television show *Jersey Shore* that showcases youths getting drunk, fighting, and other controversial behavior.[12] The fact that these reality show characters get paid millions of dollars to behave like deadbeats sends a clear message to Americans that education isn't material to fame and wealth. When over 10,000 people line up to audition for *American Idol* in a single city, the trend is clear.[13] Young Americans may have high aspirations, but many don't invest in the skills and knowledge necessary to achieve those aspirations. Some of them have been led to believe by the prevailing culture that with a little bit of luck, talent, and networking, one can become a Hollywood celebrity overnight.

Standards may be lowered or ignored for student athletes since sports revenue is important to many academic institutions. The NBA and NFL further fuel the popularity of sports as potential careers, distorting youth priorities. Even among the elite college kids at Ivy League schools, getting educated is secondary to other concerns. When I spoke to my friend Sheldon Garon, professor of history at

Princeton University, he said that in his lecture classes of 80 students, not one of them had heard of the term *collective bargaining*. "The students may be smart, but they are narrow-minded," he said. "They only care about joining the most exclusive eating clubs in order to land the right Wall Street jobs." As a result, probably far fewer Americans are pursuing the less glorified fields of scientific research, social work, and environmental preservation than if the cultural messaging and pay scales were different.

Not only do sports, entertainment, and Wall Street shape American values, but celebrity figures like Joel Osteen have also exerted a powerful influence. Preaching "prosperity theology" or "prosperity gospel," Mr. Osteen has dismantled Christian values of thrift, hard work, and the Golden Rule and replaced them with notions that individual wealth and power are virtues. He has used the Jewish success in the United States as a model for Christians to emulate, completely reversing the anti-Semitism that used to be prevalent among Evangelical Christians. Desire for individual success and improvement has always been an American trademark, but such individual pursuits were once more balanced with religious teachings from Jesus to practice modesty and to Love Thy Neighbor. Some of these modernized versions of religion downplay or ignore the more humanistic and civic virtues and instead glorify selfishness and self-aggrandizement.

## U.S. Education: D+?

Certainly, there is much about American culture to love and celebrate. But when it comes to prizing education, the messages our mass media send out to our citizens usually contradict our wiser national imperative to improve the talent base. Modern American culture that diminishes the role and importance of education in society often gets overlooked as a critical contributing factor to America's deteriorating educational system. While policymakers and politicians have talked about improving the educational system for the last ten years, nothing has changed in part because the public has not built the necessary consensus to push the issue forward. The political will just has not been strong enough, so the education challenge still remains largely under the radar screen.

When such cultural attitudes and perceptions become collectively ingrained, they become reflected in our policies, which unfortunately have sacrificed education as a national priority. U.S. public school teachers, far from being elevated and respected, receive low pay and minimal administrative support. Average teacher salaries are roughly $40,000 a year, less than what some financiers get paid in an hour.[14] A telling joke about our national priorities goes something like this: if you can't get a real job, go be a teacher. Teachers' unions block reform to weed out underperformers, and policymakers prioritize the military over our children when it comes to the budgeting process. Very few find it worth their while to champion the cause of public education. The ones who have money and influence often opt to send their children to elite private schools, again preferring to ignore the fate of the broader society.

The problem is that in a knowledge economy where ideas and other intangible assets drive future wealth creation, an educated labor force becomes the most important ingredient and key competitive advantage for a nation's future. Without an educated workforce, the freedom for a society to develop economically is limited. Even if one assumes that only 1 percent of the U.S. population is necessary to run companies, cities, states, or the nation, those leaders will not be successful if they cannot hire skilled and educated employees. Because most new job openings are in information technology, healthcare, and education, the problem of matching skilled and educated American workers with these positions is already upon us. Indeed, the National Institute for Literacy concluded that at least 4 percent of the adult American population was illiterate because they couldn't even perform the simplest literacy tasks on their survey. Not only are American corporations at risk, but even American democracy could be at risk when millions who are eligible to vote and thus influence the direction of the country's future cannot read or write.

However, despite the millions allocated to the U.S. public educational system, numerous reports document that the educational system is still falling farther and farther behind other nations.[15] America's youth population, especially among minorities, has an elevated high school dropout rate. Studies warn that 7,000 students drop out of high school every day, amounting to 1.2 million youths every year. More disturbing, graduation rates have been continually dropping. In 1969, the high school graduation rate was 77 percent, but by 2007, the graduation rate was 68.8 percent.[16] The reasons for the demise of public education are numerous, which documentary films like *Waiting for Superman* outline with compassion and detail. But that's not the end of the story.

The United States has long taken solace that its higher educational system is the best in the world. However, of the 3,000 colleges and universities in the United States, most of them underperform those in other countries. According to Dr. Robert Mendenhall, President of Western Governors University, the United States dropped from first place to twelfth in the world university rankings. And while the number of Americans with college degrees has steadily increased since 1950, the degree may be less valuable than ones earned in the past.[17] My friend Carol Irving, who teaches freshman English at the New School in New York City, asked me to help her find a teaching job in China because she was tired of babysitting her students. "These college students can't even write a sentence!" she complained to me. So while these graduates may hold a degree, their abilities upon graduation won't likely be uniform.

The repercussions of marginalizing education for the broader population can extend further. According to a Gallup poll conducted in 2009, only 40 percent of Americans believe in evolution while 91 percent of Chinese students believe in it. An overwhelming reliance on faith and lack of scientific curiosity among the majority of the population does not encourage the kind of experimentation that would lead to breakthrough innovations that can solve 21st-century problems. Worse, if antiscientific attitudes develop too far, we would not only lack a workforce that could function capably in a knowledge economy, we could even put the knowledge economy itself at risk of enormous setbacks. When religious fanatics sacked the Serapeum of Alexandria in the 4th century, some scholars believe that scientific inquiry was impeded for several centuries. So as long as the status quo prevails, the United States will gradually lose its historic attraction as a nation of opportunity and progress if its population is not motivated to pursue the knowledge, skills, and creativity to compete with an increasingly "flat world," as Tom Friedman of the *New York Times* put it.

## Proof Is in the Pudding

What can the United States learn from China in the way of elevating education in importance? The population, first and foremost, must believe that education is valuable for improving their future. Obviously to change values and belief systems can take generations, but sometimes small changes can have revolutionary effects, especially if they are sustained over a period of time. The fastest way to alter belief systems is to provide evidence. When the CCP reversed policies regarding education, millions of Chinese began to see evidence that the educated classes were rewarded regardless of family background. Likewise, the election of Barack Obama as the first black President of the United States has certainly sent a strong, positive message to minorities that America remains a nation where all dreams are still possible. He and other prominent minority figures serve as inspirational role models for those who have been impoverished to maintain hope and try harder.

However, despite the isolated successes of certain individuals, more can be done to encourage the next generation to embrace scholarly and civic-minded pursuits. For instance, perhaps the government could provide tax incentives for television producers to create programming that promotes innovation by seeking out America's greatest new inventors, doctors, engineers, astronomers, teachers, social workers, and others in the same way *American Idol* discovers talented new singers through live competition. Another idea is to showcase the CEOs of high-tech and biotech companies. The television programs could tell their stories of how they created their products and show how they are changing the world for the better. People need exposure to professions that have traditionally lacked media attention in order to imagine their own lives unfolding in roles with which they may be unfamiliar.

If the FCC regulates sex and violence on television, why not have the government mandate that television stations allocate time for airing programming that enriches the mind and soul and encourages the pursuit of higher education? Such a mandate can be part of their civic duty in exchange for the privilege of having a broadcasting license. Insistence by the media that programming should be based only on market demand ignores the reflexive nature of human behavior. Like the chicken or the egg, it's not clear what came first—media dictating pop culture or vice versa. But the relationship is inseparable, so changing one part of the equation will certainly influence the other.

Grassroots organizations can also help kick-start a counterculture in education. One group called CEOs for Cities engaged some innovative advisors and experts to develop new ideas for educating the public in the 21st century. Their report called "101 Wacky Ideas: Reclaiming a Nation of Pre-Graduates," advocates pop-up classrooms, failure labs, and career discovery camps, among many other suggestions to reach a broad public that may not have the time or money to go back to school full-time.

The possibilities are limitless, but it begins with an awareness and willingness to influence the prevailing culture as part of a comprehensive strategy to reorient priorities. The Confucian values of scholarship, endurance, and tolerance can gain traction in American society if tastemakers and policymakers work together to make the benefits of embracing such values more obvious to the general public. Policies in isolation and working at cross-purposes with culture will likely fail, but policies that harness the power of the prevailing culture just might succeed. If people learn to value education again, then half the battle to make our workforce competitive will be won.

Moreover, America's strength has always been its import of people from all races and nations who tend to be diligent and value higher education. Immigrants like Albert Einstein led much of the cutting-edge thinking that enabled the United States to catapult to super-power status. Others, such as Andy Grove of Intel Corporation, have helped create great companies that have not only employed many Americans but kept America competitive. Immigration is the part of American culture that has made us the best in the world because it brings together ideas from different parts of the world. The result is fresh thinking that can spur innovation. So we must always safe-guard this policy for the greater good of the nation, despite pressure to close our doors. To close our doors to the world would risk closing our minds to the world, a risk not worth taking given our present educational challenges.

## Honest Pay for an Honest Day's Work

In addition to education, Confucian teachings promote thrift and plain living, which fortunately (or unfortunately, depending on how you see it) stand in stark contrast to America's love affair with extravagance, consumerism, and money. Confucius thought highly of Yan Ying, prime minister of the state of Qi, who wore the same fur coat for 30 years. Fast-forward to modern day China and one will discover that the laboring Chinese have ingrained beliefs that diligence and frugality will eventually lead to prosperity while laziness and wastefulness can only lead to decline and destruction. The Chinese savings rate at over 50 percent is among the highest in the world.[18] Extravagance and reckless wasting of natural resources are actively opposed by many Chinese to the point that even throwing away a grain of rice is considered bad form. Chinese superstitions also reinforce this value. One popular superstition is that living in a large, empty home is bad luck. Too many empty rooms that are not occupied with people for daily living supposedly invite bad spirits. With such superstitions, overbuilt communities of McMansions that were typical of the U.S. subprime crisis will unlikely materialize as a problem in China.

In contrast, Americans have been accustomed to consume beyond their means and sometimes without necessarily giving anything of value to society in return. Teenagers are given credit cards by banks before they even earn a penny.[19] Introducing Confucian values of thrift and spending within one's means to young adults may reduce the risk of young adults experimenting with drugs, dropping out of school, or doing jail time. Studies have shown that youths who suffer from low self-esteem tend to use drugs as a coping mechanism for pain and stress.[20] They have not built confidence in themselves, confidence that can come from the responsibility of earning a living. Learning Confucianism can give them a life-changing opportunity to view the world in a new way that nourishes their desire to master something while delaying immediate gratification. Rather than medicating them for depression, hyperactivity, or some other disorder, it may be far safer and far less expensive to teach them a proven ancient philosophy for coping with the world. It could give people new reasons to accomplish something meaningful that is independent of monetary reward, a vital ingredient for human motivation and feelings of well-being.

The Confucian work ethic is also highly correlated with thrift and springs from its long-term orientation toward future rewards. The idea of perseverance and deferring gratification becomes second nature. The experience of a former head of Pfizer's research is typical for many Western firms operating in China. He claimed he outsourced all his work to the Chinese in China because they could be depended upon to have conference calls at 2 AM if necessary. He was completely unapologetic about giving jobs to the Chinese over Americans because he said no American would ever work that hard. With such trends, eight-hour workdays may become a thing of the past. Job security that assures employment until retirement is increasingly rare, so keeping a job means working longer, harder, smarter. In a global world, the Confucian virtue of perseverance through the most difficult of conditions will likely be as accepted in the future as Mohamed El-Erian's "new normal"—his assertion that slow U.S. economic growth will be the rule rather than the exception—is today.

Studies by MIT, University of Chicago, and Carnegie Mellon funded by the Federal Reserve have discovered that when offered significant rewards, people performed well only if the skills involved were largely repetitive. But when the same reward schemes were offered to people working on activities that involved more than rudimentary cognitive skills, such as those that involve creative or conceptual thinking, monetary incentives had the opposite effect on human performance and motivation. Study after study in psychology, sociology, and economics revealed that once people were paid enough not to make money an issue, the ones who performed the best in cognitive activity were more motivated by autonomy, mastery, and purpose.[21]

These studies lend support to the argument that innovation breakthroughs come from people who are motivated to work on a problem or an idea solely because the work is meaningful or fun for them. A desire for enormous wealth is usually not a motivating factor that comes up in biographies of inventors. The next Thomas Edison will not be discovered simply by promising millions in bonus money if he comes up with the next brilliant invention. Dr. Jonas Salk, who discovered the first safe polio vaccine, did not do his work for monetary awards.[22] In fact, he refrained from owning a patent and shunned publicity despite being hailed as a national hero for his contribution to medical science. Bill Gates and Steve Jobs likewise led the charge in personal computer innovation because they were driven by curiosity and mastery of new frontiers.[23]

However, despite being an advanced economy, the vast majority in American society work in jobs that are repetitive and are rewarded for not rocking the boat. Even people who work in highly paid positions in financial services firms engage in largely routine tasks. Though many of these professionals like to pride themselves on being smart, the fact is that the information and analyses they act upon to earn their giant bonuses routinely come from outside sources. Financial firms pay millions of dollars to access "independent" research reports, data services, investment conferences, and speakers considered "experts," but very few of them generate much original or creative thought. Television shows such as CNBC showcase daily portfolio managers who repeat the same ideas and concepts that they've heard from others in the industry. Momentum trading, a legitimate strategy followed by many money managers, is predicated on copying other traders. As a result of this herd mentality, multiple asset bubbles have been created and burst in just the last two decades alone, leaving much to be desired in the way of real human progress.

Whether it is to sell a product or trade financial instruments, most jobs in the United States that give big bonuses don't award them for creating revolutionary breakthroughs. The ones who are tasked with doing such things are scientists and other researchers, who are not given the name recognition, money, or other benefits that would be commensurate with the value of their contributions to society. The logical conclusion one can draw from these observations is that the United States rewards repetitive work but discourages the true innovation and creative thought that could dramatically improve the quality of human existence. Unless we find a way to modify this incentive system, we would be hard-pressed to create a new catalyst that will drive the type of hiring that occurred during the Industrial Revolution. A lack of a new catalyst coupled with incremental improvements in existing technology can accelerate structural unemployment in the United States and around the globe. For instance, high-frequency trading software has replaced many Wall Street traders, and artificial intelligence software is beginning to replace secretaries and nurses. Once these jobs are replaced with incremental improvements in technology, they are never coming back. Radical inventions must be created in order to put people back to work.

With this in mind, the Confucian prescription for excellence, which is detached from material reward, would be consistent with scientific findings about human performance and more in harmony with human nature. The value of a person under Confucian doctrine always prizes the character and scholarly accomplishments of a person as opposed to his or her net financial worth. The importance of this shift in value cannot be understated.

Let's imagine a Wall Street under a Confucian influence. The financial crisis may never happen again. Why? Confucian bankers would be more concerned about channeling their energies and capital toward people and ideas that contribute to society and do valuable things than with the sole purpose of getting wealthy. Confucian bankers would be better stewards of capital and the financial system because they would understand that even if they were the last ones standing in a world destroyed by greed and short-term behavior, it would not be a world worth living in. Perhaps there would be more wealthy Silicon Valley people as opposed to wealthy bankers from Goldman Sachs as a result. But for the most part, they would become wealthy because they created something useful and valuable to society, as opposed to causing enormous damage to others.

## Inconsistencies?

Of course Confucianism is not a silver bullet. Some cynically believe that Confucianism was reintroduced by the CCP to control the masses while others point to the numerous unethical behaviors that are routinely reported by Westerners doing business in China. Stories about fake Apple stores and businessmen carrying briefcases full of cash seem uncharacteristically common for a society heavily under Confucian influence. However, whether it's corruption from property developers or local government officials, Confucian values alone cannot eliminate all of society's ills. Bad eggs exist in every society, and China is no exception. Obviously not all Americans behave like Good Samaritans either. Spiritual development in the world is unfortunately in short supply regardless of religious faith or philosophy, but it doesn't mean that it's useless. In approaching anything, the aphorism, "don't throw the baby out with the bath water" applies to Confucianism as well.

What matters more is that a society and its government should strive to achieve more enlightened ways of being. Corruption still happens in China, but China's leaders recognize the problem and are making substantive moves to address it, not because they have to but because of their Confucian beliefs about their own legitimacy. Course corrections in policy can happen smoothly as long as the society and government can work together with aligned values, whether they are Confucian or not. However, the best values usually withstand the test of time. Confucian values at least have that going for them.

## Yes, Master

Americans may worry that Confucianism is too hierarchic and too deferential to elders to be appropriate for America's heritage of being irreverent and questioning of authority. After all, the Founding Fathers rebelled against authority in order to create the United States, defining the American character for generations to come.

The hierarchical relationships that are defined by Confucian teachings are not taken as literally by modern, urban Chinese. In fact, most of them interpret *hierarchy* to mean *respect* for elders, not necessarily to *obey* their elders, which is not incompatible with American culture. Though there are examples of young chief executives and relatively young people occupying high office, as in the case of Presidents Barack Obama or John F. Kennedy, most American leaders in business or in politics that garner the deepest respect remain those who have been around long enough to develop wisdom.

Respecting the more experienced isn't just a nice value but is good policy. Much wisdom can be learned from previous generations if they feel their opinions and thoughts are welcomed. The Chinese know this truth and therefore keep their elders in close quarters rather than send them off to nursing homes. Chinese adults who visit their elders when they live separately almost never even consider staying at a hotel when they return. To live at a hotel would be considered an insult to the parents no matter how small the living quarters are. It is just assumed that familial ties must be tight to ensure maximum communication between the generations. With much more frequent contact than the average American, the osmosis of knowledge between Chinese parent or grandparent and child can be more efficient and complete.

If Americans learned this one Confucian value, perhaps fewer Americans would fear growing old and becoming irrelevant in their old age. Rather than being seen as a burden on the younger generation, grandparents can act as wise and loving mentors to both their own children and grandchildren and valued as a source of history, companionship, and support.

## Compassion Calling

Researchers have documented that humans instinctively experience another's plights as if we are experiencing them ourselves. People need love, companionship, and belonging to a community; aggression, violence, or self-interest are not natural states of being.[24] Furthermore, people naturally experience empathy, not hatred, for all life on earth. Confucian values and philosophy recognize this aspect of human nature and the human dependency on its ecosystem. If

Confucianism were more widely embraced in the United States, there would be pressure to preserve more of our natural resources. We would likely reduce military arms and increase diplomacy. We also would probably empathize with immigrants and other minorities as if they were family. Finally, pursuing a more cohesive and egalitarian society might be more commonplace. Confucians' holistic ways of viewing the world could be enough to change history and compel more Americans to extend our empathy beyond our immediate circles to the entire human race and even all the biosphere.

Throughout human history, civilizations have evolved by cooperating with greater numbers of people. Solidarity between blood ties were extended to tribal members, which eventually got extended to citizens of nations. There is no scientific law that states that people are not capable of seeing the human race as one family ultimately. The fact that technology already allows a person to inseminate an egg, have a separate surrogate mother carry the baby, and have a third person raise the child demonstrates that family is merely a construct that can have a wider definition. Scientific research has long established that everyone on earth is 99.5 percent similar in genetic makeup.[25] Dominant theories about the origins of man also point to common ancestry from Africa. If this is true, the argument for universal human empathy—consistent with Confucianism—is even stronger.[26]

Reversing existing broad cultural trends in the United States may require many policy adjustments that could take lifetimes to implement. However, jumpstarting a renaissance in ethics and a realignment of priorities could conceivably be achieved through China's example of reintroducing Confucian principles in the media and through government and corporate policies to accentuate what is already innate in all people. Most Americans are generous, thoughtful, and motivated to do the right thing. Confucian principles would be a welcome contrast to the me-oriented, money-oriented consumerist philosophy that dominates American culture today. Though the notion of introducing ancient Chinese teachings to American modern culture seems laughable, major swings in what is fashionable have happened in the past. When JFK famously said, "Ask not what the country can do for you; ask what you can do for your country," America was ready to embrace moral rectitude and step up to challenges, behavior advocated in Confucian teachings. Confucian teachings in many ways would essentially represent reintroducing old American values back into U.S. culture rather than importing values and beliefs that are completely new and unfamiliar. Confucianism could help stop the slide in American education and serve as a counterweight to America's overwhelming materialist culture. By broadening its understanding of Eastern philosophy, the United States can take advantage of wisdom that has been developed over thousands of years. Perhaps we can start by creating a national holiday where we can all be Confucian for a day.

# Meritocracy

You can delegate authority, but not responsibility.
—STEPHEN W. COMISKEY

## Democracy No Guarantee

Unlike in earlier centuries when one's birth determined one's permanent economic fortunes and clout in the world, most modern societies today subscribe to the notion that individuals should have the opportunity to live up to their potential through talent and hard work. Monarchies have been largely dismantled and replaced with institutions that recruit the most able individuals to run countries. Since blood lineage is no longer the sole determinant of the extraordinary privilege of leading most countries, determining who should have those roles and the best method for vetting those individuals becomes of paramount importance. Since the end of the Cold War, many countries that were once dictatorships or authoritarian regimes have converted to democracies because many were attracted by the relative freedoms and riches that characterized Western democratic economies.

However, there is also a developing consensus that the term *democracy* can be used to shield or excuse abuses and atrocities. In fact, many democracies have had egregious records in serving their citizens. India, hailed as a democracy, for example, still suffers from extensive poverty. According to a 2007 NCEUS estimate, 77 percent of Indians live on less than a half dollar a day. Additionally, there is still an active caste system. Its human rights abuses also can put totalitarian governments to shame. Bride burning, a practice in which thousands of young brides have been burned to death by their in-laws every year due to low dowries, has hardly received any coverage from Western media.[1] Neither has its human trafficking been much reported. Around 10,000 Nepali women are brought to India annually for commercial sexual exploitation.[2] Each year, estimates between 20,000 and 30,000 women and children are trafficked from Bangladesh.[3] Finally, violence such as extra-judicial executions, disappearances, and torture of indigenous peoples by Indians in India have received condemnation from human rights organizations such as Amnesty International and the Human Rights Watch, but little else has been done by the international community to stop such life-threatening abuses.

Kenya is another reportedly democratic country whose widespread human rights abuses include life-threatening prison conditions, infringements of rights in the course of legal proceedings, abuse of children, forced labor, prostitution, wife inheritance, and female genital mutilation.[4] Perhaps this country would be disastrous under another form of government as well, but it does call to question the notion that democracy is the universal solution to human rights abuses and the best way to run nations.

Comparatively speaking, some authoritarian governments managed to deliver extraordinary improvements in quality of life that under some definitions would qualify as a human right. Lifting hundreds of millions of people out of abject poverty in China has been a stunning feat and arguably qualifies as the most far-reaching humanitarian assistance in history. Although China still has to contend with its policy of capital punishment, the surprising economic success of China for the last two decades has nonetheless prompted many nations to reconsider their governance structures. Some of them have even considered emulating China. Russia's leaders have inquired about learning China's governance methods and have formally approached the Chinese leaders for instruction.[5] Though China still needs to make more progress in other areas of human rights, the Russians are unlikely to be the only ones seeking to replicate the Chinese style of government if wealth inequality and unemployment continue to dog democratic regimes.

While some may marvel at China's success, it is certainly not the first authoritarian government to have delivered impressive economic performance. When Singapore exited the British Empire for example, the prospects for the island nation were poor. It not only had no natural resources to export, but also no manufacturing base to produce anything. However, Singapore was enormously lucky to have a far-sighted leader, Lee Kwan Yew. As the first prime minister of the Republic of Singapore, from 1959 to 1990, and one of the longest-serving prime ministers in the world, Lee had to solve many problems after gaining self-rule for Singapore from the British, including upgrading education and housing, improving its limited defense capability, and reducing unemployment.

Acting as a benevolent authoritarian, he developed and executed a national strategy based on clean government and superior human capital. Since people were Singapore's most abundant resource, he made it his priority to build an exceptionally well-educated workforce by emerging market standards. Creating a clean government would give Singapore a competitive advantage because corruption—pervasive in developing nations—has been theorized to be a leading contributor to national poverty.[6] Lee crafted a bureaucracy that was difficult to corrupt because (1) good incentives were built into the system, (2) high-level bureaucrats were given compensation comparable to the private sector, and (3) rigorous internal audits ensured compliance.[7] Today, thanks to Lee's vision, Singapore's population enjoys the high standard of living that Westerners enjoy. Though it does not confer the same level of freedoms as many Western countries and can be criticized for erecting barriers to political opposition, Singapore may not have been able to develop into its present modern state as rapidly as it has had it not been for its early authoritarian rule.

Another authoritarian government that achieved rapid modernization and economic growth was Turkey under the leadership of Mustafa Kemal Atatürk. Atatürk had the foresight to lead Turkey toward a more secular future in his attempt to modernize the country. During his presidency, Atatürk pursued political, economic, and cultural reforms.[8] Public education was elevated to the highest of priorities because he believed that the Turkish people had to free themselves from religious doctrine before the nation could attain true prosperity and liberation.[9] Like Lee Kwan Yew, he favored realism and pragmatism to guide his policies.

Although Atatürk envisioned a direct government by the Assembly and hoped a representative democracy and parliamentary sovereignty would one day take root, he did not promote such governance while he was in power. He saw that pluralism repeatedly failed because disagreements over secularism and the rules for engagement created deadlocks to conflict resolution. But even long after his death, he left a legacy of economic stability and growth in most regions. In fact, Turkey has outperformed some Western countries.[10]

The lessons to be learned are that while democracy has its merits, it can be abused in the wrong hands, and that democracy alone cannot deliver the results that a society desires, such as economic opportunity. Democracy is a lofty goal, but as Fareed Zakaria pointed out in his book *The Future of Freedom,* the ideology can be manipulated and actually cause the opposite to happen in a country if the institutions and incentives are not properly designed to ensure healthy democratic rule. He questions whether democracy is fit for America, embracing elite authoritarianism over democracy under certain conditions and arguing that democracy is not an innately virtuous system of government. Zakaria believes that democracy needs two prerequisites—genuine economic development and effective political institutions—to function properly.[11]

But as I have pointed out in the earlier examples from other countries, democracy—or any other form of government—needs above all else good people to function properly. A democracy run by corrupt politicians will result in a government unable to serve its own citizens and create laws where *legal* is no longer synonymous with *ethical*.

Although a functioning democracy should have checks and balances to curtail free reign of abusive practices, even these counter measures can be gamed when loopholes are found or introduced. Judges, for example, who are supposed to "check and balance" other politicians and policies can fail to act as the counterweight for a variety of reasons. A retired judge once told me that she received death threats that were probably supported by members of another branch in government, if she dared to rule on a case a certain way. Another admitted that some cases get pushed aside because the judge did not want to be caught in the crossfire between powerful interest groups.

## American Political Dystopia

In America today, voter participation has been steadily dropping since 1876 from over 80 percent to roughly 55 percent in the last few presidential elections. The reasons for the decline may be attributed to various factors, but when these statistics are compared to other nations such as Australia, Chile, and many European countries where voter participation exceeds 85 percent, the low turnout indicates some deep-rooted problems in the political system.[12] Lobbying is long-term policy shaping, and most voters are substantially disadvantaged for being left out, especially since unions and other civic groups that used to represent the middle class have largely been dismantled. Low participation in elections reflects in part that some citizens don't believe they are being integrated into the decision-making process and therefore can't change government.

The view that the political system has become dysfunctional through the capture of special interests is well documented in books such as *Kabuki Democracy* by Eric Alterman. Professor Lawrence Lessig of Harvard University asserts that American politicians who get elected are really front men for large corporate or other special interests who funnel large amounts of money to their campaigns.[13] Rather than represent the public interest, these politicians merely ensure that their patrons are satisfied with their voting records on particular issues.

Compounding the problem of special interests gaming democratic elections, eligible voters may not necessarily understand the dilemmas and tradeoffs required for running a complex society. According to the 2009 U.S. Census, less than 40 percent of the American population has a college degree and less than 10 percent have a masters degree. Today's complex global economy demands a higher level of education in voters in order to understand the consequences of different policies. If many of the eligible voters are unable to evaluate the issues comprehensively, they may make suboptimal political choices.

Already, we have witnessed candidates reducing their campaigns to simplistic slogans and easily digestible sound bites that fail to convey the multifaceted aspects of most problems and issues. The democratic process has taken on the character of salesmanship based on personalities as opposed to well-reasoned debate in enlightened forums followed by deliberation. Many politicians avoid being honest and realistic about proposals to fix critical problems because they fear sounding too negative to the voters who don't understand the complexities and sacrifices required.

As a result, we now have a situation in which politicians tend to focus their pandering on those people most easily swayed by lofty words and promises and who live in states that have the electoral votes to swing an election. In other words, American democracy has turned into a system that systematically caters its rhetoric to the lowest common denominator, the least informed voter. As Jacob Hacker writes in his book *Winner-Take-All-Politics*, Americans have been brainwashed through professional messaging and framing to care more about political equality than economic unresponsiveness. According to the Gini index, which measures income ranges, economic inequality is growing increasingly severe in the United States, yet addressing the problem has been absent in most political dialogue. Politicians prefer to use social issues, like gay marriage, to take advantage of the ignorant, since it is much easier to unite disparate groups through fear than it is to solve economic problems by making difficult choices.

Economic warfare has often been the precursor to revolutions. A democracy unable and/or unwilling to address the sources of class warfare risks reaching a tipping point where the uneducated and economically desperate resort to mob behavior and cease to uphold democratic values like civil liberties for minorities. Alexis de Toqueville had warned against this form of tyranny in his book *Democracy in America*.

Equally disturbing, deliberative democracy as envisioned during the Founding Fathers' time has devolved into strong-arming exercises in Congress. The *Hill,* a Congressional daily newspaper, has reported stories of both parties guilty of engaging in these tactics. Party leaders make regular use of filibusters to obstruct bills from being passed. In the 19th century, fewer than two dozen filibusters were enacted, but the number went up to 20 *per year* during the Carter administration.[14] Party leaders have also reportedly used various levels of coercion such as threats of withholding campaign funds from political action committees to force members of Congress to vote along party lines. In controversial bills such as H.R.2454 (Cap and Trade) or H.R.3692 (House Democratic Health Care), many media websites, including the GOP's, reported that Congressmen were asked to "walk the plank," a term that refers to political arm twisting in order to secure enough votes for controversial initiatives. None of these tactics are deliberative or democratic in nature. Instead, what goes on in Congress today may be quite reminiscent of the graft and political corruption during the times of Tammany Hall.

Most importantly, under no circumstances do our politicians need to prove that they are qualified for the job. By virtue of being a U.S. citizen and reaching a certain age, anyone can qualify to run for office. While this feature may appeal to some on democratic principles, the reality is that such a system may be recruiting the wrong talent for the most important positions in the nation. Just as we send trade representatives who are adept at negotiating complex deals with other nations, the United States should consider a system that will ensure that the country recruits and elects the most qualified people to represent and act on the interests of the general American population.

The U.S. political system today arguably tends to attract self-serving people who are gifted self-promoters because the media have become so central in election campaigns. It can be inferred that one's mastery of media appearances, as opposed to other important qualifications and leadership skills, can unduly determine a candidate's chance to be elected. Without some type of institutional change, we will continue this highly imperfect system in which mostly media-savvy people will choose to run for office. Do we want interest groups and political parties to endorse potential candidates using vastly different criteria than what would be considered important to the general public?

## Earned Authority

Luckily, China's model of leadership selection demonstrates great promise for being effective and has aspects that the United States may want to consider adopting. Although China's system is far from an ideal democracy, its system of meritocracy contains elements of democratic representation that permeate the entire governance structure. The Chinese believe that the privilege of leading a country should belong only to those who have proven that they can serve the country over long periods of time in a selfless way and accomplish a great deal. Thus, the process of leadership selection in China at its heart is based on merit rather than mere popularity contests during elections.

Analogous to many large corporations, China's government is hierarchical as well as broadly lateral in its scope. The Organization Department of the Party oversees the personnel appointments of several thousand high-ranking leadership positions in the Party, the government institutions, key state-owned enterprises, key universities, the military, and other institutions. Government officials serve up to two five-year terms. Each one of these officials is evaluated by peers, subordinates, superiors, and even the general public in regards to their performance in those roles. For instance, a government official who is appointed to be the president of a university must prove that the institution has improved during his or her tenure. Achievements can be shown in a variety of ways: increasing student enrollment, creating more diverse course curricula, or establishing more overseas student exchanges. At the end of a president's term, if the achievements and job evaluations are overwhelmingly positive, he or she may be promoted to a position with more responsibility, such as mayor. But if expectations are not met, the university president could be demoted to some lesser position and consequently also receive less compensation. Only after decades of increasing responsibility and achievement will a government official have an opportunity to be elected to one of the top positions. The Politburo, of which there are 25 members, and the Standing Committee, consisting of 9 members, comprise the most powerful group in China. Together, these top national officials form a collective leadership in the CCP that negotiates and compromises among competing factions to find consensus on issues that becomes regarded as their collective wisdom.

China's system of collective leadership is a significant departure from Mao's reign in which he commanded the CCP as a cult of personality. Political succession now is governed by rules that make leadership selection more objective and consistent. These institutional changes have significantly curtailed abuses of power and favoritism such as nepotism and have forced China's elites to share power through political compromises and coalition building.

Similar to the way many CEOs have been selected to head large corporations after years of service and accomplishments, China's top leaders correspondingly have devoted their entire careers to government service. General Secretary Hu Jintao's résumé illustrates this point. Hu started his career with the Party as a technician after graduating from Tsinghua University. From there, he held twenty or so posts of increasing responsibility before being appointed to the highest office in the nation, including

- Deputy Party Secretary of Sinohydro Engineering Bureau
- Secretary of Gansu Provincial Construction Committee
- Vice Director of Gansu Provincial Construction Committee
- Secretary of Gansu branch of Communist Youth League
- Vice Chairman of Gansu Provincial Construction Committee
- Deputy Secretary of Gansu Communist Youth League
- Secretariat of the National Communist Youth League of China
- CEO of National Youth League
- Politburo Standing Committee
- Secretary of Guizhou
- Party Secretary of Tibetan Autonomous Region
- Head of CPC Secretariat
- President of Central Party School
- State Vice President
- Vice Chairman of Central Military Commission.[15]

The career of Bo Xilai, a senior leader in the party and a contender for the position of premier of China, is another illustration of this principle. After graduating from Peking University as a history major, he served as a mayor, Party secretary, and then governor of

Dalian. Subsequently he was promoted to become China's minister of commerce before being transferred to Chongqing as its Party secretary. At Chongqing, Bo Xilai made his most impressive mark. The province-level municipality had a long history of corruption and was known for its prostitution and other unseemly activities. In the past, whenever people from the central government went there to investigate corruption charges, they were unable to find any wrongdoing. Nightclubs and other places where criminal activities allegedly took place appeared quite legitimate whenever the police arrived. Bo suspected that government insiders tipped off the club owners and other mafia-like groups as to when inspectors would arrive and raids would happen. So when Bo arrived, he transferred with him roughly 1,500 police officers from the previous province where he governed without telling anyone in the Chongqing police system that he had done so. With this new set of police officers aiding him, they broke up prostitution, drug trafficking, and other illegal activities, cleaning up Chongqing almost overnight. They collected enough evidence to arrest the second in command of the Chongqing police for corruption and fraud, who was subsequently sentenced to death.[16]

Without the political support of senior leaders who also toiled a lifetime for the common good, Bo Xilai and other up-and-coming Chinese leaders would have faced certain death in carrying out such courageous reforms. But China's leaders are united with a utopian goal that guides their policy making. They understand that they must remain vigilant against corruption in order to maintain legitimacy among the citizens and attract foreign investment to continue the nation's nascent development. Only then can the Chinese continue to eliminate poverty and move closer to their Communist ideal of egalitarianism through increasing productivity.

Of course, there are also many examples of relatively high-ranking government officials that have engaged in corrupt practices and have escaped censure. Corruption, defined as the abuse of entrusted power for private gain, hurts societies where lives and livelihoods depend on the integrity of the people in power. To date, no country in history has been free from corrupt government officials.[17] But these kinds of incremental improvements to minimize the extent of corruption are worthy of study. Perhaps we could even emulate them.

By the time a person is chosen by peers to become premier of China, that government official has served for decades in numerous and diverse leadership roles with a very public track record of accomplishments. Unlike some U.S. politicians who are elected to the federal government with limited leadership experience in both the government and corporate world, a Chinese leader will have served in a variety of government roles that may be as diverse as leading several provinces as a governor, engaging in trade negotiations, heading a state-owned company, and running regulatory agencies. Thus Chinese leaders have earned their titles with lifetimes of service and accomplishments for the benefit of society. The need to pander, buy votes, and give eloquent speeches to convince the masses that one is moral and capable doesn't figure prominently under this system; one's lifetime of actions speak for themselves. Someone who has not lived up to the expectations would face an extremely difficult, if not impossible, task of ascending to the top. Even if one were promoted unfairly, further promotions would be blocked because a spotty track record would not win the support of all the decision makers over long periods of time. Thus, the individual who does get elected into the Politburo already has been vetted by millions of Chinese citizens. One can safely infer that the selected leader has earned the indirect and tacit approval of the entire nation even if there was no direct election.

Unsurprisingly, the Chinese leaders who have been selected tend to have very high approval ratings from the Chinese citizenry even if they are not chosen in a formal election process. Indeed, the Pew Global Attitudes Survey (2010) reported that 87 percent of Chinese were content with their country's direction. This stands in sharp contrast to the attitudes of Americans, among whom only 30 percent were content with the direction of the United States. Other polls report consistent results. A *New York Times*/CBS News poll in 2011 showed that seven out of ten thought America is on the wrong track, nearly 60 percent disapproved of the Obama administration's handling of the economy, and three quarters of the respondents think Congress is doing a lousy job.

This data is even more remarkable in light of the fact that the Chinese tend to be more skeptical of their government since they are aware of government propaganda. Most Americans, on the other hand, get lulled into American government propaganda because many assume that the Western "free press" filters propaganda. That may have been true in earlier decades when there were more independent news agencies competing, which resulted in honest-to-goodness journalism, with a greater diversity of opinions and perspectives. However, the advent of the Internet has forced many of these firms to go out of business or get swallowed up by larger entities. As a result of this extreme consolidation, the mainstream media can no longer be counted on for watchdog journalism, as it once was. The interests, and thus agenda, for these media executives have since become more aligned with their large corporate clients, who provide revenue, and with government in order to gain privileged access.[18] But these events and subsequent internal changes in the industry have largely happened without the broader public fully understanding or being aware of its compromising implications.

Notably, in spite of the learned skepticism of its government, many Chinese still buy into the system because they believe that their meritocratic process in selecting the smartest and most far-sighted people to lead China is a key factor for the rapid economic improvement in their lives. Starting from the mid-1980s, the overwhelming majority of China's top leaders boasted engineering degrees from the country's top universities and brandished track records of achievements in government service lasting decades.[19] Though one can claim that the praise of their achievements is government propaganda, the evidence of progress and economic improvement is nonetheless ubiquitous. Popular support would likely exist even if the propaganda was absent.

Following the ascendance of the technocrats, China's entrepreneurs and lawyers are now starting to gain more political sway within the Party. Starting with the reforms under Premier Jiang Zemin, these so-called capitalists have been allowed to join the CCP and are now starting to occupy the highest positions in government. Their diverse educational and occupational backgrounds will add further pluralism to the Chinese leadership. Such a development could eventually become a precursor to broader public elections that today only exist in the lower levels of government like townships and villages.

Obviously, the principle of meritocracy doesn't free the leaders from petty politics. Like the office politicking that goes on in any organization, upcoming Chinese leaders jockey for favor and seek mentors to gain political power as well. Sometimes the horse trading and blackmailing between party members can smell pretty corrupt and even dangerous. Zhao Ziyang, a high Chinese government official who was third premier of the Peoples Republic of China (PRC), was put under house arrest when he encouraged the college students to demonstrate in Tiananmen Square. Similarly, Zhu Rongji, another once high-ranking Chinese government official who pressed for tough reforms, made many government insiders very unhappy. As a result, his right-hand man was thrown into jail on trumped-up charges to serve as a warning to Zhu not to push his reform agenda any further. Zhu understood the warning and publicly announced, "Whoever wants to kill me, go ahead." Luckily for Zhu, Jiang Zemin, China's president at the time, was powerful enough to protect Zhu. However, the damage was done, and Zhu became less aggressive with his reforms afterward in deference to the more conservative constituents within the Party. Unfortunately, just as no political system is free from corruption, no political system can exist without petty political interests interfering. But on balance, the enormous economic benefits to the Chinese citizens under this system of government have seemed to outweigh the drawbacks.

Another little-known fact is that not everyone can be admitted into the Chinese government. Government service in that country requires one to pass a national civil service exam by the time a person reaches 35 years of age. If one doesn't meet this requirement, then the person must stay in the private sector. This rule helps prevent the conflict of interest that happens when people go back and forth between the private sector and the public sector in what is known as a "revolving door." Although criticized, this practice has become widespread in the United States and other countries where private citizens get rewarded with coveted public sector jobs and vice versa as part of political patronage.[20]

While an argument can be made that the government could use the expertise of citizens who have worked in the private sector to govern effectively, this issue is somewhat moot in China. Chinese government officials can learn business skills running large state-owned enterprises in addition to running more traditional government organs such as regulatory agencies in subsequent stints of service. In this way, they learn traditional business skills without leaving the government and thus understand how to regulate those industries because they have experience on both sides of the coin. While the idea of officially mixing government and business sounds bad to free market supporters, the conflict is no different from the coexistence of the U.S. Postal Service and FedEx. Both a private and a public entity engaging in comparable activities can coexist without conflict of interest as long as the individuals are not going back and forth between the two. So when a Chinese public official is functioning as the president of a state-owned bank, there is little conflict if he does not use his connections, privileged information, and other advantages to exploit a subsequent role in a private bank. Lines are clearly delineated, and as an official, the scrutiny will remain high throughout the duration of his career.

But when government and business are enmeshed unofficially in the United States, there is more opportunity for corruption because it is less transparent. Wall Street bank bailouts and large multiyear defense contracts come to mind since private companies take advantage of government largesse while avoiding official government oversight over executive compensation and other private perks, even if they are pseudo government entities. In the book *Shadow Elite,* Janine Wedel explains in great detail how private actors regularly exploit the U.S. government with their own agendas because their unofficial and nontransparent roles let them escape scrutiny and supervision that would be mandatory if they were government employees.

Unquestioningly some Chinese government officials have also abused their positions of power in private enterprise for personal enrichment. However, minimizing conflicts of interest through more explicit government rules can be more beneficial than hurtful if the terms of engagement for government officials are clearly defined, accountable, and capable of advancing the public's interest.

## Qualifications, or Lack Thereof

Ethics violations arguably engender the most public outrage and distrust in government officials. When government officials who have been entrusted to work for the common good misuse their power by making decisions that only benefit certain special interest groups who later reward the same government officials with high-paying positions in the private sector, governments lose legitimacy among the broader citizenry. Even strong democracies can degenerate into plutocracies if the vigilance of the masses cannot keep up with the political maneuverings of the politically powerful who can manipulate government to their private advantage at the expense of the public.

Disturbingly, the United States is in danger of becoming such a plutocracy. For one, its list of abuses by public officials is already growing uncomfortably long. Even more disquieting, members from both dominant political parties can share in the blame:

- Dick Cheney left Halliburton as CEO to become vice president of the United States. He exploited 9/11 angst and the government's ineptness in capturing bin Laden to start a war in oil-rich Iraq against a dictator he knew could be blamed for anything by falsifying intelligence and persecuting the whistleblowers (Joe Wilson and Valerie Plame).[21] He then awarded a huge no-bid contract back to Halliburton to clean up his mess.[22]

- Hank Paulson left his position of CEO at Goldman Sachs to become treasury secretary. He played a principal role in setting up the Troubled Asset Relief Program (TARP) so that banks could access government funds. He also helped investment banks become commercial banks in order to qualify for support from the Federal Reserve.[23]

- Former Clinton treasury secretary Robert Rubin accepted a job as vice chairman of Citicorp after he left office. Coincidentally, he had helped Citicorp become the first U.S. bank to open an office in China while he was in office. He was rewarded with over $100 million for performing this "service."[24]

- Former Clinton treasury secretary Lawrence Summers was compensated with $5.2 million working for hedge fund D.E. Shaw after he oversaw the repeal of the Glass-Steagall Act of 1932. He also testified before Congress against the regulation of over-the-counter derivatives market by the Commodity Futures Trading Commission as part of his push to deregulate Wall Street, which led to the 2008 financial crisis. He was paid another $2.77 million in speaking fees from financial firms in 2008 just before he joined the Obama administration as the director of the White House National Economic Council.[25]

- Former Office of Management and Budget director (OMB) Peter Orszag left the Obama administration after less than two years of service to accept the position of vice chairman at Citicorp to replace Robert Rubin, who had stepped down after Citicorp received hundreds of billions of government bailout dollars from the financial crisis.[26]

- Former New York Federal Reserve Bank governor E. Gerald Corrigan accepted a position as vice chairman of Goldman Sachs. He likely played a role in preventing it from going bankrupt by ensuring the firm received help from the Federal Reserve.[27]

- Former Medicare and Medicaid Services chief Thomas Scully received an ethics waiver so he could negotiate jobs with private companies while working on the 2003 Medicare Prescription Drug Bill, which forced the government to pay full price to drug companies for all prescription drugs for Medicare recipients. Upon leaving office, he joined a financial services firm that profits from health care and the law firm Alston & Bird as their healthcare lobbyist.[28]

- Edward C. Aldridge Jr. joined the board of Lockheed Martin a month before he left the Pentagon and approved a $200 billion contract to build Lockheed planes. While on Lockheed's board, he was appointed by President Bush to chair a commission on space exploration policy. Lockheed coincidentally was one of NASA's biggest contractors and manager of the Space Shuttle program.[29]

- Former assistant secretary of Water and Science in the Department of the Interior, Bennett Raley, was previously a property rights lawyer who was also a corporate rights activist who lobbied to kill the Clean Water Act. While in office, he overrode federal protections in the Klamath River to provide agribusiness with more water, which killed thousands of endangered wild salmon.[30]

As a result, many Americans not only mistrust policymakers, but have begun to question American democracy, especially when they witness the incompetence and wrongdoing it systematically breeds regardless of party affiliation.[31] As a CBS/*NY Times* poll reported in 2010, a mere 19 percent of respondents trusted the government while 78 percent believed the government is run by special interests not for the benefit of the people.[32] There is nothing inherently democratic about a president using taxpayer money to hire cronies into the top echelons of government so that they can pad their résumés and profit from the system.

Hurricane Katrina and the Gulf oil spill reminded people how providing plum government positions as spoils to the politically connected can result in incompetent responses to unforeseen disasters. Not only were the authorities incompetent, some accused the authorities as being transgressors who facilitated the disasters by allowing companies to cut corners.[33] In the case of BP's oil spill, U.S. government officials gave BP the green light to drill without requiring them to follow proper precautionary measures.[34] Some see their lax regulatory attitudes as symptoms of regulatory capture by private industries.[35]

In addition to ethics violations, American politicians and policy makers currently do not need to prove minimum standards of competence for the jobs they seek. This is strange when most employers in both the private and public sectors specify qualifications of job applicants. It would seem logical that people who are charged with running the most powerful nation in the world have some basic knowledge of history, politics, economics, and hard sciences and that they reasonably demonstrate the ability to think critically. So when politicians like Senator Harry Reid publicly call Hu Jintao a "dictator" on television talk shows,[36] it is not only inaccurate, but rather embarrassing for the nation to reveal to the world the depth of ignorance that exists among the nation's top elected officials.

Chinese-style meritocracy is actually quite consistent with the American meritocratic culture. After all, lawyers must pass the bar exam, doctors must pass medical boards, and students still take SATs for college entrance. The fact that the United States exempts politicians and their political appointees from passing some basic competency test to qualify for office seems like an aberration when looked at from this angle. Though the U.S. Foreign Service administers a competency test for all its applicants, these positions are not elected and are not appointed. In general, the most senior government jobs are still appointed by the discretion of whoever is in elected office. These high-level and powerful positions are listed in the Plum Book. So although the rest of society has modernized to become more meritocratic, the century-old phrase "To the victor belong the spoils," still holds true for the powerful in government. While some may assert that the campaign process may prove whether one is medically and mentally fit, the process today tends to be a better barometer of one's ability to access the funds of wealthy donors, by promising that their interests will be met, as opposed to one's ability to represent the best interests of the public.

The framers of the Constitution used Senate confirmations of high-level presidential appointees as a way to prevent political patronage. However, in modern American politics, presidents have found ways to avoid the confirmation process by appointing low-level officials to run departments, officials whose positions don't require confirmation. Or they appoint people into top advisory positions—such as director of the White House National Economic Council—that may exert more power than formal heads of departments. Again, none of these positions require proving competency and/or a history of serving the public interest.

For the above reasons, the United States can and should consider adopting some of China's practices in encouraging more meritocracy in government, namely requiring a track record of serving the public interest, competency exams for anyone seeking public office, and limiting the revolving door. Determining the best criteria may take some time, and passing an amendment to accommodate these changes may take even longer, but these ideas are worth pursuing.

Independent committees can be tasked with creating the best criteria using experts from government, business, and academia across multiple institutions. The goal is to achieve some level of consensus on the basis of experience, integrity, and competence required of stewards of public office. Our current leadership selection is prone to groundless partisan attacks and mudslinging. But we can replace it with one that features more meaningful discussion and analysis of the most important issues by thoughtful individuals. Such a shift would make a big difference in the way our country governs itself. Even though candidates today are scrutinized by online blogs during campaigns, it is difficult for the average citizen to ascertain the veracity of statements made in such forums. A more uniform standard and reliable source such as a board consisting of nonpartisan experts confirming candidate qualifications could help build greater transparency and minimize the corruption that pervades modern American politics.

Another worthy practice to adopt is to make online policy evaluations available for citizens to rate job performances of their mayors and other elected representatives. These 360-degree evaluations could give everyone an opportunity to rate the progress of certain programs under a politician's purview. A tally of these survey results could be made available prior to Election Day. In this way, the United States can start rebuilding citizens' trust in government, which is currently low.[37]

China limits conflicts of interest by forbidding the revolving door practice that is prevalent in democratic countries. This policy warrants careful consideration as well. While a policy forbidding one to go back and forth between the public and private sectors is unlikely in the United States, Americans ought to demand certain protections against abusive and self-serving behavior among policymakers. Some politicians have come to treat public office as a moneymaking operation as opposed to selfless public service. Former president Bill Clinton has popularized the practice of accepting millions of dollars for making speeches. Although retired elected officials receiving honorariums for speaking is nothing new, the demand has risen significantly, as has the price tag. For lesser-known policymakers, the well-understood business model that many of them follow is to serve public office for a couple of terms and then retire as a lobbyist where they can earn millions from special interest groups and corporations who want laws passed in their favor.[38] For starters, there could be a rule that forbids policymakers from working for companies that benefited from their legislation for at least ten years after they leave office and does not allow them to receive any contracts that promise remuneration or positions during that entire period of time.

Alternatively (or additionally), the United States could mandate that in order to qualify for federal office, a candidate must have served in local government first or have donated substantial time performing qualified community service. The idea is to test a person's resolve and dedication to improving the community. We all know that smart, elite people do not necessarily have the public's interest at heart, so a long track record of accomplishments in public service or of volunteering for work that benefits the public interest should be mandatory for politicians and their political appointees.

Too often today, people occupy government positions because they want the spoils that come with holding high government office without giving to the community first. Other times, people take on government service because they have become bored with their corporate lives and want to experience the exhilarating feeling of power after they already have earned all the money they could want in their lifetimes. Restoring the credibility of government requires limiting the access of these people from holding high office. Or we could eliminate the incentives that attract these opportunists to government service. Imagine an election in which officials are chosen based on what they know and what they have done to deserve the position as opposed to who they know and their level of campaign fundraising—wouldn't that go a long way toward restoring trust in the current political process?

While it is possible that some may still find ways to work a system to their advantage, setting minimum standards to encourage more meritocracy in our democracy should be seen in a positive light. Such requirements could potentially shrink the pool of eligible candidates at first. But in the long run, this practice may actually increase the number of candidates since it could rekindle faith in our system, which might encourage more citizens to participate and engage. Charges of elitism seem groundless since its direct opposite—having no standards—could just as easily lead to undemocratic outcomes such as unenlightened mob rule. A balance must be struck between providing equal opportunity to hold office and barring unqualified talent from occupying positions inappropriate for their level of knowledge and experience. As long as our laws institute term limits, fair elections, and options for impeachment, elitist tendencies that lead to totalitarian control can be kept at bay. By keeping standards high for recruiting our nation's leaders, we will have a better chance of encouraging educated and civic-minded citizens to make a difference in our nation. Better to have people with the historical perspective, experience, competence, and selflessness in office than those who don't possess those qualities.

## Through the Looking Glass

As part of a push to ensure that the government is responsive to the public's needs, China's elites have also been promoting more access and transparency. One of the measures the government has undertaken is to publish the phone numbers of government officials—making them available to citizens—and assigning government employees to randomly call the numbers to make sure the government officials do indeed pick up the phone. As a venue to air grievances, the government also hosts public blogs so that citizens can write to government officials who can then respond. Shortly after the Sichuan earthquake of 2008 for instance, Premier Wen Jiaobao blogged about his visit to the disaster site, wrote about his grief, and responded to citizens' requests and questions online.

While the Obama campaign supporters made brilliant use of social media and the Web to get Obama elected, his administration was more elusive to the general public once he took office. Much of the transparency and integrity he promised to bring to Washington still has not come to fruition. The decision to bomb Libya, for instance, was not explained to the public until days after the bombing already occurred. Decisions to engage in warfare are significant enough that it was disappointing that the public was left in the dark for so long. While national security concerns are valid, they should not be applied carte blanche to the point where the public has virtually no say in such matters.

Finally, to underscore that meritocracy—not corruption—must rule the day in China, the Chinese leaders have encouraged their journalists to engage in investigative journalism. Overseeing more than a billion people who are experiencing rapid and dramatic social and economic changes is an incredibly daunting task. Chinese leaders simply do not have enough reliable enforcement officials to keep the peace everywhere and realize that journalists could play a decisive role in keeping government officials informed. When journalist Wang Keqin, who exposed illegal dealings in local financial markets, was protected from harm by China's then premier Zhu Rongji in February 2001, the press understood that they had gotten the green light to report on scandals and abuses that had previously been off limits.

Exposing corruption is not just limited to professional journalists in China. At an anti-corruption meeting where a superintendent was held up as a model government official, a photographer caught on camera the pack of cigarettes the superintendent took out of his pocket and put on the table. In China, the prices for cigarettes vary widely, ranging from 12 to 250 yuan a pack, which is roughly the equivalent of $1.50 to $50. The brand that this superintendent happened to be smoking was among the most expensive. Immediately,

Internet blogs were buzzing. Given the low level of his government salary, people wondered how it was possible for this government official to afford such a luxury unless he was getting bribed. The Chinese government investigated the case and reportedly found hundreds of thousands of dollars stashed all over the superintendent's apartment, including in the bathroom and under the mattresses. They even discovered that he kept several wives and bought different buildings to house them all. Needless to say, the scandal was broadcast, and the superintendent was arrested with the help of freelance journalism.

The increased freedom of speech and watchdog journalism, thanks to the Internet bulletin boards and government policies for more openness, has helped China inch toward a more democratic form of government. Although at the time of this writing the CCP still does not tolerate its citizens or journalists questioning or challenging the authority of the Chinese government as a whole, the fact that it encourages the unveiling of certain individuals who are corrupting the system and allows open debate on many policy issues represents enormous civil progress since Mao's rule only several decades ago.

As a result of such reform, journalism in China has entered a golden age, printing over 1,900 different newspapers with an annual circulation of almost 43 billion and importing 400 newspapers from around the world.[39] Additionally, millions of blogs and homegrown Twitter-like accounts called Weibo connect the billion Chinese people to opinions and events both near and far.

True, China has received much criticism for its highly publicized Internet censorship in which a network firewall selectively blocks content from certain IP addresses such as Google and Facebook. Americans interpret it as evidence that China is a threat to Western values. The Western press actually never presents China's reasons for doing so, and as all rational people know, there are always at least two sides to a story. According to my sources, the Chinese look at it this way: in the name of "security," the American government feels justified in imprisoning people without evidence or trial in Guantanamo

Bay and subjects airplane passengers flying in and out of the United States to full body scans at security checkpoints—despite its enormous invasion of privacy, harassment due to increased racial profiling, and possible increased health risks due to unnecessary X-rays. By the same token, China is justified in protecting its national security by blocking people who they view as potential subversives to national stability. When computer hackers shut down email accounts of Chinese dissidents, Google called it a suppression of freedom, but the Chinese government believes that these dissidents are no different from terrorists trying to cause social unrest.

Americans may find it hard to relate to fears of widespread revolt since we have not experienced such massive carnage on our soil since the Civil War, while the national chaos that accompanied the Cultural Revolution in China is more recent. True, Americans had the Watts riots and civil rights marches, but the unrest was more contained, and the turmoil was arguably less brutal. At least in America, there was not a wholesale rebellion of American children persecuting their own parents.

Seen in this context, it is more understandable that they liken these website shutdowns to sleeper cell raids by FBI officials or forcing people to go through full-body scanners at airports as safety precautions. In fact, the United States probably wouldn't behave any differently—or perhaps even more severely—if it were faced with a similar situation and concerns. After all, the FBI has been alleged by some documentary films to make arrests of people with Muslim backgrounds without solid proof. The main point is that China perceived these email accounts and websites as national security threats as opposed to any inherent opposition to open debate and rigorous journalism. Under international rules of sovereignty, China has complete discretion on how to handle threats within its own borders. These same rules allowed the United States to put up surveillance cameras all over New York City, engage in wiretapping, suspend habeas corpus, and pursue other activities that limit civil liberties. The United

States even renewed the Patriot Act after Osama bin Laden was killed. So unless all nations unite as one government with complete agreement on how to handle every situation, it would be difficult to judge the merits of another country's security procedures without a greater understanding of the broader context.

American journalists most certainly have in the past been watchdogs of government. But unfortunately, investigative journalism has been dramatically scaled back in America. Indeed, mainstream newspapers like the *Los Angeles Times* and the *Washington Post* have reduced their staff by as much as 60 percent since the advent of the Internet. Joe Nocera of the *New York Times* publicly stated at the 2011 Levy Conference that critiquing is difficult to do in news pages and almost all the commentary has been left to opinion-editorials where the vast majority of published opinions belong to the wealthy and the powerful.

## Hidden Agendas

Americans have also rarely questioned why Western press has been almost universally biased against China. Indeed, one doesn't even realize bias exists when only one viewpoint gets presented as if it were factual. The availability bias, a bias that develops when something is underreported or overreported, has colored Western perceptions of China because the incidence of negative reporting has overwhelmed reports of anything positive. I only became aware of this bias when I went to China and was surprised to learn that the Chinese were overwhelmingly in agreement that the West systematically painted them unfavorably. I saw that news about Tibet, for instance, was completely different from reports coming from the West, which tended to be critical of China. The Chinese reported that the Tibetan monks instigated the violence against the Han civilians with burning, looting, and killing in the Llasa violence of 2008. Chinese television even showed that the police who arrived to intervene were actually

Tibetans, not Han Chinese. The police also showed relative restraint in dealing with the violent protestors, but Western reporting did not pick up on these details. Instead, they painted the Chinese government as violent, when law enforcement was simply using tear gas and cattle prods to prevent the Tibetan violence against innocent civilians from escalating. It was a bit of a mystery to me as to why Western reporting was so uniformly negative until I had a conversation with Michael Massing, former executive editor and now contributing editor of the *Columbia Journalism Review*. Mr. Massing informed me that a reporter and friend of his who worked at the Beijing office of the *Wall Street Journal* told him that the editors in Washington regularly changed material information and opinions in his articles. Given the twelve-hour time difference, by the time his stories went to press in the West, the editors had found the time to replace all the Chinese interviews and quotes with statements from American talking heads who worked at think tanks promoting anti-China perspectives.

How widespread this practice is in American media could be anybody's guess, but according to Jill Swenson, a former journalism and communications professor at Ithaca College, this problem with corporate journalism is not unique to the question of China but has also happened in the reporting of Vietnam, as well as the reporting in Afghanistan. America's so-called free press suddenly seems more like propaganda cleverly disguised, the same way American political bribery is cleverly disguised with corporate handouts of top jobs and compensation.

The information Mr. Massing passed on is sadly consistent with other stories of distortions by American mainstream media. Tom Avitabile, senior vice president of Sid Paterson Advertising and former employee at NBC News, shared with me his experience working in the NBC newsroom. While the Vietnam War was raging, a freelance cameraman in the warzone filmed and sent back a videotape of American soldiers to the studios for airing. Before the clip was shown, the editor cut out the scene in which four American soldiers walked right into a landmine that blew up, throwing into the air their dismembered body parts. The editor said aloud, "Mr. and Mrs. Front Porch in Nebraska don't need to see this." Tom, who wished he could have stolen the cut reel, believed that the Vietnam War would have ended sooner had the war not been sanitized by the media. If the inhumanity of war was more apparent to the American people, the pressure to end it sooner probably would have been greater.

Even I have my own disappointing media experiences to share. When then treasury secretary Hank Paulson asked the Congress to give him $700 billion to bail out the banks, I agreed to a two-hour interview with CBS three days before Congress was scheduled to vote on the matter. During the two hours, I explained the notion of regulatory capture and talked about how taxpayers were getting a raw deal in multiple ways. I asked the producer if my interview could air the following day given that the topic was of enormous national importance and consequence, and he promised he would. However, the interview, which was reduced to a mere sound bite, did not air until the morning of the vote, giving Americans no time to digest the arguments and no opportunity to call their Congressmen to block the vote. When I phoned the producer to find out why they didn't air the interview sooner, he replied that the decision was made by a senior executive. His assistant, a young reporter, later confided to me over the phone that despite efforts on their part to push the studio to do more responsible reporting, the top-level staff always resisted, often he believed due to political reasons. Sadly, I discovered that this assistant was later fired. While the executive never explained why my interview was not aired in its entirety, I believe that my statements were in opposition to points upon which senior media executives and policymakers were aligned.

Americans and the world deserve better. Good governance, democratic or authoritarian, cannot last without responsible journalism that reports with accuracy, uncovers corruption, and offers a balance of opinions. Good journalism acts as the canary in the coalmine, providing fair warning before real trouble brews. However, a free independent press is hard to maintain unless genuine competition exists and doesn't become slave to special interests. In democracies UK, Sweden, and Germany, journalism is government subsidized. The BBC is arguably better than all the U.S. broadcast networks because of its broad coverage and factual accuracy. By setting the bar, the BBC forces other private British media to match its high journalistic standards in order to compete and therefore discourages them from racing to the bottom by cutting corners for the sake of pure profits.

More importantly, aside from the debate over whether only commercial versus government-subsidized journalism will yield the best outcome for a democracy, journalism backed by any source should only be allowed to report the truth and not mislead viewers by mislabeling entertainment as journalistic content. Ever since the Fairness Doctrine was repealed in 1987, news agencies repeatedly blur the distinction between political editorializing and straight facts. Canada prohibits broadcast news from airing misleading or false information within their borders. America would do well to reinstate the same standards.

Furthermore, all policy advice should be published in full and debated at length in public so that everyone who is eligible to vote understands both the policy disadvantages as well as the advantages. Voters should also know who is supporting certain policies so that hidden agendas no longer remain hidden. The best solutions to complex problems cannot be communicated effectively, let alone understood in its entirety, in sound bites and unsubstantiated opinions.

Unfortunately, the current trend toward more entertainment in journalism in order to sell more advertising doesn't bode well for informed public discourse necessary for healthy democratic rule. Media executives already have been engaging in a decade-long decimation of their foreign bureaus. They also prefer to air talk show hosts who express extreme political views—rather than more reasonable political dialogue—in order to boost ratings and profits at the expense of integrity.

It is politically and practically difficult to require commercial

American media to operate differently in the age of the Internet when they have finally found a profitable business model. An easier alternative to this problem of hidden agendas and compromised journalism would be to support WikiLeaks and similar organizations. Americans should demand that the American government let Julian Assange and others like him to run their operations unhindered. WikiLeaks is one of the most widely read journalistic publishers that does not have a commercial interest, making it a powerful watchdog with an agenda that is transparent and free of conflicts of interest. WikiLeaks claims it has been flooded with requests from individuals to submit information without compensation, lending further support that whistleblowers everywhere are not being heard in mainstream media. By blocking WikiLeaks, the U.S. government sabotages the First Amendment right to freedom of speech and Article 19 of the Universal Declaration of Human Rights recognized in human rights law.

It is interesting to note that in the aftermath of the WikiLeaks affair, Western commentators suddenly became less vocal in their assertions that China needed to offer its citizens better transparency. Perhaps they realized that criticizing China in such a way would risk sounding too hypocritical of American policies. The truth is that every country engages in censorship whether it admits it or not, and every country's leaders have information they will determine needs to be confidential for national security reasons, including the United States. But undoubtedly, for a government to win the confidence of the population, a certain amount of transparency is required. If the Chinese have made some progress with their reforms in regards to greater openness, Americans should and must find the inspiration and leadership to press for even more at home.

## It's a Party

One common misconception about China is that because it is a one-party system, true debate and dissension don't exist. The reality is that within the Party, there is an inner bipartisanship in which two informal factions provide a semblance of checks and balances to China's politics. Those in the elitist faction, often known as *princelings,* refer to the policymakers who benefited from family ties early in their careers that led to rapid career advancement. Though they still are subject to the same meritocratic reviews as other government officials, they tend to have built-in mentors. Typically they represent the interests of citizens living in the richer, coastal cities of China. The populist faction or *tuanpai* refer to those members who came from more humble backgrounds. Tuanpai folks tend to fight for resources for the poorer inland regions. While both factions share the same fundamental goals—ensuring the survival of the Party and a strong stable China—they are continuously forced to cooperate and compromise on competing policies and priorities in order to form a collective leadership that incorporates the needs of disparate social and geographic constituencies.

China's leaders and other policymakers frequently disagree and debate each other on every issue ranging from environmental protection to redistribution of resources. According to Michael Pettis, who writes a regular blog from Beijing as a Peking University professor:

> It is simply not true that Chinese scholars are largely cheerleaders for China's development policies, and certainly not to the extent that foreign observers tend to be. In fact the discussion within China is far more sophisticated, and fierce, than anything outside the country, although the ferocity of the debate is often disguised by a certain shyness on the part of most of the mainstream Chinese press.

He goes on to cite various entries by the *People's Daily, East Asia Forum, South China Morning Post, Caing,* and others that support his assertion. Whereas almost all the hotly debated issues facing government officials used to be shielded from the public, China's media now constantly air dissenting points of view so that multiple sides are heard. On any given day, CCTV, China's official news station, broadcasts the opinions of pundits who weigh in on everything from foreign policy to the economy.

The final decisions of national importance are still decided by just a handful of the top leaders of the nation who have access to all the brightest minds in the country, but rarely do their decisions come as a surprise to the Chinese general public. Indeed, the Party leadership prefers to reach consensus after careful analysis of the facts and lively debate over the differences in opinion. The Chinese officials maintain that a benefit to having a one-party system is that it frees the government leaders from election-driven thinking and allows them to focus on long-term strategic planning. Precious time and money wouldn't need to be wasted on campaign activities. They have seen how politicians in Taiwan as well as in the United States relinquish their duty to serve the public interest because they are so busy repaying all their election debts to their campaign supporters.

According to the article "Begging for Bucks," written by Peter Francia and Paul Herrnson in *Campaigns and Elections:*

> One survey in the United States found that 23 percent of candidates for statewide office surveyed say that they spent *more than half* of their scheduled time raising money. Over half of all candidates surveyed spent at least ¼ of their time on fundraising. The tactics used can include direct mail solicitation, attempts to encourage supporters to contribute via the Internet, direct solicitation from the candidate, and events specifically for the purpose of fundraising, or other activities.[40]

*OpenSecrets.org* also reported that "For the first time ever in U.S. history, the candidates for president raised more than $1 billion." In the United States, total fundraising reached $2.4 billion in the 2008 campaign.[41] This is $2.4 billion that didn't go into education, infrastructure, and scientific research that can directly benefit the general public. Instead, it went into the pockets of wealthy media executives, lobbyists, public relations, and a whole host of other professionals who profit from election-year entertainment.

But despite the obvious waste of resources around elections, the United States will never become a one-party state, even if the two parties today are more alike in substance than in form. The time and

money spent on election campaigning at the expense of real governance and policy leadership will continue to be an Achilles heel if
not addressed in some way. While the United States has engaged in a
number of campaign finance reforms, none get to the root of the problem. Though some reformers see the Supreme Court ruling in *Citizens
United* (2010)—which allows unrestricted corporate advertising in
election campaigns—as a huge setback, it actually evens the playing
field so that political action committees are not the only ones who
can spend unlimited amounts of money influencing elections. The
real culprit is the large amount of money needed for media advertising in the first place. Thirty-second commercials on television could
run into the millions and little information is communicated other
than name recognition. Reforming the process would require making
it easier for candidates to run without having to rely on money. One
solution is to require television networks to air more public debates
between candidates as a public service. Capping the amount of advertising dollars candidates are allowed to spend could be another. Finding a way so that candidates can win on their merits as opposed to
depending solely on their ability to access more campaign funds than
their rivals would be a huge step toward a meritocratic democracy.

However, it will be difficult, if not impossible, to get Congress to
change a system that gives them income security. According to the
Campaign Finance Institute, Congress raised $447 million between
January 2007 and March 2008, and less than 10 percent came from
donations less than $200. If we are unable to limit the amount of
money spent in the election process, Harvard law professor Lawrence
Lessig has advocated another way to level the playing field between
individual donations and corporate donations to political campaigns:
give every eligible voter $50 of government money to contribute to
any candidate. This would create a total of $6 billion for every elec-
tion, enough to offset the current corporate campaign contributions.
While $6 billion sounds like an enormous sum of money to be wasted
on election activities, it is a small amount when compared to the $89

billion Congress has given to corporate welfare in response to corporate campaign contributions.[42] Since our democracy today responds essentially to "one dollar, one vote" as opposed to "one person, one vote," giving citizens the ability to cast their votes with money would even out the playing field against corporate interests who are regularly large campaign contributors.

Another common concern about China's one-party state involves the ability of citizens to keep their government officials accountable if they cannot be voted out of office. Even if investigative journalism uncovers corruption and/or ineptitude, what can ensure that proper action is taken to rectify the problems? As I mentioned before, China's leaders are extremely sensitive to the fact that they could be removed from power if their legitimacy ever came into question. With tens of millions of migrant workers constantly looking for work in China's big cities, it wouldn't take much for an uprising to overwhelm security forces and cause complete chaos in the country. The Chinese have a saying that "swatting flies is easier than catching tigers," meaning that anti-corruption campaigns by government officials tend to go after the less powerful violators while letting the most powerful criminals run free. If enough of society believes this is true, the government will be quickly seen as corrupt and illegitimate. Because the prospect of being deposed keeps the Chinese leaders awake at night, they have become increasingly forceful and more willing to punish high-level officials in addition to mid-level officers who have been caught in corruption cases in recent years. The former vice mayor of Beijing and organizer of the Beijing Olympics was sentenced to death after it was discovered that he had accepted a million dollars in bribes. The regulators responsible for food safety likewise faced execution over the tainted milk scandal in the fall of 2008 where allegations were made that milk powder was tainted with the chemical melamine.

Clearly, no corruption should be regarded as a capital crime, so Beijing must find a better balance between discouraging corruption and safeguarding the sanctity of human life. Ironically, Beijing's responses have made it *too* democratic because they so readily follow Chinese public opinion, which supports the use of capital punishment to deter corruption.

But whether we agree with capital punishment or not, the key takeaway is that politicians need to be motivated to work for the common good. If U.S. politicians are too complacent because they have the support of the party machine and assume voters don't pay much attention to governing except during election time, the danger is that little or nothing gets accomplished in government. U.S. politicians in general are too preoccupied with managing their public relations image for their next election and tend to worry more about being caught with a prostitute than with failing to get an important piece of legislation passed. Even if U.S. politicians are voted out of office or asked to resign due to scandals, they often get political cover like a presidential pardon so that the consequences are minor for unacceptable behavior. During Reagan's era, he pardoned or rescinded the convictions of 393 people. Under Bill Clinton, the number was 396.[43]

Chinese leaders cite that a paramount benefit of their system is that they don't have to worry about being disqualified from serving if they represent a minority voice or hold an unpopular opinion. This principle of no dismissal for difference of opinion is similar to the reason that tenure was created to protect university professors in America from being fired over political rather than performance reasons. This provision can also make it possible to protect minority groups that don't have the financial resources to hire expensive lobbyists.

Indeed, the Chinese genuinely view their way of government as more democratic than Western democracy in the ideal sense of serving the public. They hold firmly to the belief that despite being the only party in power, they can be deposed anytime by an angry public if they fail to serve the nation's long-term interests. The chaos under Mao during the Cultural Revolution remains an augury that dense populations can be incited to destroy any vestiges of the establishment swiftly and totally. To the Chinese leaders, the lesson of the

Cultural Revolution is that the party must be united in serving the people (as opposed to ideology) and resolute in suppressing would-be minority troublemakers who can derail their important mission to eradicate poverty by turning popular movements easily into irrational mob rule. They see their one-party state today as very different from the one in the 1960s. Thus, to remain in power implies a vote of confidence from the majority of the population.

While a majority of Americans have difficulty comprehending how a one-party system can be democratic, the two-party system in America today offers fundamentally no substantial choice to voters either. Fareed Zakaria states in his book *Future of Freedom* that "political parties have no real significance in America today."[44] Using George Bush as a modern example to illustrate this point, he says, "He had the two things you need in a partyless system—name recognition and a fundraising machine."[45] This fundraising machine has primarily transferred the power of politics to a new class of elites consisting of professional consultants, lobbyists, pollsters, and activists. The result is that the American political system has produced a "hidden elite, unaccountable, unresponsive, and often unconcerned with any larger public interest."[46] Moreover, the inability of third-party candidates to get elected in American politics further highlights the point that the two-party system has become substantially one large monopoly party of the rich masquerading as two parties that more or less support the same establishment.

## Dealing with Fat Cats

The debate over whether democracy needs one, two, three, or more parties to achieve proper representation of the public interest misses the bigger question—what conditions are required to create a system that will be the most proactive in planning for a sustainable future for the greatest number of people? The conditions should include a way to pick the most suitable and qualified individuals to take the helm while simultaneously holding them directly accountable for all the results in a system that gives them instant and direct feedback of outcomes. Nobody knows when the perfect system of government will be invented. But I posit that a more effective and enlightened form of government would likely include best practices from both United States and China. Though Winston Churchill famously said, "Democracy is the worst form of government except all those other forms that have been tried," I suggest that unless we believe human evolution has stopped, we must continue to strive to develop a better system. Hank Paulson, former Treasury Secretary under the Bush administration, admitted at the 2010 Rodman and Renshaw Investment Conference in New York that the "U.S. always needs a crisis to make necessary changes." He believed that the multiple brewing crises in social security entitlements, healthcare, and military overspending will cause another financial crisis in the United States within the next ten years and that nothing will be done to avert the disasters. Why is this state of affairs acceptable or even tolerable? Deep down, we know that we must do better.

The Founding Fathers stated in the Constitution that our republic must be dependent on the people in order for it to function properly. As Martin Gilens, a professor at Princeton, has pointed out, there is a vast discrepancy in U.S. democracy in which policy follows the funders, not the Founders. The system is corrupted, but the solution lies in attacking its source, which is money. Recognizing this problem, Buddy Roemer, a former Louisiana governor who announced he would be running in the 2012 election for president of the United States, has publicly stated that he will not accept any political action committee (PAC) money because "our nation needs a president who is free to lead." His courageous example harkens back to FDR who stated in 1939 that he needed to "convince a reluctant nation to wage a war to save democracy." Today's war is not against fascists, but against funders corrupting the democratic system. Politicians who are dependent on the rich to get elected can't hear what the vast majority of Americans are saying.

To conclude, the freedoms and rights that the Chinese people now enjoy have increased tenfold from the time under Mao, and the reforms for human rights in China continue to move along a democratic trajectory. After all, it took Europe centuries to develop democracy, and the United States about one hundred years to eliminate slavery. In China, it has taken a mere thirty years for half a billion of its citizens to enjoy a relatively modern state of existence. China's system of meritocracy can serve as a wakeup call to Western capitalists to update its democracy so that it can be more effective and responsive to the public interest.

Democracy, defined as the rights of life, liberty, and the pursuit of happiness for all people, is only as successful as people make it. The institutions for a democracy can assume various forms, ranging from China's one-party system to parliamentary elections for multiple parties. But what must be preserved is the ability of any system to answer its citizens legitimately. As the numerous polls have shown, U.S. politicians have continually and consistently disappointed Americans, a state of affairs that indicates a systemic problem with American democracy. We have let mediocrity and conflicts of interest interfere with the idealistic aims of our nation, a situation that can be corrected. The content of our democratic conversation needs to be lifted to a higher level of discourse, but that cannot happen until we rethink how we put people in office. If the United States is serious about any policy reform, it must begin by institutionalizing more meritocracy into government and making politicians more accountable to the people rather than to major funders. Government of the people, by the people, for the people—must be restored to its original state in order for democracy to be saved. Leon Trotsky wrote that the whole crisis of history can be summed up as a crisis of leadership.[47] Let's try to avoid such a crisis in the United States by modifying our system so that it ensures we can consistently find the best leaders first.

# 4
# Five-Year Plans

We go where our vision is.   —JOSEPH MURPHY

## Short-Term Disease

Ask a person on the street what he or she plans to do or be in five years and the likely reaction you will receive is a blank face. The truth is that most people just don't envision themselves, let alone make plans, that far into the future. Research has shown that many often confuse medium-term with long-term tradeoffs and have difficulty with delayed gratification. A famous study by Walter Mischel, commonly referred to as the Stanford marshmallow experiment, showed that children who were able to refrain from eating a marshmallow in front of them—knowing that they would be rewarded with two later—were more likely to succeed as adults. Unfortunately, most of the children chose to eat the marshmallow immediately, giving up the prospect of receiving more at a later time. Despite the lessons taught in fables like Aesop's "The Ant and the Grasshopper," impatience for immediate pleasures often gets the better of us, and procrastination of undesirable tasks is common.

Multiplied over millions of people, we can delay to act as a society until disaster comes knocking on our door. The notion of energy conservation, for example, is an idea many embrace, but few actually find the discipline to execute. As a result, the compound annual growth rate of America's national energy consumption has been 0.4 percent from 2000 to 2009, according to the statistical energy review yearbook published by Enerdata in 2010.

Likewise, the southern economies of Europe have been facing the likelihood of sovereign default and potential expulsion from the Eurozone unless they can increase their productivity and reduce their government spending in order to balance their fiscal budgets. But even after numerous bailouts and many public demonstrations by angry citizens, these countries are still struggling to pay the price of austerity measures such as postponed retirement benefits and reduced government pay. In the view of some citizens, the costs of being part of the European Union (EU) now seem to overshadow the benefits of such membership. Reform should have taken place much sooner.

Given both the proclivity of Americans to favor short-term rewards and our current system of democracy, which records the thoughts and mandates of the voting population, the ability to meet long-term goals and objectives could be compromised. In addition, other issues naturally related to preparations for the future include problems of objectivity, judgment, and other human shortcomings. All of these, if left to the whims of an entire population, may consistently fail to put the long-term interests as a priority.

Moreover, with two- and four-year election cycles, politicians who are supposed to help craft long-term policies of the country are instead systematically forced to think about the short- and medium-term issues of staying in office and being reelected. They realize that pleasing their constituents with promises of quick fixes, like bigger tax cuts across the board, is a more effective way to win elections than vowing long-term solutions to deep, structural problems like overhauling the entire tax code.

While some studies, as reported by James Surowiecki in his book *The Wisdom of Crowds,* have shown that large numbers of people can usually outsmart an expert in guessing the correct answers to questions, the studies do not measure what happens in real life when most choices do not provide clear-cut right and wrong answers. Most national policies would produce outcomes that lie along a continuum of gray possibilities in which the tradeoffs and benefits of one set of policies over another would require much more advanced analysis and knowledge. And if everyone in the sample population is ignorant or has been methodically misinformed about something, it matters not if you ask 100,000 people or 10. As Nassim Taleb stated in his book *The Black Swan: The Impact of the Highly Improbable,* everyone in Europe used to assume all swans were white because no one had gone abroad and seen that black swans existed in another part of the world.[1]

The need to think past our collective mental predisposition for short-term gains due to shortsightedness is crucial. It has been shown that instinct doesn't work particularly well in the complexities of the modern world when people are confronted with millions of choices that are associated with millions of consequences. As Barry Schwartz pointed out in his book *The Paradox of Choice: Why More Is Less,* when faced with too many options, people tend to become less thoughtful and reflective of any particular decision and of the likely short- and long-range consequences.[2] A more systematic plan should be in place that encourages working together to make good decisions for the long term and accounts for the human temptation to succumb to short-term needs. A system of checks and balances is in order, and one with carrots and sticks would be ideal.

## Back to the Future

China's leaders have used a partial solution to address this problem of short-term thinking. Borrowing the idea from the former Soviet Union, party members through the central committee and national congresses collectively shape Five-Year Plans as part of their national goal-setting exercise for economic and social initiatives. These plans create benchmarks to evaluate the performance of the government and are intended to inform the public of the Party's strategies for economic development, growth targets, and reforms. They are further developed, executed, and monitored by the various ministries who report back to the Party congresses when they meet every year for two weeks.

These plans receive critical input from all factions of the Communist Party, and after much deliberation, they are published for the world to see as a way to provide transparency. But unlike empty campaign promises, these plans are treated like law and taken seriously by all members of the Party. When a goal is articulated in a Five-Year Plan, chances of the nation meeting it within five years is a near certainty, though on occasion, some goals are met earlier and others may be dropped.

The Five-Year Plan in many ways is similar to a strategic plan that a U.S. corporation would create. It is a document that provides a road map and focuses the discussion and analyses of all responsible parties when real results deviate from the optimum targets. But instead of meeting shareholder demands, these proposals incorporate the values, hopes, and demands of the population so that the Party is accountable to its own citizens the way a democracy should be. Each five-year plan has thus dealt with comprehensive aspects that matter to human development: capital goods, consumer goods, agriculture, transportation, communications, health, education, and welfare. The emphasis varies, but the primary elements remain largely the same.

As an example, China's Eleventh Five-Year plan spanning the years 2006–2010 addressed the following measurable goals:

*Economic growth*
1. GDP up 7.5 percent annually from 18.2 trillion yuan in 2005 to 26.1 trillion yuan in 2010
2. Per capita GDP up 6.6 percent annually from 13,985 yuan in 2005 to 19,270 yuan in 2010

*Economic structure*
1. Share of service industry's value added to GDP up from 40.3 percent in 2005 to 43.3 percent in 2010

2. Share of employment in service industry up from 31.3 percent in 2005 to 35.3 percent in 2010

3. Share of research and development (R&D) spending out of total GDP up from 1.3 percent in 2005 to 2 percent in 2010

4. Urbanization rate up from 43 percent in 2005 to 47 percent in 2010

*Population, resources, environment*

1. Population up from less than 1.31 billion in 2005 to 1.36 billion in 2010

2. Energy consumption per unit of GDP down 20 percent in five years

3. Water consumption per unit of industrial added value down 30 percent in five years

4. Coefficient of effective use of water for irrigation up from 0.45 percent in 2005 to 0.5 percent in 2010

5. Rate of comprehensive use of solid industrial waste up from 55.8 percent in 2005 to 60 percent in 2010

6. Total acreage of cultivated land down from 122 million hectares in 2005 to 120 million in 2010

7. Total discharge of major pollutants down 10 percent in five years

8. Forest coverage up from 18.2 percent in 2005 to 20 percent in 2010

*Public service, people's life*

1. Term of education per capita up from 8.5 years in 2005 to 9 years in 2010

2. Coverage of urban basic old-age pension up from 174 million people in 2005 to 223 million people in 2010

3. Coverage of the new rural cooperative medical care system up from 23.5 percent in 2005 to over 80 percent in 2010

4. New jobs created for urban residents reaching 45 million in five years

5. Number of rural laborers transferred to non-agriculture sectors reaching 45 million in five years

6. Per capita disposable income of urban residents up 5 percent annually in five years, from 10,493 yuan in 2005 to 13,390 yuan in 2010

7. Per capita net income of rural residents up 5 percent annually in five years, from 3,255 yuan in 2005 to 4,150 yuan in 2010

The Twelfth Five-Year Plan of 2011–2015, which was approved in 2011 by the National Congress, articulates the importance of addressing rising wealth inequality and championing an environment for more sustainable growth. The document proposes more equitable wealth distribution, increased domestic consumption, and improved social programs, such as providing larger safety nets for the unemployed and elderly. The plan represents China's efforts to rebalance its economy by shifting emphasis from investment toward consumption and from urban and coastal growth toward rural and inland development. The plan also reiterates objectives articulated in the Eleventh Five-Year Plan to improve environmental protection and accelerate the process of reform, which includes transforming its metropolitan areas into international financial hubs.

These long-term plans have historically been met with derision by the West because they were associated with the Soviet system of central planning, which led to their downfall. Even during the Mao years in China, officials lied about productivity in the Communist economic system because meeting the goals of the five-year plans took top priority as a measure of progress toward a Communist utopia. Numbers were systematically fudged when production failed to meet targets set by the state. The rapid disintegration of the Soviet Union and of Mao's Great Leap Forward convinced Westerners that democratic capitalism proved resoundingly to be the best economic and political system.

## Capitalism with Chinese Characteristics

China has learned to incorporate market capitalism into the central planning process so that market forces can be used to help rather than hinder the state achieve its development goals. Rather than suppress human nature and deny the natural urge for individuals to succeed and differentiate themselves from others, the Party harnessed the power of human ambition. China created an environment that triggered human productivity to be unleashed in the short term by allowing private businesses to keep profits while the state maintained a watchful eye on the country's long-term goals in a constant feedback loop about the overall economy and state of affairs. The leaders observe whether their policies achieve the desired effects. If not, they revise them.

The beauty of China's system is that market forces are permitted to flourish at the corporate and retail level, but the government's role is to make decisions independent of fleeting considerations like returns on investment. China's leaders realize that major purchases such as infrastructure require enormous sums of capital and long payoff periods, risks that private entities rarely undertake. The government thus fills the role where markets fail to work, providing an invaluable service to society.

A recent example of China's courage to pursue comprehensive strategies is its investments in high-speed railroads.[3] As soon as the rail lines were built, China invited members of the Western press to ride them. The media duly noted that the trains were largely empty, which is precisely the reason these trains had not received private funding in the United States. Commuter traffic can be erratic, and ticket pricing could be an issue for private investors who would want a quick return on their investment. However, since the enduring sustainability of the economy—not profit and returns on investment—is the top consideration for the Chinese government, it had no problem making the outlay of billions of dollars to build the rail system. The government believes that over time, the trains will be fully utilized as the population continues to migrate to the cities that are connected by the trains.

This combination of central planning at the government level and market forces for the private sector has proven to be powerful and a bit of a competitive advantage for Chinese companies. Since the Party accepts accountability for the plan, the government has been consistently able to make significant advancements in public infrastructure, both hard and soft (*hard* referring to tangible items such as bridges and roads and *soft* referring to intangible items such as education and pension systems), as well as effect necessary course corrections. Despite historically widespread corruption at the local level, Party policy is at least predictable. With this added certainty, Chinese companies know what to expect from the government and are able to move forward with their own operations accordingly.

## U.S. Government Fogginess

In contrast, there is less certainty today about what the U.S. government will do since its policies can be subject to a fickle Congress engaged more in politics than in passing legislation. Through logrolling, filibusters, and other political shenanigans, standoffs between the two parties have largely resulted in a nation of decaying infrastructure where most electrical grids and bridges have not been upgraded for almost a century.[4] Not only are ordinary citizens denied the means to improve their everyday productivity, but even corporate officials are left in limbo because they don't know whether to prepare for changes or not. According to a former staffer who requested anonymity, Hillary Clinton's policy statements when she served as Senator of New York were based on short-term public opinion polls that her staffers frequently conducted as opposed to articulating any convictions of her own. So when domestic lawmakers' rhetoric vacillates with public opinion, U.S. companies often find themselves disadvantaged vis á vis their foreign competitors, who benefit from a more stable outlook and reliable government.

A recent example of U.S. uncertainty at its best is the passage of the Financial Reform Act of 2010 (the Dodd-Frank Act). Although the document is over 2000 pages, the law does not spell out specific changes that financial services companies must make; much of the detailed rule making will be subject to the discretion of special commissions and taskforces that at the time of this writing haven't even been funded and assigned. This continuous state of limbo causes end-less confusion, wasting valuable time of executives who would prefer to engage in strategic planning over devoting their time to ensuring they meet new compliance standards.

America's lack of long-term planning also makes it difficult for the Chinese to work with U.S. government officials. In negotiations, foreign leaders never quite know whether the treaties they negotiate will ever get passed by Congress. Bilateral or multilateral agreements such as the Kyoto Protocol to address global issues are always at risk when those representing the United States don't have the authority to implement them or when changes in leadership can reverse hard-won gains. For foreign governments that are on the receiving end of America's inability to make long-term commitments, the experience is nothing short of frustrating.

The closest thing to a Five-Year Plan that the United States has now is probably the U.S. federal budget. The budget process starts with the Office of Management and Budget (OMB) making economic forecasts based on various assumptions such as population growth and antici-pated government revenue. Next OMB projects either surpluses or deficits and recommends allocations or ways to address gaps when the budget is not balanced. However, these funds do not have per-formance goals attached to them. Although accessing federal funds at times requires jumping over many hurdles of bureaucracy, which are usually designed to limit disbursements to qualified applicants, this system does not necessarily assign targets or ensure performance. It would be the equivalent of a CEO giving out money to different departments without holding any of them accountable for results that would help the company achieve its goals. If the United States wants to rein in runaway Medicaid costs for example, measurable goals, like reducing the number of unwanted teenage pregnancies, might improve the ability to get the right resources in place to achieve desirable objectives.

The sad truth is that the U.S. government used to be more proactive and forward looking. The New Deal was a great example of this. The Hoover Dam and the Golden Gate Bridge were built during the Great Depression when the nation was suffering the most. Plans for interstate highways were also drawn up then. Had the country not made such large investments in its infrastructure, the subsequent boom in the decades leading up to the 21st century probably would have never been as strong as it was, considering economic prosperity depended on goods being moved all across the nation on these highways. Through the leadership of Franklin D. Roosevelt and other individuals in that generation, America developed the political will to act beyond the short term. Was it a one-time fluke or does the United States have the ability to develop the political will to act in its long-term interests again?

## Market Myopia

Unfortunately, this shortsightedness in outlook and behavior in a democratic capitalist system infects not just the government, but also private industry. The prevalence of short-term stock price movements contributes heavily to the phenomenon of making decisions based on immediate outcomes, or what some refer to as *short-termism*. Many public companies have officers whose compensation is tied to earnings-per-share calculations.

While this compensation scheme was initially meant to align managers with the owners or shareholders for the benefit of the company, this practice inadvertently encouraged decision making based on short-term considerations because of the rise of hedge funds, and due to day traders and other shareholders, who are all more interested in quick profits than in enduring stakes in companies. As a result, these investors developed outsized influence in the stock markets. By early 2000, CB Lee, an employee at SAC Capital, stated that his hedge fund alone contributed almost 10 percent of daily volume on the NYSE. Within a decade, high-frequency trading was so prevalent that a single stock order sent the Dow plummeting almost 1,000 points within minutes for what is now famously known as the *Flash Crash* of May 6, 2010. Tying performance of a company to the volatility of the stock market inevitably leads to a greater emphasis on higher quarterly earnings reports at the expense of encouraging a more consistent, abiding approach. A byproduct of such short-term focus was shorter tenures across industries for CEOs because they couldn't meet the impossibly high standards of delivering consistent growth every single quarter without incurring some investment expenses that would hurt profits in the short run.

Maintaining the ideology that the market is always right and the voter is always right begs the question of whether the democratic capitalist system is capable of systematically incorporating anything comparable to a Five-Year Plan.

## Government Band-Aids

One thought is to leave more planning to bureaucrats as opposed to elected officials and appointed officers. Indeed, plenty of officials already carry over from administration to administration within agencies, and sometimes these individuals assist lawmakers, though it is up to the lawmakers to come to them as resources. Bureaucrats who are hired by the federal government to perform specific duties should have the required knowledge and the longevity of tenure to oversee longer-term policy initiatives. So instead of the traditional method of drafting a bill in Congress, the bureaucrats would craft the necessary language of the bill, free from the influence of lobbyists who have been hired to affect the voting of politicians. This may require amending the Constitution so that a bill would be permitted to become law if both Houses fail to veto it. In other words, the process would happen in reverse: policies would become laws by default when politicians fail to cooperate.

This process would have its own set of problems—namely, too

much power invested in people who are not elected. But the situation is not so different from what happens today since most legislation is written by lobbyists, who are clearly not elected. The difference would be that the politicians who are now held accountable for bills they pass would escape that responsibility, possibly incurring more serious damage if corrupt elite interests stepped in to advance their own measures. While this reverse process has already been used in some legislative situations and has advocates like the former OMB director, Peter Orszag, it could become more widespread if some U.S. policymakers and constituents become sufficiently frustrated and impatient with the current process of legal sausage making. But whether bureaucrats or lobbyists write policy, Congress still has to vote on the measures. The heart of the problem is that Congress feels more accountable to the lobbyists than to the American citizens.

Another thought is to create capital budgets separate from expense budgets so that politicians can be held accountable to long-term investments separately from the vicissitudes of short-term entitlement handouts. By separating the expense items that do not lead to future productivity, like unemployment benefits, from investments that can lead to the country's increased productivity, such as smart electricity grids, more transparency is introduced in the government budgeting process, which can potentially lead to better allocation of government resources.

The Obama administration has advocated the idea of a U.S. bank chartered specifically to make infrastructure loans, which is not so different from the policy banks of China.[5] Before the introduction of Western reforms, China's banking system was dominated by four large state-owned banks that conducted all its lending based on state directives. All these banks had mandates to provide funds for government projects. While these four banks are now largely commercial entities, which are more driven to make profitable loans than before the reforms took place, the Chinese government still owns the majority of shares and can issue directives to banks to loan for specific infrastructure projects and other policies that the government deems important for the country's development. Obama's infrastructure bank idea would act similarly in that the bank would borrow capital from the capital markets and relend the money to higher-return infrastructure projects that would provide stable long-term cash flows. In theory, the infrastructure bank could work. In reality, the ability of the bank to redeploy capital for an acceptable return to investors would mean that long-term planning would still be hostage to those more interested in quick returns by private actors. Perhaps the only way such a bank could be guaranteed to function is to nationalize it.

The public-private partnership (PPP) programs have been widely discussed in the United States as being a possible vehicle for funding long-term projects such as infrastructure, but have acquired a stigma among some critics. The public aversion to it seems to stem largely from the fact that many associate PPP with cash-strapped governments selling the crown jewels of public infrastructure to private financial entities such as private equity firms and bankers. These financiers, like barbarians at the gate, are circling the carcass of bankrupt government coffers to acquire public assets on the cheap. Many public assets such as parking garages, libraries, and bridges do not have accurate valuations since most of them have never been put to auction and are unusual enough that one couldn't find comparable entities to get a fair price.

The public outcry against private takeovers of public assets is not without merits. After all, when taxpayers foot the bill for something, such as a bridge, it seems unfair that due to ineffective government management, that bridge is sold to private players at a bargain price. In addition, this transaction could inflict lasting economic damage since the new private owner could charge user fees. Let's return to the example of the bridge. If a private equity fund buys it from a local government, the fund owners could levy a toll on a bridge that used to be free to cross. The citizens would then be subject to fee hikes but would have no say over the matter because, unlike the government, the private owner doesn't have any obligation to respond to the citizens. The net effect would be a regressive tax since the poorest citizens would be paying a much higher percentage of their income for use of these assets.

Unfortunately, most citizens do not understand that this would be the likely outcome if they don't have transparency and fiscal long-term planning by government officials to avoid such dire situations. Many citizens, aside from voting once every four years, absolve themselves from paying much attention to what goes on in government. Perhaps we feel too removed, too busy, or too powerless to make a difference. According to the Center for Deliberative Democracy at Stanford University, not only do Americans have one of the lowest voter turnout rates, but many also don't have basic knowledge about the workings of our government. For five years, the Intercollegiate Studies Institute has been conducting a national survey of 30,000 Americans to gauge the quality of civic education in the country. In 2011, it found that only 50 percent of Americans could name all three branches of government, just 54 percent knew that only Congress and not the president could declare war, and a whopping 49 percent answered most of the 33 questions on the test incorrectly.

Usually, when people don't know something, it reflects the low priority assigned to it because they don't care enough to find out. As a result, systemic waste and corruption that permeate the U.S. government at the local, state, and federal levels have drained public coffers dry. An example of this sort of misconduct is a New Jersey municipality where public officials paid salaries and pensions to employees who "worked" for a completely fictitious school.[6] Additionally, labor unions for government workers who help elect people into office often ensure that overly generous salaries and pensions are subsequently guaranteed to its members by the elected officials as rewards for voter support at taxpayers' expense. The *New York Post* reported that Jerry Speziale collects a disability tax-free pension of $58,000 from the NYPD while he works as the deputy superintendent of the Port Authority Police Department for a $198,500 salary.[7]

As a result of widespread government unscrupulousness, budget crises across the country from California to New York cannot meet their fiscal obligations and must curtail government services such as K–12 public education. Public assets are now being seriously considered for sale to wealthy private investors as a means to raise funds to pay for all the previous government commitments and entitlements. Private equity funds have raised hundreds of billions of dollars in recent years to prepare themselves for one of the biggest raids of the U.S. government's public assets in history. According to the January 2010 issue of *Power* magazine, "In 2004, $4 billion were raised for global infrastructure funds; in 2005, $8 billion. Between 2006 and 2008 $90 billion were raised—$37 billion in 2008 alone." These funds are waiting to say checkmate to the government when the U.S. public is so desperate that they have no other options left.

Some may find this scenario hard to believe, but in fact, American financiers have made this move numerous times in history, but in the backyards of other countries. In the 1980s for example, U.S. policymakers from the World Bank and the International Monetary Fund had required Latin American countries to open up their local markets to U.S. businesses. U.S. banks lent cheap money to foreign governments, and when banks raised interest rates on floating rate issues, the foreign governments couldn't repay many of the loans at the higher rates. When these governments defaulted, the U.S. banks and other financiers demanded that the foreign governments sell public assets as repayment for the loans. As James Henry documented in his book *Blood Bankers,* U.S. banks legally stole Latin American assets, including pension funds, ports, and other public assets for pennies on the dollar.

## Investing in America

Selling existing infrastructure to raise badly needed government revenue clearly has negative consequences for the public. Partnering with the private sector to build new infrastructure could potentially have a better outcome. The reason this second option may prove more beneficial is that the public doesn't lose anything and stands to gain if government joins forces with the right private players to create something useful that wouldn't otherwise exist. In this scenario, the government would do what it does best by providing the proper regulations and guarantees for public land use, and the private partners would do what they do best by channeling creativity and innovation to deliver a project that benefits everyone. An example of such collaboration could be a research and development facility for which the government would sponsor long-term clean energy research. Leading private architects could design an energy-efficient research facility utilizing proven but underfunded groundbreaking technology developed by private entrepreneurs who need a few large orders so that they can become cost competitive with existing technology that is less green. In this way, the government and private industry can join forces to give the local U.S. economies a helping hand while investing in the future at the same time.

Thus far, not many collaborations have materialized. One possible reason is that entrenched interests who do not want to see innovation erode their current streams of income have more money and power to block government from partnering with the entrepreneurial outfits that are rich with new ideas but low on lobbying power and capital.[8] Another possible reason is that many Americans distrust large government. They fear government waste and the shortsightedness of public officials. Finally, there may not have been many compelling projects being proposed. I used the example of a research facility because building infrastructure alone does not necessarily lead to competitiveness. In Portugal and other places, significant capital has been invested in upgrading infrastructure, but these investments didn't lead to competitive industries. Coming up with worthwhile projects would require the collaboration of many thoughtful groups, and pulling off such feats are not easy to do.

In contrast, the Chinese government systematically partners with all registered companies, and in fact actively encourages innovation and entrepreneurship by building technology parks in most of the major cities where new businesses spring up. Recognizing that entrepreneurs lack capital and time, the government acts as both venture capitalist and incubator—providing seed money to build prototypes while also supplying research facilities, room and board, and other amenities that support a distraction-free environment, such as high-quality education for their kids and supermarkets within walking distance.

Originally, the technology parks were primarily R&D centers for large foreign companies like Microsoft, but the subsequent ones that have been built were designed to replicate the support network of Silicon Valley as a way to attract and house young technology entrepreneurs from around the world. By becoming its own venture capitalist, China has been investing in the next generation of talent with an eye to commercialize the new innovations. By 2010, China had created over 150 national technology parks and technology incubators.[9] Many of them just allow general research while some focus on specific industries and applications. The technology park in Changping, for instance, will focus on everything 3-D: 3-D technology research and development, manufacturing of high-end 3-D products, check and verification of 3-D products, 3-D medical imaging services, and 3-D international conventions and exhibitions. It will also have a 3-D international research and development central area, a 3-D international enterprise park, and even a 3-D international theme park.[10]

## Intellectual Property Rights Is the New Black

The leaders also recognize that to successfully transition China's economy to one that relies less on export also requires an economy that can innovate its way out of its problems. Innovation, once a weakness for China—because it lacked intellectual property protection—has been given a boost from the government. China has historically condoned copying and stealing of intellectual property because the original Communist ideology promoted communal sharing of everything, including knowledge, which was considered a public good. Since almost all private property in China was destroyed or seized for the benefit of the community during Mao's rule, intellectual property rights (IPR) certainly had no place in the national vocabulary. But with their push to drive innovation, the Chinese leaders now realize that IPR is a crucial prerequisite for motivating people to innovate, and they have allocated more resources for IPR enforcement.[11]

Bashing against Chinese entrepreneurs originally started with the fashion industry, software makers, and media companies blaming the Chinese for copyright infringement and intellectual property violations. As a response, the Chinese government agreed to crack down on the stealing and passed laws strictly forbidding such acts. However, enforcing them has been a challenge since the legal system is still embryonic, and private law didn't exist prior to 1996, meaning that lawyers only recently were allowed to represent private clients and not just the state. To put the situation into context, roughly one out of every 260 Americans is a lawyer, while in China, there is only one lawyer for roughly every 8,000 citizens. So a shortage of qualified personnel in China's judicial system still exists.[12] But since China plans to address this issue with a "talent" plan, which I will discuss later in this section, the ratio of qualified Chinese lawyers will likely catch up to America's in the not-too-distant future.

Getting the desired effect is not without its challenges. Just as U.S. venture capitalists could demand a pound of flesh from the entrepreneurs who seek financing from them, the government officials who run the technology parks can also demand terms that border on extortion in exchange for access to technological and business resources. A sample contract would go something like this: someone with a great idea and plan receives $3 million from the Chinese technology park to prove the concept. If product development succeeds according to plan, additional funds would be needed to design further, manufacture a prototype, and bring it to market. The government would offer another $10 million in exchange for 50 percent of the company and board representation, but the entrepreneur would also have to match the funds somehow by coughing up another $10 million. Some of the traditional channels to access those funds would be through foreign direct investments and initial public offerings.

Unfortunately, the Chinese technology park model also suffers from uneven relationships, which may derail chances for success. In the case of the Chinese model, even if the entrepreneur is anointed the CEO, he or she must obey Party guidelines. A government official who seeds the company and happens to be chairman of the board could easily oust the CEO over a disagreement because the CEO has only a minority shareholding in the company that he or she created. If the relationship is good, that business manager could be blessed with contract orders from the government; but if it sours, the entrepreneur could even face the prospect of jail time. While the financial terms may not be so different from those one could get from a traditional venture capitalist, and while investors often dictate to management what to do, the difference is that a VC usually would have some technological expertise. The Chinese government officials who are put in charge, however, may not have the relevant technological expertise. But since the top leadership recognizes that this is an Achilles heel, it will likely get rectified quickly as well.

While these investments have largely focused on catching up to the West, these initiatives could someday enable China to surpass the West. Such long-term investing in entrepreneurial partnerships is starting to pay off in the form of indigenous innovations coming out of China that are beginning to compete with the best technologies coming from the United States. In some areas, such as solar panel technology, China has already outdone the United States.[13] As a result of long-term thinking and planning, innovation rates in China are approaching U.S. levels. Patent filings have been steadily rising. In

2009, 300,000 patents were filed in China, and projections estimate that the number will increase to two million by 2015.[14]

Is there a way for the U.S. government to entice American private investors to partner in a win-win situation the way the Chinese have done? Perhaps. U.S. investors who have the funds claim that they might be convinced to invest in new structures rather than purchase existing ones if the U.S. government didn't have so many bureaucratic rules. George Bilicic, director of infrastructure investments at Lazard Freres, says that private companies invest abroad in places like Chile and Argentina because regulations are less onerous. Other financiers, such as Macquarie's executive director Nicholas Hann, assert that public-private partnerships in Canada flourish because the Canadian government has standardized the process so that the government and the private sector can work together with efficiency and transparency. Streamlining the process is certainly an easier initial step for the United States to investigate and pursue. But the bigger issue—overcoming inertia of short-termism—remains.

During the 1970s, author E.F. Schumacher had a brilliant idea that could potentially reduce the role of speculation in stock markets. He proposed that private companies could partner with government; employees would receive 50 percent ownership, and the public sector would own the other 50 percent. Such an ownership structure would give both private and public stakeholders equal say in the business, and they would share in the benefits and externalities. The idea is that two long-term stakeholders are less likely to make short-term decisions and would make for a more responsible ownership of corporate action. Ironically, his idea has in large part been adopted by the Chinese. The Chinese, perhaps like the Japanese when they adopted Dr. Deming's ideas, embraced Schumacher's ideas because they didn't have established interests defending an existing capital market system.

Investment bankers, financial investors, and others whose livelihoods depend on the status quo would likely oppose Schumacher's proposals vigorously. But while his idea may be too politically unpopular for immediate adoption by the United States, less radical measures ought to be implemented. The Committee of Economic Development (CED), a think tank based in Washington DC, issued a report in 2007 to combat short-termism. Their recommendations included the following:

- Structure incentive compensation plans so that a significant portion of the income of the CEO and other top executives is tied to the achievement of well-articulated long-term performance objectives in line with corporate strategy.
- Insist that corporate reporting be redesigned to include useful non-financial indicators of value.
- Eliminate quarterly guidance on earnings per share.
- Promote succession plans that emphasize growth of managerial talent internally.

Though the report was written up in the *Financial Times* as it was published, there has not been a follow-on study to research the number of companies that have adopted the recommendations (if any), the reasons for why they did or didn't follow them, or what the outcomes were if the recommendations were indeed pursued. Such studies would require significant resources and time, commitments that have yet to be made in a short-term–oriented society.

## Local Power

Still others believe that more power should be devolved to the local level to achieve longer-term objectives. Carne Ross, executive director of The Independent Diplomat and a former British foreign service officer who served in places such as Kosovo, has argued for a form of anarchy because he believes that nation-states absolve people from public responsibility for their civic lives. If every citizen were to face greater accountability for his or her actions, then more care would be devoted toward long-term planning for the public good since top priorities for most people are their immediate environments and social circles. There is some credence to this argument. The Iroquois Confederacy, which existed centuries ago, always abided by the notion that one must keep the interests of the next seven generations in mind before negotiating anything. These were tribes who felt deep responsibility to their communities and conducted their affairs accordingly. Today, we need to find a way to replicate that level of accountability and foresight in our present political system. Anarchy may be far too radical, but if there is a way to transfer more power from the federal government back to the state and local governments, that may be our greatest hope in mobilizing Americans to care about our collective future and to act on tough political problems that continually get brushed aside.

On the surface, relinquishing more power to the local level as a solution to short-termism seems to be at odds with what the Chinese have done. But contrary to Western misperceptions, China does not act as a monolithic central government but is highly decentralized. The CCP has unambiguously empowered the numerous local officials who run the many Chinese provinces to such an extent that a common joke is that businessmen must pay 1000 yuan to dine with the president, but must pay 10,000 yuan to dine with the mayor. While the national leaders set national goals and establish public standards for everyone to follow, the actual governance is extremely decentralized and carried out almost entirely by the local officials. Most American businessmen who have conducted business in China can attest to this fact. Provincial government officials hold significant power over their jurisdictions, empowering government decision making to be much quicker and more efficient than democracies such as India's where government approval requires wading through layers of bureaucracy. Likewise, terrorist groups, such as Al Qaeda, can be extremely effective in carrying out their missions because they are decentralized networks that do not require any hierarchical approval for action.

## Talent Poaching

In order to engineer a smooth transition away from an economy that relies on cheap exports to a more balanced knowledge economy, China understands that it must develop its talent pool. Without cultivating and attracting talent, China will never catch up with the United States. China may have a population of 1.4 billion people from which to draw talent, but given America's stellar track record of absorbing immigrants from all over the world, it can rely on the expertise of 7 billion people. China is keenly aware that of the 1.62 million Chinese who traveled to the United States to study since 1978, only 497,000 of them have returned. The U.S. Energy Department supported China's worries with a report which stated that 92 percent of the 2,139 Chinese nationals who received science and technology doctorates from U.S. universities in 2002 were still in the United States in 2007.

Thus, to address this deficit, China's leaders have created a separate Ten-Year Plan to develop talent as a national strategy. They define *talent* as those who can create something new and original with their own intellectual and creative abilities. By 2007, the CCP adopted a strategic plan for the years 2010–2020, which was advanced to the Party Congress and finally approved by all the top government officials by April of 2010. This document detailed many objectives they wanted to accomplish. The six major categories that they wanted to develop were (1) political leaders, (2) business entrepreneurs, (3) technical professionals, (4) highly skilled tradesmen, (5) agrarian expertise, and (6) professional social workers. They also created a separate program to address scholars in the humanities to engage in philosophy, cultural heritage preservation, and the arts. For each of these areas, they drew up specific numerical targets. For instance, they want to increase the total talent pool from 113 million to 180 million by 2020. They also want to raise the ratio of their population who had received higher education from 9.2 percent to 20 percent. And they expressed a commitment to raise the amount invested in human capital as a percentage of GDP from 10.75 percent to 15 percent.

In specific industries, their goals to be achieved by 2020 include the following:[15]

- more than 5 million people working in information technology, biotechnology, equipment manufacturing, and other industries requiring highly technical skills
- more than 8 million working in the service industries of law, education, media, healthcare, public relations, and disaster prevention
- at least 3 million social workers to handle mental health, trauma victims, senior citizens, and the impoverished
- at least 3.8 million research and development professionals
- at least 100 CEOs on the Fortune 500 list

The methods for achieving these lofty goals will come in various forms. More of the government budget will be allocated toward national research and development and national education. The CCP will also actively engage in recruiting globally to fill top positions in state-owned enterprises, which have historically been occupied by government-appointed officials. Additionally, Chinese citizenship will be eliminated as a requirement for holding top positions in major state-owned enterprises. A recent example of this was recruiting the chairman of Deutsche Bank Asia, Zhang Hongli, to become vice president of ICBC, China's largest state-owned bank. Even before the Talent Strategy was approved, the Thousand Talents Program was initiated in 2008. To attract 2,000 high-level overseas professionals to relocate and work for the Chinese government, the CCP provided generous relocation costs and guaranteed competitive salaries. By

January of 2010, 1,100 had already been hired. While roughly 50 percent of these were Chinese foreign nationals, the CCP actually hired the balance from other ethnicities and nationalities, which included British and Germans.

But just as important as having an entrepreneurial spirit, the government realizes that steering the country toward a more service-oriented economy away from its recent industrial past will again entail much knowledge transfer. In recognizing the need for know-how to transition successfully, China has been actively recruiting talent from the entire globe. The Chinese government hosted numerous job fairs in New York City to recruit Mandarin-speaking talent with Wall Street experience for Chinese financial firms in insurance, brokerage, and banking. Cities such as Shanghai also invited overseas Chinese young professionals to visit multi-day receptions to network and learn about service-oriented opportunities that the government was promoting. Packages offered to top professionals often included competitive salaries, housing, relocation, and other benefits. Just as corporations poach competitive firms for strategic talent, China's leaders have taken it to an international level, showing extreme foresight and vision for their future.

The takeaway message is that America's leadership should at least articulate its national goals so that voters can have objective benchmarks to measure whether their politicians are delivering. Reaching worthy goals often requires careful planning. If these objectives are memorialized in writing, the public is less likely to forget them and can also see whether government officials keep their promises. Plans are not laws, but they will have institutional backing complete with personnel, budgets, and accountability.

## An Industrial Talent Policy Wanted

The United States can also formulate a talent development policy not too dissimilar from China in order to address the long-term demographic challenge of an aging population coupled with the relentless pace of technological innovation and globalization of markets. Any job that can be automated will be done by computers and robots in the coming years, so the United States must begin thinking about how to reintegrate back into the workforce people whose jobs will disappear at ever-faster rates in the not-too-distant future. In the recession following the 2008 financial crisis, most of the jobs lost were in high-wage sectors, and the jobs created were on the low end of the pay scale according to the Council of Competitiveness. Furthermore, the Council cites that between the years 2008 and 2018, senior citizens will account for 90 percent of the labor growth. The United States has not addressed the issue of how it will train mature workers, let alone younger workers, whose skills have been atrophying during long periods of unemployment. Arguably, the need for mid-career training may be just as essential for America's competitiveness as K–12 education.

Without a national policy, employers will continue to react to short-term demands for profitability and fail to develop our talent pool for the future. The U.S. Head of Deutsche Bank's legal department, for example, explained that as a client, he was only willing to pay top dollar for the time of senior partners in Western law firms but would not subsidize the training of law firm associates coming out of law school. For low-level legal work, he was only willing to pay the hourly rates of roughly $20 an hour charged by Indians in India. Obviously, it would be hard for Americans to swallow paying $1,200 an hour to a Washington law firm for any work done there on behalf of a client. There are certainly tradeoffs in both cases. Private companies will always be driven to behave in their own short-term self-interest to meet profit targets, which will be at odds with the national goal of devoting time and resources to cultivate future generations with the necessary skills to compete in an increasingly competitive world. The U.S. leadership must find a viable solution to bridge the gap between short-term economic behavior and long-term talent development. Unless the U.S. government takes a more proactive role in closing the gap, it is likely that more and more young Americans will leave the United States to work abroad, further draining talent from the United States.[16]

## Swimming with Sharks

Foreign companies that enter China believing it is a big market opportunity often get burned because they are wholly unprepared for the competition. In America and in Europe, large companies who have large market shares are used to executing at a much slower pace because they have already created huge barriers to entry for those who want to compete in that space. However, in China, the markets are a free-for-all. One must be prepared to swim in shark-infested waters to operate in China. The Darwinian concept of survival of the fittest is exemplified in its purest form among Chinese businesspeople, who undercut in price, poach key employees, and engage in other aggressive business behavior simply to survive. Unfortunately, the General Electrics of the world, who enjoy protections in their home markets due to their political power, cannot replicate those cushy conditions in China. These large multinationals cannot hire lobbyists to persuade Chinese politicians to grant them the same special privileges, provide American-style bailouts, or pass unfair laws to ensure that they can profit in China in the same manner that they have in the United States. Whereas large foreign multinationals have used their market positioning to buy shelf space; their financial power to buy politicians, ads, and regulators; and their political power to blackmail potential competitors, they have become bitter that Chinese companies have beaten them at their own game. The CEOs of these companies who have been spoiled for decades in their home markets with uneven playing fields that favor them are now screaming at politicians to do something. Western CEOs must realize that the best defense is to have a good offense, and the secret to a good offense is to always anticipate the future. Even Wayne Gretzky has said, "A good hockey player plays where the puck is. A great hockey player plays where the puck is going to be." The irony is that the future is less certain for large corporations when fresh competition is coming from everywhere, Five-Year Plans notwithstanding. With the Chinese government as a deep-pocketed financial backer with long-term goals, entrepreneurs in China may for the first time since the Industrial Revolution have a shot at changing the world. This could eventually force American corporate executives to stop listening to short-term, earnings-oriented analysts on Wall Street and re-start long-term investments in research and development for a change.

Last but not least, some will argue that long-term plans make sense for China because they have the United States as a model to emulate, but that such plans are less useful for developed countries who are pathfinders that are not trying to catch up with others. In other words, long-term plans may not speed up economic growth for advanced countries like the United States whose incremental improvements come from discovery of new frontiers and not from racing to beat a forerunner. I agree that a pathfinder must invent its future and make decisions under real uncertainty. But encouraging long-term planning and path finding aren't mutually exclusive ideas. In fact, these two go hand in hand because path finding requires much research, and research requires advance planning and long-term budgets that are shielded from short-term considerations in order to invent the best possible future in the face of uncertainty. Growth rates in the West have been unnecessarily hamstrung by special interests blocking entrepreneurs. Short-term profits have consistently trumped longer-term investments as priorities. But rapid growth rates can reappear for pathfinders when they hit upon the next taproot invention that sets off the next explosion of exponentially increasing productivity. Just as Thomas Edison was a pathfinder in his day, we need to budget and plan for more people to perform Edison-like path-finding work.

Currently, America is not optimizing our democratic capitalist system because of our collective tendency to think and work in the short-term without comprehending the effects on the entire ecosystem. Thinking laterally and seeing beyond immediate boundaries have been further handicapped by entrenched interests who protect their turf by blocking solutions that could lead to more sustainable outcomes. As a result, balancing interests between different people across time is not functioning the way our Founding Fathers had envisioned. Although we have attempts at longer-term thinking such as the No Child Left Behind Act, we need to incorporate more of such thinking into our current system. When Goldman Sachs was still a partnership, legend has it that its employees were told to be "long-term greedy, not short-term greedy." If the United States follows this advice, long-term greed could be interpreted as developing the conditions today for ensuring long-term health and wealth for tomorrow. Not only should we consider the long-term well-being of our own nation but of all nations since, like passengers on the Titanic, we ultimately all share the same ship called Planet Earth regardless of how rich or poor we are. The consequences of short-term behavior will catch up with all of us. So whether we tie more measurable objectives and timelines to budget line items or devolve more power to the local level so that citizens can see the tradeoffs more clearly and appreciate how their own behaviors shape those tradeoffs, we must begin acting now while we still have the luxury to think about the long term. As economist John Maynard Keynes famously said, "In the long run, we are all dead." Let's not wait until death is upon us before we think about changing course.

# 5

# Special Economic Zones

Don't be too timid and squeamish about your actions.
All life is an experiment. The more experiments you
make the better. —RALPH WALDO EMERSON

**MAO'S SUCCESSOR DENG XIAO PING** famously said, "It does not matter if the cat is black or white as long as it catches mice," signaling that he no longer demanded that the country adhere to strict ideology, but wanted pragmatism to inform policy. His pragmatic statement was not only revolutionary during his time given the Communist ideological orientation in China back then, but it is even revolutionary today here in the United States as it relates to economic policy.

## Fraud Called Economics

For decades, the study of economics in the West has been based on empirical observation of society and extrapolated into a broader theory in an attempt to turn a social science into a harder science. Mathematical formulas were further created to describe an economic theory or "law" in much the same way that mathematical formulas were developed for the hard sciences of physics or chemistry. The problem with economic theories is that economics isn't a hard science no matter how much economists would like it to be. In the hard sciences, scientific experiments can be replicated. Atoms and chemical reactions are predictable. Humans however are not. Humans have the freedom to choose, and while humans may often make economically rational decisions, they are also just as likely to make choices based on other factors. Humans also can behave differently based on cultural influences. The best economists can do is create models or abstractions to use as a guide to understand the system. We cannot assume, however, that these economic models will ever represent the entire truth.

Moreover, mainstream economists cannot control conditions the way scientific experiments can be controlled in laboratories by isolating variables. Economists have taken surveys and sometimes do controlled experiments to research a single variable, but most of that research doesn't shed much light because they have not been able to control enough of the other external conditions to ensure an apples-to-apples comparison. Oftentimes, modern Western economics is based on one theorist who makes a generalization after making some observations about an economy. The theorist then has a sophisticated mathematician develop a complicated model that is supposed to describe the theory in mathematical terms. Since the theorist may not be as strong at math as the mathematician, the theorist may not be able to verify the accuracy of the model. Conversely, the mathematician doesn't know whether the theory is valid because his specialty is in economic modeling, not theorizing. Thus the two most important pieces in the economic theory cannot be relied upon with certainty.

To make matters worse, large economic organizations like the International Monetary Fund often use these economic models to make forecasts and economic policy decisions. The economists who use these models for forecasts often have neither the mathematical ability to fix the formulas to make them more accurate nor the research ability to test the original hypotheses. Since the models may be flawed, any inputs and outputs from the model are thus also flawed. Yet billions of dollars regularly get spent on policy decisions that affect billions of people based on potentially wrong data. For instance, macroeconomic models at the Federal Reserve today don't incorporate microeconomic models that take into account incentives, fraud, and other factors in human behavior. Their models also don't take into account the banking moral hazard of "too big to fail" (TBTF), which I go into in greater depth in chapter 6. While economist Hyman Minsky's models are not used widely and are only macroeconomic, at least they took into account irrational behavior. Such deficiencies explain in part why economists are consistently wrong on their forecasts and why many economic programs prescribed by such economic organizations have failed miserably to fix the economic problems they were supposed to fix.

Add to this toxic combination the fact that most economists with PhDs have never spent any time working in the economy they purport to understand. Most of these economists went straight into graduate school studying only the theories and mathematics of predecessors, who also never worked outside of academia, creating an echo chamber where their ideas are not challenged by real-world experiences. It begs credibility that these people could explain human behavior when they themselves have not understood how economic players game an economy, how information truly gets distributed and shared, and why people respond differently to the same conditions because of cultural biases or other beliefs and values.

Every nation and its people grow up with differences—depending on their values, educational opportunities, and other circumstances that shaped their normative behavior. There are many factors that economists often fail to consider when they draw broad, sweeping conclusions. For instance, on the question of whether poverty leads to violence, they typically do not consider a variety of issues, such as whether the prospect of a more promising future deters violence in one nation versus one whose population feels more hopeless. Does the level of exposure to violence have a greater influence than poverty? What effect does it have for one to be raised by one's own parents versus one where disasters like tsunamis or devastating earthquakes render such an upbringing impossible? What's the verdict of neuroscience on violence?

Arguably many economists cannot control for all these considerations when they do a study. Contrary to what they want the public to believe, there is much room for advancement in our knowledge in all areas of economics. Economists' current level of understanding may be on par with the era when doctors applied leeches to patients for curing disease. When economists develop macroeconomic theories based on observation, they can be quite sophisticated and convincing in their methodologies. But in the end, they may also be no different from the people who believed that the sun and planets revolved around the Earth before Copernicus came along to prove that the conventional wisdom of the day was wrong. As societies, we obviously must make do with the current level of economic understanding, but we must also remain cognizant of how little economists know and comprehend, especially across economic disciplines, and act accordingly.

One of the most blatant failures of economists was the financial crisis of 2008. Economists, including chairman of the United States Federal Reserve Board, Alan Greenspan, exerted enormous weight over the economic policies of the United States and the world, yet none of them have acknowledged their roles in creating the disaster. Either they did not believe the crisis was possible, they gravely underestimated the danger of selling credit derivatives to the world, or they secretly understood the riskiness of the situation but chose to hide knowledge of imminent disaster from the public. This third possibility would clearly show public malfeasance and criminal behavior on the part of these economists, which cannot be ruled out, especially if politics drove policies.

In the late 1990s, technology stocks surged, and 2000 was an election year when rates raised quickly and sharply. The tech bubble burst right before the election. When a new party was in the White

House in 2001, rates were quickly lowered and held there to stimulate growth. Eerily, a similar pattern had appeared in the early 1990s with the real estate crash. A nascent recovery began after 1992, but the Federal Reserve raised rates just before the election in 1994, causing a double dip in the economy that prompted a change of control in Congress. Did politics drive policies in these cases?

However, if we choose to believe that economists were merely objective actors who relied on economic models that failed to predict the 2008 crisis, then the economists' theory of efficient markets, the market's ability to self-regulate, and a whole host of other economic assumptions were obviously wrong. Yet these premises have been accepted as fact by economists for years and incorporated into national public policy as if they were indisputable.

It is difficult, if not impossible, to separate economics from politics. That which benefits one group routinely harms another one. To pretend that economics is scientific in the way it has been practiced in the West is one of the most sophisticated hoaxes of the 21st century. Karl Marx understood that economics under the capitalist system would inevitably divide societies between the haves and have-nots. That the capitalist system is a natural law doesn't hold water when other systems such as kibbutzim have also worked in modern society. More accurately, capitalism is a system as imperfect as those that preceded it, but it had better support from influential political advocates. Communism wasn't necessarily doomed to fail. It was the way in which it was implemented by corrupted Communist Party leaders in the former Soviet Union and China under Mao that condemned that economic ideology to failure.

## Economic Lab Experiments

China's leaders, starting with Deng Xiao Ping, were astute and practical enough to recognize that it was not ideology that made one set of economic principles trump another. Rather, it was the tactical implementation at the microeconomic level that would determine if the economic policies would succeed or not in achieving a set of economic objectives. For too many decades, Mao had used the people to serve the Marxist ideology rather than the other way around. But after Deng had seen that a group of farmers had succeeded in increasing food output through profit retention, thereby flouting communist orders, he was wise enough not to punish the farmers but instead engineered a 180-degree course reversal at the PRC. Fortunately for the Chinese, Deng made public service to the people of China the number-one priority of the Party.

China's leaders wanted to learn how to best serve the people, but they knew that sweeping policy changes would risk derailing the country, which was still shell-shocked from the brutality of World War II and Mao's reign of terror. So they decided to embark on a much less risky approach by systematically testing different economic theories in small, contained regions. The regions that would be chosen to test these economic policies were called Special Economic Zones.

Special Economic Zones (SEZs) are geographic regions ranging from villages to provinces within China that were granted special privileges and allocations of national capital for a specific period of time to experiment with a new economic policy in order to test the merits of the policy. Ever since technocrats have run the country, their collective thinking has been shaped by a scientific approach to problems, even though they knew that assessing social policy is far less precise than conducting scientific experiments. Nonetheless, China's leaders have placed primary importance on collecting as much empirical evidence as possible. Following Deng's lead, pragmatism overruled ideology, and so to verify whether their hypotheses were correct and policies had the intended effect, limited populations piloted programs before they were launched on the wider public.

Most SEZs are used to test tax incentives and rules regarding foreign direct investment within different cities and provinces. Experts and policymakers would often be brought together to observe and analyze the outcomes in order to determine the right courses of action on a broader level. Invariably several provinces are designated SEZs at the same time in order to have control groups, and if economic outcomes are inconclusive, policies would be slightly modified for further observation. Furthermore, to avoid conflicts of interest, many of the experts are chosen on the basis that they have no self-interest in the interpretation of the outcomes, such as academics from other countries. Much like scientists in a lab collaborating to discover the right answers with repeated experimentation, China has created the first real-time economic labs in the world.

The concept behind SEZs is statistical experimental design, which underpins most scientific research today. Statistical experimental design is very mainstream and used by many sophisticated thinkers in research organizations. In fact, it is used for optimizing factories, product designs, marketing strategies, and countless other human endeavors. Above all, the concept is safe; we use it in everyday life in the West, so this method cannot be accused of being threatening, Communist propaganda.

It might be fair to say that China not only invented economic labs, but it has also turned itself into the largest pilot project in human history. By testing out different political and economic theories simultaneously throughout the country with well-managed plans and teams of experts who are entrusted with monitoring the developing situations, China has managed to turn the soft social science of economics into a much closer cousin of the hard sciences. Their economic experimentation has sped their understanding of human dynamics and institutions, which has translated into a model that has challenged the Washington Consensus for economic and societal development.

The first SEZs took place in Guangzhou, Shenzhen, and Shanghai back in the 1980s when the leaders decided to experiment with free trade after decades of centrally planned economies. One of the earliest and the most famous SEZ was Guangdong. Located in proximity to the thriving cities of Hong Kong and Macao, Guangdong had been plagued with low arable land, deficient energy and transportation infrastructure, and significant structural damage from the Cultural Revolution. Xi Zhongcun, a revolutionary hero from the 1920s, had been assigned to govern Guangdong in 1978 after Mao passed away. The vibrancy of Hong Kong contrasting sharply with the moribund Guangdong prompted Xi to contemplate the reasons for the disparity, especially since over 80 percent of Hong Kong citizens had come from Guangdong. After researching different hunches, he eventually concluded that economic governance was the dominant cause for the huge economic differences. Xi pleaded his case to China's central government to permit Guangdong to accept capital from Hong Kong and Macau in order to upgrade farming technologies. When they granted him permission to set up an SEZ, Deng warned that Xi might be risking his life by going down a road less traveled. Although worried about his lack of experience, Xi nonetheless made it his mission to attract the finance capital from outsiders to modernize everything in the province. The last thing he worried about was being accused of resorting to capitalism. He is remembered among the Chinese for saying, "As long as you can boost the economy so that the people can enjoy a better life, just go ahead and make it happen. There are good things we can learn from capitalism too."

According to the U.S. Census, China's trade with the United States was a mere $7.7 billion in 1985. The Chinese government arbitrarily set interest rates and exchange rates. Even though the mainland Chinese knew very little about how to conduct business with the outside world, they quickly learned from the overseas Chinese businesspeople from Taiwan and Hong Kong who were among the first to venture into the country. These Chinese businesspeople recognized the vast opportunity that an awakening China represented, so they poured foreign investment over the borders to create factories of every stripe and color. By 2010, China's trade with the rest of the world topped $3 trillion.[1]

The SEZs became enormous successes. Within ten years, the economies in those provinces were completely transformed, drawing more workers and more employers with every passing minute. The Chinese leaders, encouraged by the initial successes, gradually opened more provinces to the same rules, and China was off to the races.

While I was teaching at Peking University in the spring of 2008, I had the pleasure of speaking to a visiting professor from the University of Washington who also stayed at the guesthouse on campus. She told me that she was working with the Chinese government on a project evaluating the "tragedy of the commons" economic theory. She said that some villagers were given a section of a forest to own and manage. Before the project commenced, the social scientists assumed that the villagers would chop down the trees, sell the wood, and keep the profit for themselves, thereby destroying the forest. To everyone's surprise, the villagers preserved the forest because they discovered that they could earn more money harvesting and selling the pine nuts, thus receiving an income in perpetuity rather than chopping the trees for a one-time gain. This project was just one of thousands of such socioeconomic experiments that continue to this day.

## Modern-Day Apprenticeships

While SEZs have had a dominant impact on economic development, another related policy also utilized by the CCP that underscores its pragmatic approach to development is the joint venture (JV). The JV has been used extensively in China to foster robust but careful economic growth. One well-known saying in Chinese is "Cross the river by feeling the stones" (*mo shi guo he*). In other words, it pays to move toward your goal slowly and carefully, even if it means taking one step back for every two steps forward.

Former president Jiang Zemin made a historic decision authorizing companies to go bankrupt and consenting to open competition by entrepreneurs. Private businesses competing with the state-owned enterprises (SOEs) enabled innovative ideas to be heard and implemented, even though it threatened the existing government-owned companies. However, the fall of too many SOEs would have threatened the stability of the country by making too many workers unemployed. Instead, a compromise structure was developed. The leaders realized that old companies could learn from new companies by tethering them to each other. Such an arrangement engendered osmosis of ideas and best practices through information sharing while causing less disruption and trauma to the workforce than letting all the old companies suddenly go bankrupt without the appropriate social safety nets in place.

Back in 2007, engineering students at California State Polytechnic University invented a car that got 1902 miles per gallon.[2] Imagine that they were given support to start their own company and then asked to team up with General Motors. It is very possible that through this kind of collaboration, GM could have sped up its development of a competitive line of cars and avoided the crisis and government bailout money that eventually led to its bankruptcy anyway. Instead of bondholders fighting over the remains of the company, the workers at GM could have saved their jobs and started a new chapter in American innovation. Obviously, other issues such as cultural and generational incompatibility could make such a partnership highly problematic, but the main point is that such economic experiments through government mandate could yield new discoveries, insights, and productivity that would otherwise not take place.

## Politics Rule

As mentioned earlier, this approach to economic development was a natural outgrowth of China's leaders whose ranks were composed entirely of highly educated engineers. In contrast, the U.S. House of Representatives in 2009 was composed of 225 lawyers but only 16 doctors.[3] While lawyers, like engineers, will use logic and supportive evidence to make their arguments, their style of arguments may be quite different. Because engineers see the world through a scientific lens, they notice such things as the need for redundancies in the event of unforeseen failures in systems. Lawyers are more likely to view the world as a set of competing interests over political issues. Their proclivity is to win an argument rather than simply let the evidence speak for itself. Engineers, on the other hand, are more apt to analyze the facts dispassionately and refrain from using the rhetorical devices of pathos and ethos, since few have been trained in the art of speech making. These differences in the ways these two sets of leaders see the world have no doubt influenced the policies and character of these two political and economic systems.

Some would argue that the United States already has some version of SEZs because it is composed of 50 laboratories of democracy, each with some level of autonomy and its own laws, but the American approach is more organic than systematic. Certainly the health care reform bill was based on a system that was pioneered in Massachusetts under former Governor Mitt Romney. However, the program had not been tested in other states and was not studied by objective experts who could have testified to its merits or drawbacks with solid data. Moreover, alternative health care solutions that were proposed by various candidates were not first tried in other states to determine if they worked better than the system in Massachusetts.

Should the United States adopt China's systematic approach to testing out programs, much waste and political dysfunction could possibly be eliminated. Conducting these trials doesn't require any ideology to dominate despite the differences in opinions between *saltwater* and *freshwater* economists. (Saltwater economists refer to those macroeconomists who practice at universities situated along the coasts, whereas freshwater economists comprise those associated with universities surrounding the Great Lakes. They disagree primarily on the effectiveness of government spending on the economy and how to account for irrational behavior.) Rather, more microeconomic research needs to be incorporated into macroeconomic theories and models. While they are considered mainstream, both dominant macroeconomic views suffer from incompleteness and ought to be tested simultaneously since the United States is large enough to have control groups. But piloting programs does require the willingness to seek truth from facts, which unfortunately may put those with established interests on the defensive. After all, the large multinational banks in the United States would hate to admit that the trillions in bailout money did not result in economic growth for the country. In fact, they continue to argue against more regulation even after inflicting the worst financial crisis in history upon the world.[4] The beneficiaries of existing policies understandably would not want policy changes even if proof of the destructiveness of existing policies was borne out.

After watching numerous congressional and senatorial hearings, many Americans have largely concluded that U.S. politics trump economics and social justice. In surveys conducted by Pew Research Center in 2011, as many as 84 percent of Americans polled cared most about jobs, but only 23 percent are satisfied with current national conditions.[5] Clearly, the political rhetoric in Washington that has been aired daily on television has not satisfied the American public. Real reform of the root causes that led to financial crisis and the derailment of the American economy has remained elusive. For instance, despite the passage of the Dodd-Frank Wall Street Reform and Consumer Protection Act, large banks that pose systemic risks to the financial system still exist. Debt levels remain elevated in both the private and public sectors in the United States. Quantitative easing measures are used despite public pronouncements from the government and the Federal Reserve that the economy is improving. More troubling is that all these indicators mirror the economic situation in the United States right before it entered World War II. As larger and more serious problems appear on the horizon, such as world resource constraints, rising unemployment, and growing trade tensions, the United States can ill afford to continue to paper over problems with political rhetoric.

## A Way Out

With a little political will, the United States can try to incorporate the SEZ model by offering incentives to states for trying out various economic programs. By working closely with states to avoid violating states' rights, the federal government can arrange for nonpartisan groups to develop and oversee the programs alongside state representatives in order to achieve consistent oversight and metrics.

A prime example for study is the EB-5, which is a visa that allows foreign nationals to get green cards. To obtain the visa, individuals must invest $500,000, creating at least 10 jobs. In its current state, it is rife with corruption. Often, authorized EB-5 centers take foreign money and invest it in projects that are unprofitable and don't generate employment while falsely advertising that their investments are guaranteed by the U.S. government. Foreigners routinely hand over millions to these unscrupulous EB-5 operators thinking they will receive green cards only to find out that they have lost their money and cannot live in the United States. This widespread fraud damages the reputation of the United States while spoiling a real opportunity to create jobs for Americans. However, such a policy, if better designed and implemented with the appropriate supervision, could be tried in several states over several years with careful surveillance by outside academics to determine the efficacy of the program. If it worked according to the original intent of U.S. job creation, the policy could be rolled out slowly on a regional basis until it became uniform across the United States.

Similarly, the joint venture, already used by some corporations to limit their risk, can be encouraged more consistently by the U.S. government. The United States could offer lucrative tax incentives to encourage more large corporations to join forces with an entrepreneurial outfit every two years to ensure that the speed of innovation doesn't slow down. Corporate internal research, while also valuable, may not operate at its potential when organizational politics and group thinking can override innovative hunches. Once acquired, entrepreneurial companies run into the same risk of losing their innovative capabilities when they are absorbed into a larger organization where the dominant culture might be antithetical to more independent thought and creativity. According to Professor Geoffrey West of the Santa Fe Institute, in order to maintain steady growth, corporations and cities must continually reinvent themselves and innovate at faster and faster rates to avoid obsolescence and death. If corporations fail to do so, they will go bankrupt. Most companies that were around a hundred years ago no longer exist today, so he surmised that Google or Facebook will also disappear one day if they fail to innovate continuously. If cities fail to do so, New York can easily look like the slums of New Delhi because population and pollution growth will add strains to the existing infrastructure that are unsustainable unless innovations can accommodate these changes.

The entrenched interests would predictably revolt against such an idea unless the government subsidized these ventures. Currently, the U.S. program that is the closest to the Chinese-style joint venture would be Defense Advanced Research Projects Agency (DARPA), which has a portfolio of Defense Department investments in private companies that could have military applications. By supplying capital, sharing knowledge, and offering a market to these entrepreneurs, the government is providing a smoother transition from prototype to a viable company. The obvious drawback in this program is that the investments focus specifically on espionage and means of destruction—such as robots capable of deception and human memory-erasing programs—rather than explore broader applications for enhancing sustainable living on the planet.

The only reason there is even such a program in the United States is because the military industrial complex has become so powerful that the defense budget has grown 9 percent annually on average since 2000, while spending on other budget items either decreased or were subject to freezes.[6] This relentless increase in military spending guarantees crumbs for a few entrepreneurs lucky enough to attract attention from government venture capitalists who have mandates to find technology with possible military applications. But for the majority of start-up companies, the door to government contracts is closed. Military administrators in charge of granting contracts tend to award them to large companies where they are ensured jobs upon military retirement. Small entrepreneurial companies that may have more compelling technology are rarely given a chance at securing a government contract because they are frequently too limited in their resources to hire retired military employees as favors in return.

## The Story of Elastol

Consider the story of Jerry Trippe, CEO of General Technology Applications (GTA). For 30 years, he tried to respond to the growing environmental crisis, but to no avail. His company sold a substance called Elastol, a nontoxic chemical polymer that can be combined with any number of other materials to solve some of the world's most insidious problems. When Elastol is added to an oil spill, for instance, it causes the oil to separate from the water and form a thin film that can be easily be skimmed off the surface. It can clean oil spills at a fraction of the time and cost of the conventional methods. Moreover, Elastol leaves the environment much cleaner and is much safer to use than other existing methods. Finally, the recovered oil can actually be restored to its original form by running it through a machine that will reliquefy the oil.

Sadly, despite having positive results after nine years of testing with the Environmental Protection Agency (EPA) and other international organizations, such as the Environmental Department of Canada and the Mineral Management Service off the coast of Newfoundland, the substance is never used. GTA found itself being defeated by Big Oil. The oil lobby had convinced the EPA to allow dispersants to be used to treat oil spills. Dispersants are highly toxic chemicals that cause the oil to break apart and disappear from the surface although it remains in the water and never gets cleaned up. Dispersants are produced by big industry including some of the oil companies such as Exxon. By using dispersants on oil spills, oil companies can not only make money through the revenue of selling themselves the dispersants, they can also make the oil disappear from sight before the media can report on the accident.

After the Exxon Valdez spill, which garnered significant media attention, Congress passed the Oil Pollution Act in 1990. OPA 90, as it is called for short, was supposed to require every oil company to create a new response capability to hydrocarbon liquid accidents. GTA responded by contacting the oil companies to sell them Elastol. But during the eleventh hour while negotiating the contracts with two oil companies that were required to comply with OPA 90, the oil companies were informed by their lawyers that they no longer had to comply. The chemical and oil companies had lobbied hard and won, although the quiet defeat was never reported or explained to the public.

Even with the cost of the BP disaster running into the billions, oil companies would rather not acknowledge the existence of Elastol, since doing so would mean that they would have to take responsibility for it and deal with the public backlash of ignoring a superior solution to the problem. Furthermore, pretending the capability doesn't exist would exempt them from cleaning it up. And evading a problem by using highly toxic dispersants is always cheaper than stockpiling Elastol and using machines to clean up the mess. Their attitude is environment be damned since the only thing important to big industry is dollars and cents.

Even more perversely, when crews are summoned in to clean up oil that has polluted protected estuaries, beaches, and other important areas, they refuse to use Elastol because the cleanup crews are handled by private companies that get paid by the hour and therefore have no interest in increasing their operational efficiency. These private companies have long-standing contracts with the government and threatened GTA employees never to bring up Elastol again unless they wanted to die an untimely death at the bottom of the ocean.

Unless a constituency is formed to improve cleanup, it will not be the people affected by the pollution who call the shots, but the responders who make money from the spills.

Elastol has other miraculous properties as well. Mixed with sawdust, it will enable birds covered with oil to clean themselves off naturally without taking off the protective coating of natural oils underneath their feathers. Cleaning birds with detergent removes the natural oils from their skin and often causes birds to die from hypothermia with the onset of cold weather. Yet despite documentary coverage by the Discovery Channel and the Smithsonian, none of the environmental groups in the United States or Canada have openly embraced the solution. Mr. Trippe asserts that the EPA, again, was a blocker, citing that birds are not worth the money in rescue activities. Indeed, the failed bird rescue efforts following the BP oil spill appear to support his claim.[7]

*The Toxic Cloud: The Poisoning of America's Air,* a book written by Michael Brown in 1987, details how crop spraying contaminated the air with toxic chemicals that traveled hundreds of miles. Again, Elastol could have prevented this from happening because the polymer inhibits vaporization when added to the insecticides. By keeping the poisons from evaporating into the air mass, toxins could have been prevented from spreading. Yet, not enough people read the book, so there was effectively no public pressure for the crop sprayers to change their methods. The only institution in the country that did any work to introduce new technology to this field was the University of California at Davis, but that was only because the agriculture sprays affected the neighboring vineyards.

Critics may argue that GTA didn't know how to market Elastol or suffered from other execution problems. It may be true that GTA could have possibly found an ally or a customer in another country. But Mr. Trippe was no naïve entrepreneur. Having worked in the State Department for many years, he knew who to approach in the government to sell his products. He also managed to get shows like *Nova* and

*Beyond 2000* to broadcast his groundbreaking technologies. He was rewarded 16 patents for these new discoveries, and he didn't give up for 30 years.

Ironically, the *Economist* reported that X Prize Foundation has set up a $1 million prize for anyone who can come up with a solution for cleaning up oil spills. Such prizes are disingenuous public relations ploys that mislead the public into thinking nothing has been done because of lack of know-how when, in reality, solutions already exist but are actively ignored by companies and even regulators. Indeed, many entrepreneurs who have tried to submit their solutions reported that their applications had been firewalled from the submission website.

It is entirely possible that Elastol has drawbacks that Mr. Trippe did not convey to me. But even with drawbacks, one would think that an open marketplace would allow for more than one solution to address problems. The sad lesson we learn from the story about Elastol is that when new technologies are developed for markets that are already occupied by strong, entrenched powers, these innovations face strikingly low odds of succeeding due to powerful political resistance.

Just as we know that working out once a month doesn't take off excess weight, we should acknowledge that following existing economic prescriptions, which are often piecemeal, will continue to fail if we don't make some real adjustments. To quote Einstein: "The definition of insanity is doing the same thing over and over again expecting different results." If Americans want to fix the structural impediments to our economy, we must leave outmoded assumptions behind. We need to test new economic policies and develop fresh theories of what is possible. Some of these theories and policies may seem radical—such as demanding that that the U.S. government levels the playing field for new entrants. But we must be open to experimentation in order to save our future. China's SEZs have demonstrated that this technical model has worked in a country of over a billion people. Isn't it time that the United States give it the old college try too?

# 6

# Real Economy First

The chief value of money lies in the fact that one lives in a world in which it is overestimated.   — H. L. MENCKEN

FOR DECADES, THE U.S. FINANCIAL SERVICES INDUSTRY has played an important role in allocating capital to great businesses and ideas. Analogies have been made that financial services is akin to the circulatory system, circulating money to different industries and companies. In the process, financial firms assist in creating great wealth, producing world-class companies all over the world today.

But because money is used in every industry, financial services, unlike other industries, affect the entire ecosystem. This special trait therefore puts the financial industry into a separate category from all other industries. As such, a watchful eye must oversee its activities and abilities so that the financial industry doesn't overstep its boundaries given its unique power. Returning to the circulatory analogy, cash, like blood, is integral to the economic system. But if a patient receives too much blood in a blood transfusion, the patient dies. In other words, the financial services industry, if too powerful, can negatively impact other industries in the economy. In 2008, the world discovered that is exactly what happened.

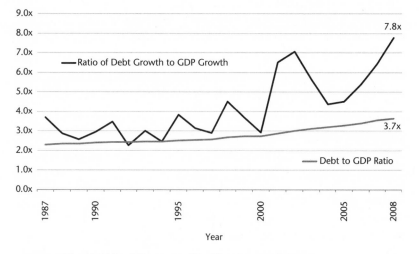

**FIGURE 2**  The Bubble: A Portrait of Inefficiency and Waste

Source: World Bank; Federal Reserve; Westwood Capital

## Masters of the Universe

Simon Johnson, a former chief economist at the International Monetary Fund, wrote in his article "The Quiet Coup" (*Atlantic Monthly,* May 2009) that Wall Street elites had captured Washington DC. At the time, most Americans were just beginning to make sense of what had happened to the nation. Simon's accusations—the U.S. government had become a banana republic thanks to financial elites who overpowered democracy—came to some as a surprise. Shortly thereafter, Matt Taibbi, editor of *Rolling Stone,* wrote more colorfully that Goldman Sachs was a vampire squid sucking up humanity. In other words, he was describing how Goldman Sachs had used its unprecedented reach and power to defraud millions of people around the world and get away with it. Since then, much has transpired that has reinforced their views and those of many others who have written countless books and articles about the financial crisis.

Contrary to what the news media reported, the Dodd-Frank Act of 2010 was not nearly as sweeping and radical as the legislation that came out of the Pecora Hearings after the Crash of 1929. Back then, the U.S. government enacted the Glass-Steagall Act, which separated commercial banks from investment banks so that speculators could not use money from depositors for speculative purposes. Lawmakers also created the Federal Deposit Insurance Corporation (FDIC) to protect bank depositors and the SEC to monitor fraud. But in 1999, during the Clinton administration, the 1933 Glass-Steagall Act was repealed. Consequently, large commercial banks such as Citigroup undertook speculative activities that ultimately required billions of dollars worth of taxpayer bailouts to save them from bankruptcy. The Financial Reform Bill that was signed into law by President Obama did not reinstate the Glass-Steagall provision. It also didn't put into place any of the critical measures that could prevent another large-scale crisis from taking place again, such as forcing the large banks to split up into smaller banks to avoid the moral hazard known as "too big to fail" (TBTF). Advocates of real financial reform, who claim that banks outspent them in lobbying dollars by a ratio of 100 to 1, maintain that the "reform" was mere window dressing to appease the financially illiterate public. The legislation did not change the rules that precipitated the crisis, but only instituted token changes that would not deprive financial institutions of the freedom to operate as they wish. The environment we have created can be summed up in one word: *financialization*.

What is financialization? Here are just two of the various definitions offered by academics:

- "a pattern of accumulation in which profit making occurs increasingly through financial channels rather than through trade and commodity production" (Greta Krippner of the University of California, Los Angeles)
- "a process whereby financial services, broadly construed, take over the dominant economic, cultural, and political role in a national economy" (Kevin Phillips in his 2006 book, *American*

*Theocracy: The Peril and Politics of Radical Religion, Oil, and Borrowed Money in the 21st Century)*[1]

Whichever definition one uses, financialization describes a classic case of the tail wagging the dog. In theory, financiers are supposed to help the real economy operate more efficiently by finding the best uses of capital. But in today's reality, the real economy has been hampered by financiers who have become too powerful. Rather than Wall Street serving the real economy, Wall Street has enslaved it. Financialization has put the cart before the horse.

The evidence for financialization is everywhere. In 1987, financial services accounted for 5 percent of the S&P 500 total market capitalization. Twenty years later, the financial services market makes up more than 20 percent of that index. At the same time, trade-sensitive industries, such as manufacturing, have declined in economic importance. According to the Bureau of Economic Analysis, manufacturing was 21 percent of GDP in 1980 but has fallen to 12 percent in 2008. Finally the U.S. Department of Commerce reported that financial services, at $241 billion, were among America's highest export categories in 2009.

Even more disturbing is the prospect that there may be nowhere in the world to escape its pernicious effects. According to McKinsey Global Institute's annual global mapping report, the interconnectedness of world financial markets has been growing exponentially. Just prior to the credit crisis, cross-border capital flows exceeded $6 trillion, almost quadrupling since 1995. Moreover, debt in the form of cross-border lending between banks and non-financial institutions was the largest component, accounting for a whopping 42 percent of total capital flows. In contrast, cross-border mergers and foreign direct investment together only accounted for 15 percent of total cross-border capital flows. Rather than greasing the wheels of global commerce, financialization has already proven that it can induce the entire world economy to fall off a cliff as we have witnessed in the aftermath of the Lehman Brothers bankruptcy.

Crisis is a natural state of affairs for financialization since the problem is never solved—it merely moves around geographically. Starting in the 1980s we had the Latin American crisis, followed by the Mexican crisis, the Long-Term Capital Management scandal, the Asian crisis, the Russian crisis, and the dot-com bubble before we finally had the subprime crisis, which hit the whole world. Although the central banks of the world came together to avoid a liquidity crunch to keep the world from falling into another depression, none of the underlying problems were fixed, the most egregious one being too much capital from too much leverage. That leaves the granddaddy of all crises—a reserve currency crisis—looming before us.

The root cause is deregulation of the financial system that empowered financiers to overstep prudential rules that originally ringfenced them. Deregulation enabled financiers to control the means of production and the economy rather than merely assist in the process. Interestingly in the United States, both political parties supported financial deregulation. Under the Clinton administration, Glass-Steagall was revoked and over-the-counter derivatives were allowed to multiply freely without being subject to the same scrutiny as stocks. Under the Bush administration, the SEC raised the permissible leverage ratios for banks. The cumulative effect of restrictions that were dismantled heightened financiers' abilities to grow exponentially wealthier with far greater ease than the rest of the economy. This became possible because financiers had access to vast amounts of leverage without having to pay the consequences. To build a factory and turn a profit selling tangible products could take years, while amassing a fortune through a single financial transaction took only seconds to complete.

Great wealth begets great power. By 2008 when the financial crisis hit, the financiers at the largest firms had become so powerful that all the rules were changed on the fly.[2] Like sovereign nations, they can't go bankrupt.[3]

When assets and the means of production can be easily separated from the original owners who have invested hard-earned savings and sweat equity into their assets, it creates a situation in which the new owners, the financiers, do not have the same interest in the success of these assets. Without an emotional stake, they are likely not to give the assets the same level of care as the original owners. For the person who uses his or her own capital, sweat equity, and valuable time to build an asset, there is nothing more demoralizing than to see a financier use the power of leverage to seize control of the same asset through financial means. Whether such financial means are called leverage buyouts, private equity, distressed investing, or hostile takeovers, such financing behavior can sometimes border on legal theft. Though legal, these methods allow a person or group of persons to take possession or control of someone else's property via financial sleights of hand based on terms that the original property owner would not have agreed to had the negotiating power been more equal.

## Private Equity Pirates

Private equity firms like Kohlberg Kravitz Roberts & Co. (KKR), Carlyle Group, and the Blackstone Group, as well as all the large multinational banks like JPMorgan and Citigroup, have taken over both public and private companies by borrowing large amounts of money from the bond markets to fund their purchases. According to Thomson Reuters, there were 1,382 transactions in 2007, representing a 30-fold jump in private equity deal volume between 1995 and 2007. The amount of money followed a similar trajectory. In 1995, only $28 billion was engaged in this kind of financial activity. By 2007, it had reached $797 billion.

A vast majority of these transactions are done for purely financial reasons, which are often at odds with the national goal of creating jobs or driving innovation. The financiers typically target cash-rich companies in order to extract the cash from the company's balance sheet. They do this by paying themselves large dividends once they control the companies. As soon as these financial players take control of a company, they temporarily hire turnaround artists from restructuring firms like Alvarez and Marsal to fire employees at the newly acquired company. Firing people is the preferred method of how these financiers "add value" and "increase profitability and efficiency" because cost cutting is the easiest way to increase profits of a company in the shortest amount of time.[4] Increasing sales, on the other hand, is usually a much more difficult task and requires much more specialized knowledge. But since these financial players are primarily interested in quick profits through financial engineering, they customarily sell the same acquired company back into the public markets or sell it to another company for a profit once the costs have been cut to the barest minimum. Avis is an example of a company that was bought and sold over a dozen times between various financial players. Every time the company was bought and sold, the company experienced employee turnover. The company is arguably no better off than when it started.

Since the 1980s, these financiers have popularized and replayed this same cookie-cutter transaction thousands of times over with companies they claim they have "improved operationally." The reality is that what the vast majority of these financiers have accomplished is the equivalent of furniture rearranging. While they reaped larger and larger profits for themselves, millions of American employees were fired, and future investments in research were sacrificed. Furthermore, the investment portfolios of these financial elites not only include ownership of entire companies all over the world but increasingly include public assets like stadiums, bridges, and ports. Taken to its logical end, it is possible that they could eventually own entire states, as desperate governments around the world have no choice but to privatize public assets in order to raise cash for the their now-empty public coffers. After all, Citibank alone, whose offices span 140 countries, made more money in 2010 than the poorest 10 countries combined.

## Traitorous Traders

Another highly disruptive financial activity involves *carry trades,* in which a trader from the developed world—namely the United States and London—borrows money in the cheapest currency and reinvests it in higher-yielding or higher-return investments for a quick profit, usually through hedge funds and large multinational financial institutions. An example of a carry trade is the money U.S. banks have been borrowing from the U.S. Federal Reserve at essentially zero interest rates. These financial institutions take the interest-free money and reinvest it in Treasury bonds, stock markets, corporate bonds, derivatives, other currencies, or commodities. The large amount of borrowed money that goes into these other financial markets artificially drives up prices for every financial instrument and commodity around the world. The money used for such purposes has reached hundreds of trillions of dollars—many times the entire world's GDP—because printing money via leverage requires nothing more than a simple computer keystroke. The only limit to such activity would be through financial regulation. But since regulators in developed nations, particularly in the United States, have been fairly liberal and permissive to the entities they regulate, the capital at the disposal of these financial institutions has become virtually limitless.

Inevitably, when the rich nations provide their financial institutions loans—that are tantamount to free money when interest rates are held near zero—to invest in however they please around the world, this *hot money* as it is known, can cause serious economic harm. In the United States, financial institutions were loaned over $2.5 trillion by the Federal Reserve to rebuild their balance sheets.[5] But instead of using these funds to provide loans to real economy businesses in the United States, these financial institutions lent the money to hedge funds or used the free money to speculate in various financial markets for easy profits.

Some of this hot money has been used to purchase long-dated

U.S. Treasuries (Treasuries with long maturities) and riskier corporate bonds. These large bond purchases have driven bond yields so low that borrowing costs for corporations returned to the same rates as it was just before the 2008 financial crisis.[6] Many expert observers believed that credit risk was being systematically mispriced once again. Even more have become skeptical of the Federal Reserve's credibility as a guardian of stable monetary conditions. Announcements of quantitative easing by the Fed were viewed as mere money-printing exercises fueling more dangerous economic bubbles.[7] Rather than help solve the problem of America's overreliance on debt in our financial system, the Federal Reserve has been increasingly seen as the source of the problem.[8]

Other hot money has gone into stock markets, artificially driving up stock prices so that the wealthy who own the majority of these assets will accrue the majority of the benefits. The artificially rising stock market also encourages more speculation from people who would otherwise find work with regular pay. When average citizens feel that they can make more money gambling in the stock market than in working at a real job, they are more likely to withdraw from being productive citizens in the real economy. A look at online brokerage data supports this trend. Prior to the 1970s, day-trading was practically nonexistent among small investors because of long settlement dates and higher commissions. But according to quarterly reports several decades later, TD Ameritrade, Schwab, and Etrade together account for about 16 million customer accounts and 540,000 trades a day. The total number of online accounts and daily trades may be multiples higher since many retail brokerage firms such as Fidelity and Scottrade also offer day-trading platforms. The total U.S. labor force is only about 150 million, according to the June 2011 report from the Bureau of Labor Statistics. If this trend persists and day-trading becomes more popular, America could become a nation of gamblers with no one left willing to work.

Hot money has also flowed into global commodity markets causing harmful inflation everywhere on the globe.[9] Skyrocketing prices for precious and base metals can hurt manufacturing profits and drive companies out of business for everything ranging from autos to medical devices. Rapidly rising food inflation is causing starvation among the poorest populations in Asia, Africa, and the Middle East, prompting widespread riots and protests.[10] While the Federal Reserve may deny responsibility for creating these speculative hot money flows, the trouble is that nothing, not even weather disruptions, can explain the coincidentally sharp rise in everything around the world since the Federal Reserve began its unprecedented money printing of trillions of dollars.

Finally, hot money has flowed across nations' borders swiftly, causing much economic instability to developing nations offering higher interest rates. While some U.S. regulators, like the Federal Reserve, have argued that it is good for developing nations to receive capital, they fail to distinguish between the type of capital that is harmful and that which is beneficial to economic development. Harmful capital is the hot money that is extremely short-term in nature. The money comes in to buy foreign currencies and sovereign debt, causing import and export prices to change so dramatically that businesses are unable to establish terms of trade for any length of time. Such currency volatility hurts cross-border trades of real goods and services. International trade can again grind to a halt as it did in the years leading up to World War II when businesses had difficulty pricing items due to rapid currency debasement from Western countries seeking to make their exports more competitive. Instability in these markets can also lead to widespread bankruptcies that leave millions unemployed. The local businesses in these developing nations have no effective way to protect themselves from persistent volatility other than to buy foreign exchange contracts that guarantee specific prices. But the financial contracts themselves can be priced expensively so that buying them essentially would have the same effect as passing all the hard-earned money in the real economy back to the financiers.

In any case, the economic situation for these developing countries has been rigged to favor the financiers under the mantra of "free market capitalism."

## The Secondary Effects

Having too many financial professionals has led to shortages of other professionals. The *Yale Daily News* reported as early as 2005 that many of its science majors were "selling out" for higher-paying business jobs such as those in finance. A whopping 58 percent of Harvard's 2009 graduating students went into banking, a career choice that could certainly help pay off their large student loans. According to Reuters, Wall Street paid cash bonuses of $20.8 billion, the fifth-highest on record in 2010.[11] That number translates to an average cash bonus of $128,530 per person, which is *in addition* to the base salary. The compensation at some financial firms was even more extreme. The average worker at Goldman Sachs, which includes secretaries and recent graduates, earned $498,000 in 2009 and $430,000 in 2010.[12] Fred Merkel, a high-frequency trader for Bank of Montreal, surmised that even in 2011, large multinational banks were still handing out employment contracts to individuals with upfront guarantees of millions of dollars in compensation. In contrast, the Bureau of Labor Statistics reported that the average salary for engineering managers of all types was only $125,000 in 2010.

Such a brain drain out of the sciences comes at a cost to technological and scientific endeavors that produce real goods and services. The creation of things such as preventative drugs and clean energy can improve the standard of living for more people than would the creation of more financial contracts. For example, according to *National Review* columnist Jerry Bowyer, the United States cannot afford to implement a universal health care program because there are not enough medical professionals in the country to service the additional 80 million uninsured patients. Similarly, the *Washington Post* and the

*Wall Street Journal* also reported that the shortage of doctors has fallen below the safe ratio of 2000 patients per doctor. Fewer people are choosing to practice medicine largely because they do not feel adequately compensated for their time and risk when compared to Wall Street professions. The insurance industry, for instance, has largely usurped the profits that would otherwise be used to pay healthcare professionals. Dr. Klaus Lessnau who oversees pulmonary research at Lenox Hill Hospital and New York University resents that hospital management makes more money than the most senior surgeons. As a result, the supply of workers in areas such as the medical profession that deliver goods and services of real value to the economy have been curtailed by the financial industry.

If financialization is left unchecked, America will lose its competitiveness, its innovative dynamism, its way of life, and will slowly transform into a society that may more resemble a caste because social mobility will become increasingly difficult. According to Stephen Kaplan, professor at the University of Chicago, there are "more than twice as many Wall Street individuals as Main Street individuals (non-financial top executives) in the top 0.5 percent and the top 0.1 percent of the adjusted gross income (AGI) distribution." It is no surprise then that the city with the most billionaires in the world, with a total of 45 according to *Forbes,* is New York City, dubbed by CNBC as the finance capital of the world. Once upon a time, the robber barons dominated their respective industries and amassed enormous personal fortunes. Today, the financial elite have become their equivalents in modern society. The difference is that the robber barons at least built great infrastructure for America, such as railroads, while Wall Street titans have left nothing of lasting value for society.

Furthermore, wealth is highly correlated to power. According to G. William Domoff, professor of sociology at the University of Santa Cruz:

> Power is defined as the ability or capacity to realize wishes and reach goals even in the face of opposition. . . . Wealth can be seen as a

"resource" that is very useful in exercising power. That's obvious when we think of donations to political parties, payments to lobbyists, and grants to experts who are employed to think up new policies beneficial to the wealthy. Wealth also can be useful in shaping the general social environment to the benefit of the wealthy, whether through hiring public relations firms or donating money for universities, museums, music halls, and art galleries. . . . Certain kinds of wealth, such as stock ownership, can be used to control corporations, which of course have a major impact on how the society functions. . . . The United States is a power pyramid. It's tough for the bottom 80 percent—maybe even the bottom 90 percent—to get organized and exercise much power.[13]

## Say No to Finance

All of this capital havoc had been wreaked on nations, especially poor ones, for decades until China came onto the scene. During the Asian crisis of 1997, China watched closely how financial capital affected the real economy of all their neighbors from Malaysia to South Korea. With the wisdom of that experience at hand, the CCP was determined to ensure that such instability would not be allowed to dismantle the hard work and fortunes of its own people. Rather than listen to the Washington consensus, they decided to delay the development of their financial system and focus instead on developing their real economy first. As a result, their industrial sector grew rapidly, protected by an environment of stable prices due to a tight rein on the financial sector and a pegged exchange rate.

China's solution to financialization is to turn hot money into *patient capital*. Patient capital is direct investment in the real economy, such as building infrastructure and creating businesses that offer products and services people need for survival. For example, foreign direct investments by American companies in China to build research and development laboratories, manufacturing plants, and retail outlets have been granted the right to enter and exit the country unhindered. Unlike financial capital or hot money, patient capital doesn't slosh around the economy looking for the next big payoff. Patient capital can enter and exit across borders without causing economic harm because it assists the growth of the real economy rather than undermining it.

Another reason that China has flourished so remarkably is that its citizens had limited opportunities to speculate and squander their savings. The only way out of poverty for most was through old-fashioned ingenuity, hard work, and long-term planning. As an example, hedge funds were illegal in China before 2010.[14] As a result, millions of real economy companies and trillions of dollars worth of goods and services were created. According to China's official statistics, China's GDP was only $306 million in 1980. By 2009, China reached a GDP of $4.9 trillion, surpassing Germany as the world's largest exporter and third largest economy in the world

China does have rapidly growing stock markets and a burgeoning bond market where unsophisticated citizens can speculate. There are even brokerage firms that host individuals who just want to day-trade their savings all day. But compared to the United States, the trading in financial markets in China is miniscule, accounting for less than a quarter of its GDP. In contrast, U.S. trading of its stock markets in 2000 was 145 percent of its GDP. By end of June 2010, U.S. trading in financial derivatives was $583 trillion, while its GDP was only $14.8 trillion.[15] In other words, trading in the over-the-counter derivatives market alone was 40 times larger than the nation's entire GDP for a year.[16] This trading doesn't even include the trillions that are traded in the equities, bonds, and foreign exchange markets. With so much money that can easily be made trading other people's money, what economic incentive is there to build anything of value? Why become an entrepreneur in America, which would require years of labor that could still yield no material success, when it is so easy to become a trader or an investment banker and earn millions, or even billions, a year with relatively little effort? The choice is clear, and the U.S. government and Federal Reserve have been tacitly supporting this choice to the detriment of working people.

To put it in stark terms, there would be no China miracle if China followed the same monetary and fiscal policies as the United States. Unquestioningly, its economy would be ruined like the economies of so many other nations that have let Wall Street get ahead of the real economy. While China's pegged exchange rate has been accused of being manipulative, China certainly was not the first nation to follow such policies. During the era of Bretton Woods, shortly after the end of World War II, Singapore, as well as Japan and Germany, experienced rapid economic development due to pegged exchange rates. Bretton Woods was a system of fixed exchange rates that 44 Allied nations adopted in an attempt to avoid the currency manipulation that preceded World War II. This idea has been resurrected as a topic of conversation among those in financial circles who do not see monetary policy by the Federal Reserve as legitimate. With a fixed exchange rate, financial institutions cannot interfere with the development of the real economy through foreign exchange markets and their derivative products. Arguably, the Industrial Revolution would not have been possible in the United States and Europe had it not been for the stabilizing effect of the gold standard during the period before World War I. With major currencies pegged to gold, central banks and financiers didn't have the power to manipulate currencies to their own advantage. The real economy flourished with innovation and prosperity for the benefit of the larger population during that time. So from a historical perspective, keeping finance in check and developing the real economy makes great empirical sense.

China's foresight became obvious to me when I went back to Shanghai in 2006 to do some research on China's State Administration of Foreign Exchange (SAFE). While meeting with representatives from Credit Suisse, Deutche Bank, and other firms, I had discovered that the Chinese officials were deliberately moving slowly on initiatives to develop the financial sector. Aside from the fancy stock exchange that was built, the Chinese dragged their feet on other financial proposals for futures trading and the liberalizing of other derivative markets. Submissions to government authorities would seemingly land in the wastebasket as getting government responses to these banks frequently lasted two years or more while responses to other industries were markedly more prompt.

I later learned that China had set up specific research arms that were independent of banks and brokerage units to investigate the likely effects and possible unintended consequences of permitting such financial products into the financial marketplace. In many ways, the Chinese method of financial regulation is similar to the process used by the U.S. Food and Drug Administration (FDA) to approve new drugs. Before a drug can be commercialized in America, the drug must undergo rigorous testing from clinical trials and be evaluated against a long list of safety measures. Likewise, the Chinese financial regulatory authorities independently conduct investigations on financial products and policies. Once researched, they review the results before giving approvals. But in the United States, new financial products are invented daily and sold to investors who are willing to purchase them. Financial innovations are not subject to reviews or approvals by United States financial regulators so long as the financial products do not violate existing laws. As a result, the alphabet soup of credit derivatives worth trillions of dollars escaped regulatory scrutiny from all the U.S. financial regulatory authorities. These were the same financial products that almost caused the collapse of the global financial system in 2008.

In addition to precautionary testing of financial products, the Chinese also require that loans reach maturity before their bankers are paid for the transactions. This policy ensures that bankers are not disaggregated from the borrower and will retain responsibility for the loan quality of the loans underwritten. A major problem with the securitized products leading up to the financial crisis of 2008 was that bankers were paid a commission for simply processing a loan application. If the loans went south, the bankers did not have to assume any responsibility for the losses. Making sure that financiers have skin in the game would help rein in irresponsible risk-taking behavior.

The Chinese government also announced in 2010 that it plans to open up other industries that were formerly closed to private investment, such as infrastructure, health care providers, and even certain types of banking. The number of people who will participate in these opportunities for wealth creation will multiply. By ensuring that other non-financial industries have a chance to flourish without outsized influence from financiers, the Chinese government will help create an economy that is entrepreneurial, diverse, and robust.

## Currency Manipulators

China's strong economic engine as a result of its peg to the U.S. dollar has been a blessing for the entire world except to the financiers. After the 2008 financial crisis, China single-handedly brought the world out of recession, assisting countries from Brazil to South Africa to resume strong economic growth comparable to pre-Lehman levels.[17] Had China not been in the picture, the world would have most definitively hit depression levels because no other country was strong and large enough to drive demand when demand vanished from American and European consumers mired in crippling debt. China was able to engineer this feat because the financial institutions in China were heavily controlled and regulated by the Chinese government. Financial institutions like hedge funds were outlawed, and banks were prohibited from gambling with depositors' money. Instead, the financial institutions were directed by the central government to lend to real economy projects that would generate millions of jobs for the Chinese people immediately as well as far into the future. This included many plans for infrastructure, such as additional passenger terminals at airports that put people to work in the short term while laying the groundwork for future economic activity.[18] These projects in turn required importing many resources from countries around the world which kick-started those foreign economies as well. Two years after the crisis, thanks to China, the economies of most developing countries had returned to growth levels comparable to pre-crisis levels. As the IMF reported, emerging market economies rebounded into positive territory in 2009 while developed countries experienced negative growth, and by 2010, emerging market economies exceeded their 2008 growth rates, growing on average 7 percent per annum.

But despite the enormous role China played in saving the economic fortunes of the world, including those of many U.S. businesses that were able to return to profitability by selling to the growing Chinese consumer class instead of indebted Americans, Washington and Western media have been relentless in filling the airwaves with vituperative accusations of China being a currency manipulator. Washington needed a scapegoat to blame for the enormous economic woes the nation suffered from the hands of its own Wall Street cronies and decided to use China as the convenient whipping boy. Even more sinister and outrageous, on March 2, 2011, the Pentagon went so far as to suggest that foreign countries such as China could have damaged the Western financial system.

Anyone who has worked in China knows this is impossible due to China's complete lack of financial sophistication as well as its extremely conservative stance toward its financial reserves. The author of the report making such claims is Kevin Freeman, who said on the record that "the two major strategic threats, radical jihadists and the Chinese, are among the best positioned in the economic battle space."[19] He jumped to these conclusions when he admittedly had no evidence about the two unidentified traders he claimed caused the stock markets to go down and no evidence that they even happened outside U.S. borders.

Given the number of hedge fund managers, such as David Einhorn of Greenlight Capital, who were calling for Lehman's demise publicly, it is certainly possible that the traders were in fact U.S. institutional money managers with trillions under management. These money managers could have borrowed amounts that were several times the worth of their net assets under management from the large multinational banks who offered prime brokerage services. Then they could have used this borrowed money to make risky bets that included shorting financial stocks.[20] (Shorting a stock is a trading strategy that enables one to profit if a stock falls in price.) By using both their own assets and the borrowed capital, these money managers could have placed bets and increased their profits exponentially if trades moved in their favor. Hedge funds alone had around $2.2 trillion under management in 2007 right before the credit crisis, according to International Financial Services London, a UK lobby group. Naked short selling, an easy strategy by stock traders to drive down share prices of stocks, was widespread in the United States, especially among hedge fund managers, up until September 2008 when the SEC restricted the practice in response to the financial crisis.[21] Short selling was illegal in China.[22]

## Financial Warfare

The inverse situation, however, is far more likely. According to Marc Chandler, head of currency research at Brown Brothers Harriman, the financial research arm of the CIA is producing simulation games of financial warfare, hiring currency specialists who work in private investment banks to provide expertise. Furthermore, Wall Street has had decades of practice outsmarting and neutralizing developing countries with financial warfare through financialization and is ready to make China its next victim. China represents the last and final frontier for the financiers to prey with abandon, and Wall Street can't wait. Sophisticated Western hedge funds and investment banking proprietary traders dream of the day they can initiate a financial attack on China's currency the same way George Soros famously broke the Bank of England in September of 1992. On the day now known as Black Wednesday, Soros walked away with billions. Financiers have more recently tried to break up the euro, but their efforts have been continually thwarted by China's opposite move to save it by its large purchases of Spanish and Greek bonds.[23]

One hypothetical scenario is that the U.S. government will continue to pressure China to make its currency float freely on the foreign exchange markets while at the same time run up its fiscal deficit unsustainably in tandem with the Federal Reserve's inflationary money-printing activities. By monetizing Treasury debt and holding short-term interest rates below global inflation rates, the Federal Reserve encourages speculators to drive up the prices of most everything in the world. If China is forced to decouple its yuan peg to the U.S. dollar due to painfully high inflation that it is importing as a result of loose U.S. monetary policies, sophisticated hedge fund managers and other currency speculators will pounce on the opportunity to attack China's currency.[24] Speculators can easily drive the value of the yuan to extreme highs or lows since they can all make the same one-way bets. In 2010, currency traders drove the euro down from $1.50 until it was almost on par with the U.S. dollar by responding to speculation that the euro would break up.[25] These speculators also are permitted much higher leverage in their currency trades (400 to 1)[26] by brokerage firms than most retail stock traders get (2 to 1). This arbitrary rule gives traders more firepower to force a currency to move according to their whims. Such a political move against the wishes of the Chinese government by the U.S. government would be quite effective in taking down China's economy without necessarily hurting large U.S. multinationals. The reason is that large U.S. companies could simply buy reasonably priced financial instruments from the American financial firms to protect themselves from a wildly fluctuating exchange rate while Chinese companies would be at the mercy of American financial firms who could discriminatorily charge outrageously higher prices for the same financial protection. Chinese financial firms have yet to gain permission from Chinese regulatory authorities to offer a variety of sophisticated financial hedging products to their customers. Although slowly catching up, they also do not have a deep bench of financial experts to compete with the likes of Goldman Sachs. If Chinese companies cannot protect themselves from wildly fluctuating prices from foreign exchange volatility on everything from imported commodities to exports, they would all be unable to conduct international business and thus go bankrupt.

The current foreign exchange market structure still makes it impossible to prevent speculative attacks. Unlike a stock exchange, foreign exchange is unregulated and conducted in over-the-counter (OTC) markets all over the world, which means that the trading happens over the phone, fax, or electronic network in a decentralized manner because there is no exchange or meeting place for this market. The lack of a centralized market place, the lack of transparency, and the lack of technology to enable central banks to deter currency attacks make foreign exchange markets a particularly vexing problem for governments everywhere, except the United States because of its reserve currency status. Speculators can attack a currency by launching trades in various geographic locations hiding behind and acting through multiple banks. For instance, Soros's fund could launch a currency attack on a country by placing separate trades with Deutsche Bank, Goldman Sachs, Credit Suisse, and others to sell a currency at any price. As a client of these financial firms, Soros's firm's identity is protected and unknown in the vast currency marketplace. The currency in question could start falling in value, and no one would be able to trace the trades back to Soros. So without a sophisticated system in place, central banks have no way of monitoring in real time what is happening. By the time an attack is detected, it is too late to do much of anything, while the attacker could walk away with billions of dollars in one day and be ready to come back for more the next day. Since some large speculators, such as Duquesne Capital Management or Quantum Fund, remain unregulated, their speculation can increase volatility in prices and cause the value of a currency

to deviate far from its fundamental value while escaping any regulatory demands to stop such harmful behavior. This manipulation of
currency value could disrupt trade, distress many domestic Chinese
companies, cause economic recession, and even induce a civil crisis or
depression in extreme cases.

Soon after the 2011 earthquake in Japan, deputy finance minister
Fumihiko Igarashi said, "The yen's rise was driven by speculators. If
we caved into such speculators that took advantage of people's misfortunes, the Japanese economy would be ruined, and the whole world
economy would be harmed."[27] In response, the G-7 Finance Ministers and Central Bank Governors admitted that government intervention in exchange markets is justified when "excess volatility and
disorderly movements in exchange rates have adverse implications
for economic and financial stability."[28] The effect of a rapidly rising
yuan would be no different. In simple terms, without a sophisticated
system in place, foreign hedge fund managers could walk away with
billions of dollars of reserves that were earned by real economy businesses operating in China.

Why would the United States potentially favor such a scenario?
Historically speaking, the rise of a nation that challenges the power
of another has often provoked great insecurity that leads to instability and wars. Today, with unemployment stubbornly high and the
U.S. Army still guarding the same Korean border that saw vicious
fighting with Chinese forces in the 1950s, the danger of kicking off
World War III is remote but not impossible. One could argue that one
way to diffuse the economic tensions that can lead to war would be to
destabilize China's economic situation so that it will never have the
economic means to catch up militarily to confront the United States.
Compare this to how Israel is suspected to have used a cyber-attack
through computer viruses to neutralize Iran's nuclear program without launching a full-scale war.[29] In a scenario using financial speculation to attack China, it would be more difficult to pin blame on the
United States for victimizing China in this way since the terrorist

speculators would be almost impossible to trace. Repeated speculative attacks could slow China's economic advance dramatically as top government officials are forced to divert attention away from other issues in order to deal with the currency problem and the resulting economic upheaval that could arise from such destabilizing economic forces. While currency attacks could be as destabilizing as a permanent revaluation, the difference is that large foreign multinationals could shield themselves by purchasing foreign exchange derivatives from large Western multinational banks that are all too happy to win additional foreign exchange business. Nonetheless, if this scenario were to unfold, it could severely damage China's economic efficiency and force the Chinese citizens to suffer a worse fate than the Japanese, who already enjoyed a much higher standard of living comparatively speaking when their economy crashed in the 1990s.

Such may be the sad reality in the end if the United States pursues this foreign policy strategy, causing the whole world to lose a productive force. If China had never opened its doors to the world, hundreds of millions of people probably would not have escaped poverty. Indeed it was only about a dozen years ago that the *Economist* had a picture of Africa on its cover with the title "Hopeless Continent." Chinese foreign direct investment in this continent turned things around. After the financial crisis, China had an integral role in preventing a worse catastrophe, which was a great blessing for every nation, including the United States, whose companies hit record profits selling to China in 2010.[30]

## Dark Ages—Again?

Against the backdrop of the growing wealth inequality and economic stagnation in the United States, innovation—widely accepted as a necessary ingredient for sustainable economic growth and wealth creation—also shows signs of heading in the wrong direction. Jonathan Huebner, a physicist who works at the Pentagon's Naval Air Warfare Center, studied the rate of significant innovations as catalogued in *The History of Science and Technology*. According to Mr. Huebner, the rate of innovation peaked in 1873 and has been declining ever since. He calculated that in terms of important technological developments, the world's current innovation rate is roughly seven per billion people per year, comparable to the rates back in 1600. If extrapolated, by 2024, innovation rates will have stagnated to the same level as it was during the Dark Ages.[31] Indeed, at the end of the 19th and the beginning of the 20th century, the world produced many inventors, including Thomas Edison and Alberto Santos-Dumont, as well as pioneering scientists, such as Marie Curie, who created life-changing inventions and made breakthrough discoveries that don't have their equivalents today.

While authors such as Ray Kurzweil and Matt Ridley would argue that innovation is increasing exponentially based on past trends, anecdotal evidence in everyday life doesn't appear to bear out their claims. After all, isn't it odd that it's always the same handful of companies—Apple, Google, Microsoft—that are most frequently cited as leaders in innovation when the United States can boast hundreds of large industrial companies? Are these other companies innovating at the same level? How come we haven't had a medical breakthrough like a cure for cancer after decades of research and billions of dollars later? Why was it that during the Industrial Revolution inventions spawned giant companies across multiple industries, yet, since then, only the information technology industry has followed that pattern a century later? Aside from those in information technology, why haven't there been more revolutionary inventions—revolutionary meaning that they fundamentally change the quality of life and serve as taproots for entrepreneurial offshoots? After all, more information, talent, and money exist now than ever before in history, yet we still haven't journeyed to distant galaxies, traveled through time, discovered the secret of immortality, or enjoy the easy life that science fiction promised us.

Two theories have been advanced by Huebner for why innovation rates are slowing to a crawl. The first is the low-hanging fruit theory: early innovators plucked the easiest-to-reach ideas, so later ones have to struggle to crack the harder problems. Or it may be that the massive accumulation of knowledge means that innovators have to stay in education longer to learn enough to invent something new and, as a result, less of their active life is spent innovating.

Former neurobiologist Paul Roossin worked as a researcher in the Human Language Technologies Laboratory at IBM's T.J. Watson Research Center. He doesn't believe that massive knowledge accumulation is the limiting factor. He said that sciences are rather easy to understand, given that most of them follow a certain logic that is consistent across scientific disciplines. Just as the social sciences are interrelated, so are the hard sciences. He claims his knowledge of chemistry is just as relevant to understanding biology and physics as was learning the rules specific to those disciplines. His ability to consult across sciences in equal fashion is not unusual.

The student exhibits at the 2010 World Science Festival held in New York City seem to lend support to Paul Roossin's claims. There, public high school students who had won a science contest displayed their own original scientific research that was on par with some of the best research labs in America. For instance, searching for the gene responsible for a certain type of cancer, one junior wrote a software program that simulated biological functions hundreds of times faster than if one were to record that behavior through empirical studies.

Today's potential inventors do have many advantages and tools that past inventors did not have, such as computer-aided design software at their disposal, which can speed up innovation. The exponentially faster and higher computing power available in the modern era should more than offset the greater time required for one to accumulate more knowledge. After all, information can be accessed and analyzed so much more quickly than a hundred years ago. Moreover, according to Paul Hoffman, author of *Wings of Madness,* the morality of scientists a century earlier drove them to conduct experiments using themselves as subjects. This had the effect of shortening their own life spans when compared with scientific inventors today. This further renders Huebner's explanations less plausible.

A theory Mr. Huebner did not consider is the systematic suppression of innovation in most industries. Austrian economist Joseph Schumpeter popularized a theory about the destruction of established companies through disruptive innovation called creative destruction. Could this be what is happening in limited circumstances? Mr. Schumpeter posited that the entry of innovative entrepreneurs would succeed in gaining market share in a capitalist society and thus destroy the profits and position of established companies while powering the economy ahead.

But the obstacle to creative destruction is described in Mancur Olson's book *The Rise and Decline of Nations*.[32] A leading economist, Mancur Olson describes how lobby groups organize over time to alter polices in their favor. Coalitions form to prevent change that would hurt its members. Since the burden is shared by the entire population and therefore unlikely to meet public resistance, these benefits initially seem inconsequential; but over time, the growing number of lobby groups and the benefits accrued to them end up stifling the nation as a whole.

It is clear that large established companies would not have any interest in seeing their market share or profit disappear to upstart entrepreneurs such as those behind Elastol that may have superior, innovative solutions. They would fortify their positions as much as they could by insisting on laws and policies that would protect their turf. The large and growing number of lobby groups in the United States—more than 17,000 in 2007—supports this hypothesis.

The United States is certainly not alone in experiencing this phenomenon. In some places in Latin America, a single company may monopolize an entire industry. The sons and daughters who take over control of a company from their parents ordinarily are not particularly innovative but have the financial resources to create laws that block new entrants from challenging the monopoly. Inefficiencies begin developing because there are no competitors to force improvements. When the established monopoly player cannot keep up with international competition, production starts sliding and domestic workers get laid off. As a result, the entire economy of the community suffers.

If the United States doesn't want to lose its competitive edge and experience this very predictable fate, it must give power to the entrepreneurs in the real economy. This, above all else, requires overcoming the inordinate amount of power that Wall Street has garnered over the years.

## Back to Basics

The United States could take a page out of China's playbook by restricting banks to traditional banking activities—making loans and taking deposits—as one possible solution. As Paul Volcker vigorously pointed out, the Glass-Steagall Act that separated investment banking from the more utilitarian, commercial banking kept the United States safe from a financial crisis reaching Depression-like levels up until the law was repealed. In some ways, China's financial regulatory system resembles the United States before Glass-Steagall was dismantled. The Chinese separate the functions between commercial banks and investment banks and have distinct regulatory agencies to govern them.

Lawrence Summers and others have argued that such a separation is unnecessary because that would not have prevented the fall of Lehman Brothers. Lehman, when it collapsed, was not also acting as a commercial bank. This argument has serious problems, however. Although Lehman remained an investment bank, the financial innovations that developed after Glass-Steagall was repealed blurred the distinctions between investment banking and commercial banking.

Furthermore, when Lehman Brothers went down, just about every other financial institution was in danger of collapsing as well. Had the Federal Reserve not intervened with historic emergency measures like guaranteeing money market funds, Lehman's downfall could have potentially wiped out the entire financial system. Even if we assume that Lehman couldn't destroy the financial system, the bankruptcies of Citibank, JP Morgan Chase, or any of the other multinational banks that conducted both commercial and investment banking activities because of the dismantling of Glass-Steagall would most certainly have done the job. Due to the elimination of Glass-Steagall, the existing multinational banks have all become TBTF, a problem that didn't exist before.

Reinstating lower leverage limits would also help solve the problem of TBTF. Part of the reason Wall Street became too powerful was the access to large amounts of leverage that they didn't used to have. The debt-to-net capital ratio—or leverage ratio—used to be 12 to 1 but was lifted to 40 to 1 for broker dealers when Christopher Cox headed the Securities and Exchange Commission. Less leverage would translate into smaller balance sheets. While this would certainly hurt the profitability of large banks, the net benefit is that financial capital would not overwhelm the real economy.

Financial institutions also used to be more conservatively managed when they were private partnerships. When partner capital was at risk, financial speculation did not run rampant because few would put their entire net worth on the line. But in more recent years, access to public markets and other innovative legal structures meant that financiers had free options. In other words, bankers and traders were rewarded for any profits they made from risk-taking behavior but did not have their wealth taken away if their actions resulted in losses. Like gamblers playing with other people's money, financiers had payoff profiles that encouraged speculation as opposed to prudent investments. If we balance the risk/reward tradeoffs more evenly, financiers will likely exercise greater self-restraint.

Proposals to reduce executive compensation have been advocated by populist groups. However, legislating such changes could become too arbitrary and create new problems. Under such a scenario, bank executives could find loopholes for compensation while regulations fail to reform the problem of a flawed incentive structure. A more straightforward way to reverse the brain drain into financial services is to follow the above prescription: limit leverage, increase personal accountability, and separate financial activities to provide more transparency and easier regulatory scrutiny. The consolidated effect of these three rule changes will naturally reduce the outsized profitability of financial services. Less profitability eventually will lead to lower compensation.

Finally, advocates for free-market capitalism should distinguish between capitalism for the real economy from capitalism for the financial community. China practices the former, encouraging capitalism to flourish in the real economy, which creates hundreds of millions of jobs and real wealth. Capitalism in the real economy enables large segments of the population to lift itself out of poverty into the middle class through real wealth creation. However, too much freedom in the financial economy can have the opposite effect. The failure of lawmakers to recognize the difference has contributed to the ascendancy of the financial sector to the most dominant position in the nation's economy at the expense of many other industries. Today, a significant percentage of the powerful and wealthy rely on financial markets to make a living, creating too much capital being sloshed around the global economy that can set off another financial crisis. They must be weaned from borrowing capital as their main line of business and source of income. It will be challenging, but the world can't afford another crisis of global magnitude.

If Americans want a healthier, more diverse economy, we should follow China's example of limiting the power of the financial sector while investing in other industries that have been neglected. Green technology has had vocal supporters. But the amount of money that has gone into green technology research from the federal government is negligible compared to the trillions that have been lent to the nation's largest banks with essentially no strings attached. Likewise, science funding to programs like NASA should be increased. Europeans have invested in a long-range plan to achieve energy independence by installing solar panels in North Africa, whose energy will be transported back to the European continent.[33] Americans have made no equivalent investments.

Many of us have been misled by government and industry spokespersons who claim innovation is alive and well by pointing to the successes of the information technology industry. A closer examination of the facts reveals that the high-tech industry gave birth to many successful start-ups only because it was an area that was largely unoccupied. Information technology was so different from traditional forms of media that the early entrants, such as Bill Gates of Microsoft, sneaked through under the radar before anyone could stop them. The challenge is to allow entrepreneurship to flourish in more established industries.

The nearly insurmountable obstacles that handicap disruptive entrepreneurial activity are bad enough, but the enduring effect of these practices is the continual brain drain out of industries that need innovation to sectors that arguably don't. As I briefly mentioned earlier, when people realize that it's too difficult to buck the system, they eventually abandon the good fight to follow the path of least resistance. Furthermore, the people who receive large compensation packages from big established firms inevitably drive up the cost of living. It becomes increasingly difficult for real economy entrepreneurs to start and sustain technologically innovative companies without regular incomes that keep up with inflation. Technological innovation often requires far more time and resources than would creating a service-oriented company like a hedge fund. The risk/reward ratio is so unfavorable that fewer entrepreneurs will be willing to stick it out. Eventually, most won't even consider a career in scientific fields and Mr. Huebner's prediction that the world will enter a period that parallels the Dark Ages will surely become realized.

We may never know to the fullest extent what the collateral damage of this systematic stifling of innovation has done to America. However, it is highly likely that the dearth of new start-ups with disruptive technology has exacerbated the growing problem of unemployment. Small and medium-sized enterprises (SMEs), which are defined as under 500 employees, have been significant sources of employment in America, accounting for roughly half of the workers in the private sector.[34] The taproot innovation called the Internet produced millions of small businesses that hired millions more. Where will the next taproot innovations come from if big industry conspires against the bright minds that dare to innovate and revive the economy?

The U.S. government can follow another of China's practices by creating government-backed incubators of technology. Private venture capital firms in Silicon Valley and Silicon Alley in New York City have provided incubator space, business advice, and funding for social media start-ups, but U.S. venture firms do not typically extend the financial and social support to the families of entrepreneurs. Supplying living quarters and other amenities means that tech entrepreneurs can focus on developing new inventions and filing patents worldwide without the worry of eking out a comfortable living. China recognizes that such support is crucial to attracting entrepreneurs, especially older ones. As the Council of Competitiveness concedes, people in their fifties start twice as many technology firms than the stereotypical tech entrepreneurs in their twenties. Following China's example would be a small investment relative to the potential payoff of starting the Third Industrial Revolution.

## U.S. Government Hatchery

The United States currently has no such comprehensive innovation program in place. It has a Small Business Administration (SBA) that provides small business loans and has a program for creating Small

Business Investment Companies (SBIC) that was supposed to provide government funds for venture capital. Unfortunately, the small business loans largely go to mom-and-pop shops, not to disruptive technological companies. The SBICs also have been known to funnel government funds to Certified Capital Companies (CAPCOs), which were originally conceived as an economic tool to create jobs by providing venture capital funds to small businesses unable to access traditional financing. However CAPCOs have largely proven to be scam vehicles for investors to arbitrage government funds for a profit without investing in a single company.[35] Even if these government programs worked according to plan, they still do not offer the same comprehensive capital and security that the Chinese incubators offer.

U.S. private capital in the form of angel investors and venture capital have historically stepped in to fund promising entrepreneurs with great ideas. Thanks to a handful of visionary venture capitalists, a number of great American companies such as Digital Equipment Corporation (DEC) and Fairchild Semiconductors have created hundreds of thousands of jobs and substantial wealth to Americans and the world with their inventions.

But leaving it solely to private industry means that perhaps many more great ideas never get funded because the time and capital required to turn a great idea into a commercial product could be more than private investors are willing to give. Most of the major venture capital investments after the dot com bust have been in social media rather than in engineering, which characterized previous venture capital investments. These investments provide much quicker financial return to the private investors. However, save for the ability to connect and coordinate large numbers of people quickly—as in the multiple Middle East demonstrations in 2011—the real material benefit to society is much less consequential than a radically disruptive new invention that could revolutionize our lifestyles. Even the average investment to bring an incrementally improved medical product to market could require upward of a billion dollars and ten years, an investment horizon often too risky for most private investors and indeed most established companies.[36] But investments in taproot technologies are the most important and most needed investments for our collective future. Acknowledging that private investment has its limitations and that we need radical new inventions to save civilization, we must have the government step in to bridge that gap.

## The Long and Short of It

Modern commerce has no doubt been profoundly shaped by the theories of John Maynard Keynes and Milton Friedman on how to manage economies. The former emphasized both fiscal and monetary policy, while the latter gave money a starring role, by suggesting that monetary policy can affect economic growth through manipulating the money supply. We now know that these strategies have reached their limits since the boundless use of both has failed to resuscitate U.S. employment in any adequate way and may, in fact, derail any possible recoveries with the threat of unacceptable levels of inflation. Thanks to financialization, these theories no longer apply.

The lesson we need to relearn from China is that we must not let the financial services industry become too powerful. China does not have a better financial system than ours, but it does have one that is not all powerful. As Americans, we knew the wisdom of curbing financial power back in the 1930s. We need to reinstate those financial regulations in order to nurse the global economy back to health. Following China's example, we also ought to provide incentives for pursuing productive real-economy activities because these activities are at an inherent disadvantage when compared to the relative ease and high compensation of financial services. Fostering true wealth creation will take more effort, ingenuity, and time to develop than financial activities. But relying on China alone for the next inventions will be too risky a proposition. China may be forging ahead, but to save the world, America must join in the race.

# 7
# Soft Power

Ultimate excellence lies in not winning every battle but
in defeating the enemy without ever fighting.   —SUN-TZU

**JOSEPH NYE STRESSED IN HIS PROGNOSTICATIONS** about power in the
21st century that the capacity to coerce will become less important
in the modern age, while the ability to set agendas and the terms of
debate will be relatively more useful. In this context, economic power
and moral authority may hold greater sway than military force. In
other words, the future of global negotiating lies more in the carrot
rather than the stick.

## A New Deal

As China has grown in economic power, it has acquired the means
to redirect entire nations in brand new directions. Though the Chinese could have easily pursued similar colonial practices that the
Americans and Europeans once used in Africa and throughout Latin
America, the Chinese have opted to create a different kind of empire.
Rather than exploiting and brutalizing people, keeping them in ser-
vitude, and denying them education, China approached people in

developing nations with an entirely new proposition. In exchange for the natural resources it so desperately needs for its own domestic economy, China has offered developing nations billions of dollars to invest in infrastructure as well as Chinese management and labor to help poor nations get their hard and soft infrastructure projects off the ground.

## The Brutal Truth

This kind of business deal differs dramatically from those offered by Western nations. In the past, Western nations simply looted natural resources while they enslaved the native population. The British, French, and Dutch extracted millions of tons of natural resources when they colonized Africa in the 1800s while forcing African men, women, and children into backbreaking labor. When the cost of maintaining colonies outstripped the material benefits during the 1930s, modern American corporations subsequently went in to buy up natural resource rights at deep discounts from the African governments without providing an ounce of help in return.

Former African colonies, stripped of natural resources and traumatized for generations under the hands of Western Europeans, lost much of their sense of identity and pride. Deadly dictators seized control with brute force when the departure of the colonists left a void. The U.S. government offered token sums of aid money amounting to less than 1 percent of the national budget, while large multinational companies such as Exxon and Chevron extracted crude oil off the African coasts. The dictators pocketed whatever aid money entered the country and used it to buy more military weapons to keep themselves in power. Through sophisticated public relations campaigns and spokespeople like Jeffrey Sachs, aid money was marketed as proof of America's benevolent and generous nature, when the truth was quite the opposite. Even Haiti, a country much closer to the United States and a recipient of over $20 billion of foreign assistance over decades, still remains one of the most corrupt and underdeveloped nations in the world.[1] Government handouts function more precisely as diplomatic cover for the United States and other Western companies to rape and pillage countries that are too weak to defend themselves.

Studies by Professor William Easterly and others have exposed development aid money for what it was—money earmarked for commercial access and/or military alliances with countries.[2] Some of this money comes from private donors, but much comes from government budgets that direct funds to various nongovernmental organizations (NGOs).[3] According to Tim Schwartz, who wrote *Travesty in Haiti,* many NGOs were riddled with fraud and hidden political agendas. These NGOs claimed to help in various humanitarian ways, but many were merely vehicles created by the politically connected to fill their own pockets. Rich, well-connected friends of elected officials would set up NGOs as personal piggy banks to receive government aid money, which was supposed to provide poor nations with food, education, and other necessities. However, most of the billions of dollars that get allocated every year never make it to the dispossessed.[4] Though the accounting is difficult to trace, it has been alleged that significant portions of the money went straight into the personal bank accounts of NGO heads, who enjoyed being overpaid for work that had no accountability to any government, client, or shareholder. Most of what's left goes to pay for the extravagant lifestyles of expatriates. Very little—some estimates are as low as .02 percent—goes toward humanitarian purposes. According to some former NGO representatives at a conference held at Columbia University's School of International and Public Affairs, U.S. aid money represented the biggest scam in history, as billions were wasted on Americans more interested in helping themselves than in helping the desperately poor and disadvantaged Africans. After roughly fifty years of aid money, there was nothing to show for it. Millions of Africans were still starving and dying from disease, and Africa had been written off by Westerners as a continent with no future.[5]

Westerners ignored the Africans until the Chinese started making deals with them. The State Department, right-wing think tanks, and anti-Chinese factions in the United States began sounding alarm bells when it became clear that the Chinese were winning over many African nations. Between the years 2007 and 2009, China provided Africa $5 billion worth of preferential loans and exports buyers' credit and extended another $10 billion for the years 2010 through 2012.[6] The loans financed major infrastructure projects such as airports, housing, bridges, railways, telecommunications, and hydropower. By the end of 2005, the number of projects assisted by the Chinese exceeded 700.[7]

As UK's *Guardian* reported: "China's fast, efficient, 'no strings attached' bilateral approach is popular in the [African] region, as is the PRC preference for infrastructure over governance projects." It further reported:

> During a February 8 lunch, Kenyan Ambassador to China, Julius Ole Sunkuli said he and other Africans were wary of the U.S.-China dialogue on Africa and felt Africa had nothing to gain from China cooperating with the international donor community. Sunkuli claimed that Africa was better off thanks to China's practical, bilateral approach to development assistance and was concerned that this would be changed by "Western" interference. He said he saw no concrete benefit for Africa in even minimal cooperation. Sunkuli said Africans were frustrated by Western insistence on capacity building, which translated, in his eyes, into conferences and seminars. They instead preferred China's focus on infrastructure and tangible projects.

The cable further states:

> South African Minister Plenipotentiary Dave Malcomson echoed the same reservations in a February 9 meeting. He opined that although governance, peace, and security are crucial to African growth, they must be accompanied by measures to reduce poverty and build infrastructure. China's emergence in Africa as a counterbalance to U.S. and European donors has been very positive for Africa by creating "competition" and giving African countries options.[8]

The African point of view was later further confirmed by an announcement on February 2, 2011, from Norway's government minister for international development pledging to support investment in Africa by Norwegian companies. According to the newspaper *Aftenposten,* Erik Solheim, minister representing the Socialist Left Party, said that he had kept a close eye on China's increasing interest in the region and hoped that business would cast aside traditional stereotypes and begin to view Africa as a place of opportunity.

China's strategy of soft power in this instance was particularly effective. When Chinese businessmen started arriving, the skeptical, bitter Africans expected them to behave in much the same way as their Western predecessors. By surprising the Africans and treating them as equals, the Chinese were able to convince them that they were in the same camp. They did not offer aid money—a gesture that the Africans associate with condescension and corruption—but instead offered medical assistance to a number of poor countries, scholarships for training young Africans in China, and guaranteed low-interest or no-interest loans to build necessary infrastructure long neglected by Westerners.[9] The loans had no strings attached, and the Chinese also forgave over $2 billion of debt from former loans.[10]

When there was no project management expertise to oversee large infrastructure projects, the Chinese provided technical assistance. Oftentimes, Chinese laborers traveled to Africa to work alongside Africans on these projects. The Chinese dug the same ditches, slept in the same bare huts, and ate the same plain food as the Africans, according to Dr. Deborah Brautigam, who spent roughly the last 30 years following the actions of the Chinese in Africa. She argues in her book *The Dragon's Gift* that the Chinese had instituted a win-win model of development, which is fostering a better economic future on the African continent.

In 2010 at an event for the book held at New York University's Wagner School of Public Service, Americans shared their experiences at the U.S. Agency for International Development (USAID) in Africa.

Apparently American officials sat in lavish surroundings watching soap operas. Those who occupied offices were utterly unhelpful to anyone who wasn't a superior. One attendee recounted, "The behavior of American diplomats and ambassadors was totally disgraceful. I was embarrassed to call myself an American there." The Chinese soft power stands in sharp contrast.

China uses soft power not only with Africans, but also with Latin Americans. China is not only one of Latin America's biggest trade partners but also one of its largest investors.[11] Chilean UN representative Heraldo Munoz, who wrote the book *Open Face of Latin America,* said in an interview on June 11, 2009, that Latin America is no longer an "unconditional" friend of the United States as China increases its presence there. He recalled that U.S. presidents have had a history of dictating terms to Latin Americans as opposed to listening and engaging in dialogue with them to achieve qualitative change. He believed that the United States needs to acknowledge the past repression of South American countries that were often carried out as silent wars against democratically elected presidents by overthrowing them through CIA armed coups. He cited a democratic movement against the dictatorship in Brazil that was stopped by the United States.

Similarly, Bolivian President Evo Morales accused U.S. officials of instigating insurrection in his country.[12] Stephen Forneris, U.S. citizen and principal at Perkins Eastman who travels to Latin America frequently for business, confirmed that the U.S. special forces were doing almost all the fighting in Colombia and that Latin Americans are not impressed with recent American overtures to help now that the Chinese have done so much investing there.

Soft power can take years to develop, and it can take even longer to undo past relationship damage. The problem for the United States is that many leaders in Latin America have socialist leanings, so they've been viewed and treated as foes. But Latin Americans want to be treated as equals, and the Chinese have done that. If the United States would like to make nice with Latin Americans, it can start by not acting against their wishes. Invading Iraq, for example, did not endear us to our neighbors to the south.[13] The United States can also enter into more free trade agreements that are accompanied by higher standards in labor and the environment to show fair and equal treatment of Latin Americans. Chris Sabatini, senior director of policy at the Council of the Americas, which promotes free trade in Latin America, has publicly stated that contrary to what conspiracy theorists believe, there are no military or political designs against the United States by the Chinese. The Chinese simply have sought an economic relationship with the Latin Americans that has worked out very well. Examples include the Chilean company Rein, which has been importing fleets of Chinese electric cars that cost under $9000.[14] There is no reason that the United States couldn't approach the Latin Americans in the same way.

Beijing's particular form of development aid has been surprisingly effective in furthering Chinese political and strategic interests in raw materials to fuel its growth, but it has also elevated its global diplomatic presence and created a basis of support for its policies on developing countries. Aid and trade partners were treated humanely and given respect. This convinced them that it was unlikely that China would behave like another member of the rich countries club. These nations feel that China understands their problems with poverty and sympathizes. In return, these countries have obeyed China's requests on the international stage. For instance, when China asked its allies not to attend the Nobel Peace Prize awards ceremony for dissident Liu Xiaobo, at least 19 countries responded to its request to protest, including U.S. allies Colombia and Egypt.[15] This growing allegiance with China shows that China's soft power is steadily paying off.

By expanding the number of people China welcomes into its fold in a nonthreatening and nonjudgmental way, China has been steadily building good will with poor, developing nations. Although this strategy certainly furthers its own interests, it also may be paving the road for truly global cooperation between rich and poor countries.

## The Green-Eyed Monster

The Western press, however, has predominately painted a very one-sided view of the Chinese as rapacious thieves stealing natural resources from developing nations and supporting genocide by cutting deals with Sudan and other human rights' violators. Yet the press conveniently ignores the hypocrisy of U.S. foreign policies supporting regimes that are equally vicious and repressive. By and large, they neglect to report that China's moves are in some ways the response to the lack of U.S. interest in a region. Shortly after it was reported that China signed an oil deal with Venezuela, a senior Senate Foreign Relations Committee aide reportedly said on condition of anonymity, "They [the Chinese] are taking advantage of the fact that we [Americans] don't care as much as we should about Latin America."[16]

As much as Americans bristle at the knowledge that China is doing so much in Africa, Latin America, and elsewhere, we must realize that China was *invited* by the host countries to come in to do something. Rather than complain, the West could learn from the Chinese and replicate what they have done. But if America continues to enter these countries with pure self-interest, as it has done for decades, it will never win the trust of these other nations or be welcome within their borders. Those who create employment will be thanked, and China has been doing a great job doing just that around the world.[17] In response to China, America should start to develop a longer-term vision of how it will be accepted in an increasingly multipolar world.

Like the Bill and Melinda Gates Foundation, China has provided medical assistance to parts of Africa that have either been underserved or have never received such aid at all.[18] No matter what critics say, the healthcare system that China brought to the Africans was better than none at all. As a result, China can pull strings without firing a single shot. China practiced *engagement with noninterference* meaning that it will maintain diplomatic dialogue and relations with everyone, including enemies, because engagement is the only way to have a positive influence over anyone. *Noninterference* means that one respects the sovereignty and differences of another country even as one engages in dialogue. China may despise the genocidal actions of particular dictators in Africa or disagree with religious rule in Iran, but it still maintains an open dialogue with the leaders of those countries as well as other national players because it knows that world peace requires everyone to get along and that politics is dynamic.

## Our Money in the Middle East

Rarely is the public aware that U.S. aid money went to support highly unpopular dictatorships in the name of "U.S. interests," a euphemism for military and financial support for despots who make agreements, for example, to avoid confrontation with Israel. It is worth noting that, since the signing of the peace accords with Israel, Egypt has been one of the largest recipients of U.S. "aid" money to the tune of $1.5 billion a year. As was reported by the *Wall Street Journal,* most of the aid had been earmarked for Mubarak's security forces, blocking democratic dissent to an oppressive regime for thirty years. Rather than mandating that the money be used for humanitarian reasons, U.S. officials knew that it was specifically used to support military forces suppressing opposition, which increased anti-American sentiment among Muslims in the Arab world. The anti-government protests that have erupted everywhere from Yemen to Egypt were in direct response to the U.S.-backed dictatorships that have impoverished majority populations of the Middle East.

China's aggressive deal making has alarmed some who fear that China may not be a responsible stakeholder in the global order, but the evidence is more to the contrary. Unlike the belligerent tactics used by the United States—embargoes, military force, and CIA subversion—China's leaders have for the most part tried to avoid creating enemies by seeking to understand the problems of other nations and then offering concrete results in the form of business deals that include technical assistance. China's leaders have sympathized with underdogs, whoever they may be. They exported help that followed the same formulaic economic model China uses at home, which they continue to refine domestically. Their economic model of state-guaranteed loans, technical training and support, and measurable results have proven to work again and again in generating prosperity for its own citizens, as well as their friends in the developing world.

## Policy Overhaul

Rather than become defensive about its current foreign policies, the United States should instead learn from China's charm offensive. China's ability to deliver on its promises and provide what foreign developing governments need most—which, more often than not, are food and jobs—go a long way in winning the friendship of those governments as well as their citizens. African citizens cannot see U.S. aid money that goes into dictator bank accounts, but they can see hospitals, football stadiums, trains, and schools that the Chinese built. Aside from the developed nations, America's allies remain allies only by propping up the corrupt elite who run their countries like police states. Citizens around the world, such as the Pakistanis, are frequently oppressed and angry at their American-backed governments. By choosing to uphold corruption and oppression in the name of national security, Americans ironically undermine our own security more than if we were to remain completely neutral. American foreign policy designed to oppress millions in foreign lands will only boomerang, causing death and destruction at home—9/11 is proof of that. Our current foreign policy of using hard power to intimidate our perceived enemies will only stoke more hatred for the United States and increase their resolve to destroy us. Time after time, outrage from a sense of injustice is what fuels uprisings and wars. Instead, America would be better off overhauling foreign policy and using some of China's tried and true methods of winning diplomatic friends around the world.

In addition to revamping foreign policy, the United States could also reform some of its political conventions. For instance, ambassadorships are currently used as rewards for political support.[19] This practice is not only ineffective because it puts ignorant people in strategic places, it is also demoralizing to members of the U.S. Foreign Service who understand other cultures and speak foreign languages. Exchanging ambassadorships for political donations means that these ambassadors are always wealthy and thus socialize with the elite in other nations, as opposed to spreading positive impressions of the United States among the vast majority of foreign populations who are less privileged.

USAID needs revamping so that U.S. representatives and other NGOs do not pay for their own luxurious lifestyles with the government money sent to aid development. Consider the contrast when the people in developing countries can see the Chinese work alongside them digging ditches and engaging in other back-breaking work to build badly needed infrastructure. Indeed, the strongest public relations move the United States can make is not merely to put a new spin on such potentially embarrassing situations, but to staff these agencies with people who will get things done. If China is sending Chinese workers to help the Africans build badly needed infrastructure, why doesn't the United States hire American construction workers who are looking for work to build new infrastructure for these nations?

More importantly, the United States should recognize that its investment in soft power has been continually eclipsed by its over-reliance on the military or what is known as *hard power*. No one disputes that having a strong defense is critical to maintaining peace and enforcing rules. The issue arises over how much investment in the U.S. military is really necessary. Today, the United States does not face a superpower military threat. Yet it still outspends the next 10 countries combined every year on the military. The military is the only part of the government budget that has never experienced cutbacks since the end of World War II.[20]

Even during the Cold War, a number of U.S. scientists and policy-makers, who understood the Soviet Union's true capabilities, deemed that the U.S. arms escalation in nuclear warheads was wholly unnecessary. The supposed need for an arms race was exaggerated by Reagan and his spokesmen, and the media simply reported the lies that were told. The collapse of the Soviet Union came as no surprise to U.S. scientists, engineers, and certain State Department officials. Years before Reagan declared victory, they knew that the Soviets did not have the technology or the resources to keep up the arms race. The hundreds of billions spent on the military could have been safely scaled back substantially, had rational minds prevailed. Instead of warheads, the U.S could have redirected those funds to domestic uses, which would have arguably yielded the same Soviet collapse.

Undoubtedly, the entrenched interests of the military do not want to see their budgets pared even one iota. Their raison d'être is to fight and kill, regardless of the reason or justification. If there is no credible threat, they can make one up just to protect their own salaries, jobs, and power from being diminished. When budget cuts were being bandied about by a newly elected Republican Congress in 2011, the Department of Defense decided to announce coincidentally that the Chinese have new fighter jets, and that China's increased military spending posed a potential threat to the United States. Interestingly, experts on China who don't work directly for the U.S. military largely agree that China represents no such threat given its low level of military investments. China's military spending is less than 2 percent of its GDP while U.S. military spending is 4.7 percent of our GDP.[21] In absolute terms, China's published military spending is $91.5 billion, while America's total defense spending was $1.35 trillion in 2010.[22] Though some believe China's military spending is higher, the highest estimate comes from the U.S. Department of Defense—$150 billion—which is still only a tenth of what the United States spends on the military. Even if the Chinese increase their military spending into the double digits every year, it would still take years for them to catch up to the United States even if we stopped spending altogether because China is coming from a much lower base and possesses far less sophisticated technological expertise.

More importantly, China's military spending is predominately a response to absorb its growing unemployed. According to my friend Ajit Pai, who immigrated to the United States from India, it would cost just as much to incarcerate a youth in India as it would to give the person a job as a uniformed police officer. Every country knows that the most efficient way to reduce unemployment is to give its citizens government jobs. Given China's extraordinary government expenditures all across the board to save the economy after the 2008 financial crisis, its 14 percent increase in military spending in 2009 when compared to its increases in other areas such as research and development—which had budget increases of over 25 percent— does not stand out as abnormally high as a percentage of its GDP.[23] China's leaders faced extraordinary pressure to create jobs wherever they could, and the military was not immune. Finally, in this nuclear age, the odds that China would be the first to attack would be close to nil because doing so would be tantamount to suicide given their inferior military technology.

As Gideon Rose wrote in his latest book, *How Wars End,* the United States needs to craft viable end games before it goes to war. War serves two purposes: first, it is supposed to end the tensions that built up before the war, and second, it should replace the original system that created the tension with a new system that eliminates it.[24] Unfortunately, the United States has consistently dealt with the first purpose of war, but not the second. The costly U.S. wars in Iraq and Afghanistan demonstrate incontrovertibly that without an end game in place, having a strong military does not guarantee national security, peace, or stability. If anything, the wars possibly fomented even greater insecurity as the number of terrorist attacks and insurgencies has only swelled since the days of 9/11, leaving tens, or perhaps even hundreds of thousands dead or wounded around the world.

Is it possible that all this needless bloodshed could be avoided if the United States were to follow China's practice of soft power and stopped making enemies? Americans actually did play this diplomatic card well after World War II through the Marshall Plan. By generously helping the Western European economies rebuild after the war through humanitarian aid, foreign investment, and other technical assistance, the United States won valuable allies who still support us today. It is a terrible shame that America has failed to repeat that policy initiative in its subsequent dealings with the rest of the world. Many reasons account for that, but one particularly powerful force is the military-industrial complex that President Eisenhower warned about in his Farewell Address to the nation on January 17, 1961. The complex today is stronger than ever and should be reined in if the United States wants to avoid another unnecessary and costly military confrontation. Furthermore, the U.S. military, by law and design, is a highly undemocratic institution. Allowing its power to grow unchecked could even turn America into a military state.

Despite grumblings about the Chinese military, the Peoples Liberation Army (PLA) hardly has the clout that the Department of Defense does. They have not fought a war in the last 30 years, and no senior Chinese official in the Standing Committee has a military background. Most of the military spending on the PLA has been to provide basic needs for soldiers, such as improving their living quarters so that they didn't have to live on dirt floors. Even if the PLA had upgraded their military capabilities significantly, the personnel still possesses little to no experience in real combat.

The United States, in contrast, can count a number of ex-military officials holding top cabinet–level positions. Ex-military personnel like Donald Rumsfeld have had outsized influence in the White House. Their dominance seems to correlate highly with the number of wars the United States has engaged in since becoming a super-power, averaging about one per president. If the United States is a peacekeeping force as it claims to be, then why has it invaded places like Iraq and conducted secret wars in Yemen and elsewhere?

"Think of how India and Brazil sided with China at the global climate-change talks. Or the votes by Turkey and Brazil against America at the United Nations on sanctions against Iran. That is just a taste of things to come," wrote Gideon Rose in a piece published by *Foreign Policy*.[25] The logical conclusion to the two foreign policy tracks the United States and China presently pursue is that China slowly wins over hearts and minds with its soft power, and the United States becomes increasingly feared, isolated, and dangerous. If the United States continues to lose friends this way, it will be severely disadvantaged, since even the most powerful military couldn't manage multiple threats without the help of enough loyal allies.

## Fair- and Foul-Weather Friends

But aside from Israel, the U.K., and Canada, most countries around the world are not beholden to the United States. The assumption that Australia and Europe would always remain strong allies may be tenuous. Australia owes its recent robust economy to China, and over 70 percent of Australians view the relationship with China as highly beneficial.[26] Likewise, some Europeans have grown more distant from the United States, particularly after the financial crisis of 2008. Most Europeans have much more socialistic and progressive views than Americans, and these differences have surfaced during G-20 meetings whenever financial reforms have been discussed.[27] While northern Europeans still preach solidarity with the United States, cracks have been appearing. Iceland's support of WikiLeaks and Julian Assange has been a slap in the face to the United States who has been trying to prosecute the Web publisher for disclosing damaging and embarrassing state secrets.[28] The Germans have been developing closer relations with Russia, a historic enemy of the United States.[29] Last but not least, the closer ties of Spain and Greece to China since the outbreak of the slow-motion Euro crisis could also signal future defections of European nations to China from the once-solid U.S. diplomatic camp.[30] As a European Central Bank (ECB) official told me over lunch at the Levy Economics Institute's 2011 conference, "There is no special relationship between the United States and Europe. We are, shall we say, *faux amis* (false friends)."

Americans can reverse this trend if they stop responding to the fearmongering from national security hawks who constantly paint a scary picture of the world. People tend to live up to expectations, and this truism would apply whether it pertains to individuals or nations. Charles Kupchan, associate professor at Princeton University, wrote in his book *How Enemies Become Friends* that the way nations turn hostility into friendship must be through active courtship initiated by the nations' leaders. Economic activity between two nations alone can't prevent war from arising as in the case between France and Germany leading up to World War II, but if the leaders of two nations decide to become friends, then warfare between two nations can be eliminated. Professor Kupchan followed the relationship between Britain and the United States, which was once hostile but became friendly after both sides decided it was in their best interest to make amends.

Some may suggest that the United States and the U.K. were exceptions because of their shared cultural heritage. However, the same could be said of the United States and China since the Founding Fathers looked to Confucianism for guidance in designing the new nation.[31] But shared cultural heritage may not be a relevant factor in decisions about alliances anyway since there are also examples in which people of shared cultural history often can become worst enemies such as the tensions between the Shiites and Sunnis.

The relationship between the United States and China may be best described as an analogy to a male/female courtship. As the book *Men Are from Mars, Women Are from Venus* describes, both may seem different on the surface and experience bouts of misunderstanding that can lead to frustration and hostilities, situations that define every close relationship. But underneath the tense exterior, the two share similarities and a strong underlying bond of respect and attraction that can draw them together to work out their differences, if they both let their guard down just a little.

By keeping such relationships in perspective, the United States ought to adopt an attitude of tolerance and goodwill toward the rest of the world, including China, whom it increasingly sees as a growing threat to its interests. Instead of viewing and treating other nations as threats and playing a zero-sum game, the United States should acknowledge that China has been adept at winning friends and should consider modifying its existing approach to nations around the world. The problem with the United States is that the entrenched interests who benefit from belligerent actions have a loud and powerful voice in Washington and they have much more to lose if foreign policy were to become less hawkish. The cooler heads in the rest of the country, whose immediate economic interests are not threatened by more friendly foreign policies but have the long-term interest of world peace at stake, have not been as vocal or as organized as the entrenched military interests. Nothing short of electing a supremely courageous and visionary leader to become Commander in Chief would be required to offset the very powerful special interests that now control the country. Perhaps even then, the chances of restraining their power and influence are slim.

## A Seat at the Table

However, it can be done. In China's case, the Red Guard that brought revolution to China was eventually dismantled because more rational leaders were promoted to positions of power. Over time, the number of doves outnumbered the number of hawks, and China turned 180 degrees from an ideological wasteland to become one of the most dynamic, productive nations in the world.

If an American president wanted to diffuse military power, he should appoint more diplomatic experts and give them seats at the table so that military solutions to overseas problems do not dominate policy conversations. Diplomatic experts do not have to be merely bureaucrats from the State Department. Ex-military whistleblowers have valid perspectives and should not be repudiated. Former Afghanistan commander Army General Stanley McChrystal, who was asked to resign for calling the Afghanistan effort a failure, could impart important lessons from the front lines that could balance pro-war views. As someone who risked his life and his soldiers' lives, he understood the importance of building alliances. Without the trust of locals, who could be abetting the Taliban, American forces were handicapped in the field. Taken to a larger level, the authoritarian pacts that the United States made to ensure national security objectives could prove unreliable as waves of democratic movements intent on unseating unpopular dictatorships sweep the Middle East and possibly elsewhere.

As the United States ought to know through its haphazard alliances, a country who was once a friend can become an enemy and vice versa. During the Iran–Iraq war, the United States sided with Iraq, but a couple of decades later, the United States invaded its former ally and deposed its leader, Saddam Hussein. Similarly, the United States fought the Germans and Japanese in World War II and now has them both as allies. The same may be said of the Vietnamese in time.

Going forward, former allies, such as Egypt and others in the Middle East, could become enemies if the United States does not engage with the players in the region who may ascend to power. These players could include the Muslim Brotherhood and militant jihadists. The United States would ignore them at its own peril however. Groups such as these have gained followers.[32] Whether the United States likes them or not, they are legitimate and could likely come to power through democratic means. The United States will have to face them one way or another, and it would be much more prudent to follow China's example and begin building relationships with these groups now so that we understand the enemy. If the United States chooses not to build connections with these people, then when they come to power, they will owe us nothing and could turn a bad situation worse. The United States, as large and powerful as it is, is not an over-lord of these countries, and can only make suggestions. Controlling the situation through military means would be a mistake. Similarly, in a region where the population will no longer tolerate another fig-urehead and would be satisfied only with substantive reconstruction, any attempts at cosmetic change would be tantamount to standing before a dam about to explode. As we are learning the hard way, the Iraq War has lasted longer than anticipated and has stretched U.S. forces to their limits. Military involvement in another Middle Eastern country now would be courting disaster.

U.S. foreign policy has historically rejected the policy of engage-ment with noninterference by calling it *appeasement,* which has had a long negative connotation, including the attempts to negotiate with Hitler at the beginning of World War II. These negotiations were dip-lomatic policies aimed at avoiding war by providing concessions to preserve peace at all costs. Over the years, critics of the policy claim that appeasement failed to prevent war, so redressing grievances peacefully through disarmament and agreements had no credibility in their eyes.

The problem with this analysis is that appeasement was used as a last resort to a hostile aggressor. Negotiating in weakness has never worked, and that is not what the Chinese are doing. Noninterference engagement simply means that a dialogue gets created between two parties that can help normalize the geopolitics and will more likely sow conditions that can bring positive political change.

No-fly zones could have potentially been an effective soft-power tactic for the West to limit civilian casualties during the Libyan upris-ings. However, the West squandered that opportunity to show moral leadership when it used no-fly zones as a thinly veiled excuse to send its own military into Libyan airspace to bomb Muammar el-Qaddafi's military forces, killing Libyan civilians in the process. In the eyes of many, the end did not justify the means, and some even question the proclaimed "end" that was used as justification for the unprovoked violence.[33]

Sanctions, while a nonmilitary tactic, have such hostile overtones that they alienate a country, giving the ostracized leader and citizens more reasons to oppose the country that imposed them. Sanctions not only breed hostility, they often drive the ostracized country to the arms of other nations who are willing to work with it. The U.S. embargoes of Iran, for example, have only enabled the leaders of Iran to strengthen their base during its three decades of isolation from the West. Through its business interests with Turkey, Russia, and China, Iran developed firm control over its economy so the U.S. policy refusal to engage with Iran backfired. Similarly, the Bush administration's refusal to reconcile with Syria was also a missed opportunity to secure U.S. interests in the region through diplomacy.[34] Syria could have been an important transport corridor and is central to the region. Had the United States begun a strategic noninterference dialogue with the Syrians, thus garnering an ally, the political landscape might look less threatening.

Another common complaint from U.S. officials is that China has essentially been economically blackmailing its Asian neighbors by procuring their loyalty in exchange for access to their market for trade. If these smaller nations run to the United States for help, China would shut them out of its economy.

Whatever tactics China uses with its neighbors, China remains a nation looking after its own security interests. Like the United States, China does not want hostile forces in its own backyard, and like the United States, China could resort to Realpolitik if forced by necessity. But unlike the United States, China has shown much greater restraint in deploying its military to express its displeasure with uncooperative foreign actors. It may have used economic threats in rare instances when it has felt another nation has crossed the line, but China still sends a consistent message that it intends to refrain from military responses as solutions to threats.

The genius of soft power is that China has teamed up with many nations to carve out win-win economic solutions, so that cooperating with China means greater benefits than drawbacks. Any fight with China would result in mutually assured economic destruction in the same way that neither the United States nor the Soviets could win in a nuclear exchange. By giving these nations an economic stake in their future, China helps minimize the threat of war among nations, who would all prefer to advance economically than to engage in more bloodshed. Had China followed the example of the West and used military interventions to force its partners to cooperate, China would no doubt be fighting bloody battles on multiple fronts today.

## Civic Ties

China is trying to build not only business connections across the world, but also civic ties. It has invited and sponsored thousands of African students to study in China to learn Mandarin.[35] China also actively invites academic experts from all nations to exchange ideas with their Chinese counterparts. While I was teaching at Peking University, I met dozens of local professors, as well as those who traveled from every corner of the earth to be there, either to teach, research, or both. There was a professor from Greece, who was invited to help the Chinese restore their dilapidating national treasures, such as the Summer Palace. I also befriended a physics professor from New York who worked with the Chinese in search of black holes and invited me to take a tour with her to see one of China's superconductor facilities. As a matter of fact, during my teaching stint there, the Chinese facilitated more meetings between the multinationals on their campuses than I have ever encountered during my time teaching at American universities.

More recently, the CCP has opened Confucian Institutes (CI) around the world. Like the Goethe Institut, Alliance Française, and Instituto Cervantes, CI was launched as an effort to bridge the cultural misunderstandings between the East and West. Given the strong influence these values have in Chinese culture, CI was initially conceived to educate those who have not been exposed to the writings or philosophy of Confucius. However, in response to assertions from some Western critics that the Chinese were using CI as a propaganda tool, most CIs today have limited their offerings mainly to Mandarin speaking instruction.[36] Nonetheless, the language outreach alone can stimulate a growing interest in China. "Languages as carriers of culture and communication tools are bridges for different civilizations," State Councilor Liu Yandong told the fourth conference of Confucius Institutes in December.[37]

Despite the controversy, the CCP has opened 316 CIs and 337 Confucius Classrooms in 94 countries and regions as of July 2010.[38] Starting with the first CI piloted in Tashkent, Uzbekistan, in June 2004, the Office of Chinese Language Council International, otherwise known as Han Ban, currently has plans to set up 1,000 CIs by 2020 and award as many as 3,000 scholarships to foreign candidates to study Chinese teaching by 2013.[39] True to its goal of spreading cultural understanding, each CI must be affiliated with a hosting university or cultural institution, with the partner required to match funding from Han Ban.

This strategy of bringing students from other parts of the world to China is similar to the strategy Julius Caesar used when he conquered Gaul. Since Caesar didn't have enough Romans to run the region, Caesar took the sons of the conquered elites and raised them as his own instead of throwing them into jail. By caring for them in such a way, he turned the Gauls into Romans who could be trusted to run Gaul for the Roman Empire.

The United States has also used this form of soft power very well by admitting international graduate students into top American universities for decades. In the process, many young Chinese have become similar to young Americans, who love to consume American products, adopt American dress, and have American ideals. But since 9/11, entry by foreigners has been curbed with immigration laws becoming tougher, thereby somewhat blunting the influence of American soft power.[40]

China's soft power is not only coming from official diplomatic channels. Its average citizens have also been ambassadors for the country. As mentioned earlier, Chinese laborers worked alongside African laborers, showing the Africans solidarity rather than superiority.[41] Many Chinese students have gone abroad to study, and in the United States, many of the PhDs in the hard sciences have consistently been Chinese foreign nationals.[42] According to the National Opinion Research Center, China was the country of origin for the largest number of non-U.S. born doctorates. Wherever the Chinese diaspora land, much evidence, anecdotal as well as statistical, confirms that the Chinese tend to become productive members of society without the help of affirmative action. In these cases and others, average Chinese civilians engage in public diplomacy as citizen role models.

## Media Megaphone

Notably at a conference in Bangalore in 2010, India's minister of state for external affairs said, "It's not the size of the army that wins; it's the country that tells a better story."[43] No nation understands this more than the United States, who launched the most successful soft power in history. From the Peace Corps to Hollywood, the United States has spread its culture and democratic capitalist values through every channel available. English is the current lingua franca, and American fast food and brands like Coca Cola can be had anywhere on earth. In fact, the dominance of American culture is so pervasive that Americans take it for granted.

The U.S. media have played a central role in American soft power too. They have been creative in exporting U.S. culture and values. While the U.S. government has an official news channel called Voice of America (VOA), the private sector has had a much bigger impact in spreading American culture. During my time living in Beijing in 2008, a number of Chinese television channels carried English-speaking programs such as the comedy series *Friends* and reality show *American Idol*. These shows subtly—and not so subtly—promoted the American way of life and its values toward individualism, consumerism, celebrity, humor, and other defining aspects of American and Western culture. Egyptian economist Samir Amin theorized that the ascent and decline of a nation is largely determined in our age by global monopolies, one of them being the media.[44]

But U.S. soft power that has been so reliant on the media for its public relations internationally will suffer a giant blow in credibility if our actions contradict our messages and if America consistently fails to deliver on its promises.

Regarding the first point, the Internet enables social media to connect people who were once unable to communicate with each other. The rise of television stations like Al Jazeera also allows hundreds of millions of people to scrutinize American actions more closely. This sort of transparency may develop public opinions that are antithetical to those that the American government and media would prefer. Most Americans did not have access to Al Jazeera's live television coverage of the unrest that unfolded throughout the Middle East. This puts in question the notion that free press guarantees the best coverage, or even open coverage. The United States remains practically the only market in the world where the Arab network is barred. Even if allegations of anti-Israeli and anti-American bias are true, the American democratic system demands that everyone has a right to be heard, including minority voices that may be deemed unpopular. In contrast, China, a government that has been accused of being less open than the United States, accepts Al Jazeera broadcasts within its borders. If America moralizes but fails to eliminate its own policy contradictions, other nations will increasingly view us as hypocritical about our democratic ideals, and fewer people will want to emulate America's model. Like China, it can be accused of spreading propaganda, but unlike China, it cannot claim consistency in its message. Breeding distrust will be the fastest way to lose influence and thus soft power.

## Selling Snake Oil

On the second point, Americans, from politicians to businessmen, are among the world's most expert salespeople. Many American CEOs and other public figures have received extensive public relations training in which they have had hours of practice speaking in front of television cameras. They hire advertising firms to craft logos, corporate messages, and advertisements that bombard multiple media outlets. Their sales teams have been carefully recruited and trained to entertain their clients in order to win deals. In other words, almost everyone can fall under the sales charm of America.

But sales need to be backed by real deliverables. To use an analogy, when a person oversells himself in an interview and résumé, an employer will eventually find out the truth on the job, and the subsequent firing of the employee is never pleasant. This American cultural habit of overselling and underdelivering is particularly acute in American politics, exemplified by President Obama who many feel has underdelivered with his promises of change. This cultural habit could have a more detrimental spillover effect in international relations as well. For example, as the largest polluter per capita in the world, the United States should show some leadership in environmental protection initiatives. U.S. government officials such as Suresh Kumar, U.S. Assistant Secretary of Commerce and Director General of the U.S. and Foreign Commercial Service, rattled off platitudes about investing in innovation and supporting clean-energy initiatives at an event hosted by New York University, but the numbers didn't support the claims. The United States has plans to invest a total of $366 million in building energy innovation hubs around the country, while China has already invested over $400 billion in clean-energy research and development with announced intentions to invest another $753 billion in this area.[45] When questioned about why the United States has failed to meet China on this challenge, Mr. Kumar responded with "The U.S. remains the most innovative place in the world," again without any facts or figures to back his assertions.[46]

Note that Mr. Kumar was speaking to a large multinational audience, including many foreign students. When I asked some of these students what they thought of the presentation, many were derisive of the speaker, disappointed that a U.S. government official had wasted their time blowing smoke and offering no concrete assurance that the United States was investing in the future. Such perceptions by the young and educated, if widespread enough, could trigger youth demonstrations not unlike what happened in Egypt and elsewhere. Indeed, the youth in America and around the world don't want lip service; they want results. As the most educated in many generations, the global youth population, particularly in the United States and Europe, has begun to realize that what was promised to their elders, such as steady jobs and retirement plans, may never materialize for them.[47] Not only are job opportunities rapidly shrinking, many have had to rely on financial resources from their parents well into their mid-thirties. As youths become increasingly desperate, they will grow steadily angrier at the status quo and government unresponsiveness. We've already seen signs of this in the 2011 London riots and Occupy Wall Street protests.

And the rest of the U.S population has grown increasingly cynical as well. The U.S. "strong dollar" slogan has not been matched by actions, as Warren Buffett would say. The U.S. tactic of relying on great public relations and sales will have run its course when there are no more people left to con. As an old Wendy's commercial put it, "Where's the beef?"

Cultivating soft power requires the good old-fashioned delivery of honesty and integrity. Glamour and the allure of lofty talk will attract short-term admirers and some alliances of convenience, but real friends and allies require trust built over years of delivering on promises. China has gone about accruing its soft power by offering financial generosity, knowledge, and human labor over decades to people and nations who have been pilloried by the West. Patient, efficient, and reliable to its partners, China invested in the idea that actions always speak louder than words. Could the United States be as effective as China on the international stage if it didn't rely on its military for results to complex foreign issues? That is the million-dollar question—and a trillion-dollar challenge.

# 8
# Cocreating a Better World

So, let us not be blind to our differences—but let us
also direct attention to our common interests and to
the means by which those differences can be resolved.
—JOHN F. KENNEDY

**FUTURISTS OFFER DIFFERENT PREDICTIONS** about what will happen
in the coming decades. George Friedman of Stratfor has speculated
on the domination of the United States in geopolitics. Ray Kurzweil
believes in singularity and that humans will one day achieve immortality. George Orwell and Franz Kafka wrote about authoritarian dys-
topias ruining everyday lives. All of them or none of them may come
true. But the future begins now because what happens in the future
always begins as thought in the present.

## Let's Get to Work, People!

Today we have an explosion of ideas and opinions that appear on
the Internet, on media airwaves, and in daily conversation. Sorting
out truth and priorities can be daunting, especially when consensus
is difficult to achieve. But it's important to recognize that the most
vital things to our lives commonly appear to be the least urgent and
sometimes require the most work. For example, reconciling difficult

relationships or studying for exams can offer great payoffs when the proper time and care are invested, but breaking the inertia in order to genuinely begin the hard work often becomes the biggest stumbling block. The problem is that the world cannot afford to procrastinate on solving the mounting global problems. We need to develop the political will and wisdom to work with all nations of the world to come up with agreeable and actionable solutions. That work will prove difficult to do and easy to put on the back burner, but humanity is at stake. In a hyperconnected world, it no longer will be sustainable for the minority international elite to thrive while billions of people suffer and die unnecessarily. The poor of the world will know and will not tolerate the present state of affairs. Change will happen whether we take a proactive position or not. I suspect that taking a proactive stance will help make the inevitable transitions smoother and less radical in the long run.

Acknowledging the fact that there are millions of worthy causes in the world, we should make every effort to match up each problem with the best people who can solve it. One would think this is easy with the connectivity of the Web, but as we know, old habits die hard. As I have articulated in the earlier chapters, the continual importance of who you know over what you know in politics, as well as in many other spheres, will always undermine a nation's ability to produce optimal results. If America does not want to lose its competitive edge, it must demand meritocracy at every level, but especially at the very top leadership circles where personal relations seem to play the most pronounced role. Putting the people in charge who will be able to deliver consistently on their promises is the best way to develop trust within the system as well as with other nations and foreign organizations.

Talk alone is not enough. An action plan must be drawn up. Whether it's a 5-year plan or a 25-year plan, a roadmap must exist and hold groups accountable for achieving agreed-upon milestones that are both meaningful and measurable. The Millennium Development Goals that were agreed upon by all the member states in the U.N. have at least articulated a shared agenda, but with four years left until the deadline, hardly any progress toward the eight goals have been made. The success of many of the goals has been uneven, and measuring progress has been challenging. Without clear accountability and binding agreements for achieving them, the goals will have been a pointless exercise and a wasted opportunity. The United States and China can take up this issue as a reason to redesign the role of the United Nations, which has come under frequent attack for being too weak, and propose a more rigorous system. But in the interim, the United States and China should not waste any more valuable time and figure out a way to work cooperatively together on global issues because war is not a viable solution. The United States has enough confrontations in the world already, so it would be better off not adding China to its growing list of adversaries. A partnership is essential because a conflict will exhaust or destroy both nations.

Given that the world is in danger of slipping into another Dark Age if World War III results from rising international tensions over a possible Malthusian catastrophe, the world desperately needs another nation to soldier forward in order to save humanity from the dysfunctions that financialization has created. The most likely contender for that role today is China, and its success or failure in this role could very well determine the fate of everyone. A more stable, peaceful, and benevolent world must be developed, and China appears to be quite adept at this kind of dialogue.

## Eradicate Extreme Poverty and Hunger

Many of the Millennium Goals have been officially embraced by China through its Five-Year Plans and pursued with determination. For instance, China has already made significant strides in the goal of poverty eradication by reducing its own poverty rate from 65 percent of the population in 1981 to just 4 percent by 2007, a reduction of over half a billion people.[1] Additionally, it has made significant contributions to alleviating poverty in African and Latin American nations by investing billions in developing their infrastructures.[2] The *New York Times* reported, for example, that China was selling cheap solar panels to be placed on African rooftops.[3] This source of cheap energy has enabled many impoverished Africans to have electricity for their homes for the first time in their lives, powering lights, radios, and fans.[4] The United States should step up to the plate with similar programs either through the World Bank, USAID, or other ways to meet China halfway.[5]

China's labor wages are also rising quickly at a rate of about 20 percent per year while U.S. wages have on average been declining 3 percent per year, thus impacting the relative labor costs of about 23 percent per year, which is roughly equivalent to a 23 percent increase in the exchange rate of yuan against the U.S. dollar every year.[6] This increase in labor wages should translate into a bigger middle class and thus greater consumer buying power. Additionally, China is changing policies to boost consumerism domestically as the developed markets overseas have dried up.[7] In other words, China's leaders are taking significant steps to address global imbalances by targeting sources of inequality while the United States, the richest country in the world, has not been pulling its weight.[8]

Moreover, while the leaders of China receive much of the media attention and are credited with many of the positive changes happening in China, the ones who make the economic miracle happen are the hundreds of millions of Chinese entrepreneurs who are unafraid to dream big and make risky bets. Millions of these ordinary citizens have scraped their life savings together to travel to China's coastal cities to start businesses. Most of them have very modest operations. Some simply lay their wares on streets and sell stuff as you would at a garage sale. Others sell food, such as green onion crepes or barbecued scorpions, to other working-class citizens. However, the most sophisticated ones, who were diligent, smart, connected, and lucky, have started companies that now amazingly compete with the most successful companies in the world.

Today there are thousands of companies in almost every industry in China vying for a piece of the proverbial pie. The competition
is fierce, like Wall Street on steroids, so these businesspeople hustle
around the clock putting deals together, cementing the necessary
relationships, and meeting growing orders from customers. Only
the largest can access bank lines; the rest usually find capital through
informal channels to grow their business. A steady stream of them
has tapped the U.S. financial markets either through an initial public
offering (IPO) or a reverse merger.[9] Getting a listing on a U.S. stock
exchange holds huge prestige for the Chinese, so they will bend over
backward to meet the stiff U.S. regulatory requirements, even when
their limited resources would be better spent getting listed on other
foreign exchanges. But as these companies get created, they create
more jobs and wealth for others in a virtuous cycle that can get bigger
and faster over time.

Tens of thousands of these Chinese companies have been established in the last decade and have experienced double-digit growth
every single year. Given the Internet-like growth rates, there has been
a rush in recent years by investment bankers to take these Chinese
companies public. Investors who have been disenchanted with the
stagnant growth of developed markets have flocked en masse to
emerging markets, particularly China. The momentum of capital
flowing into China has been increasing as investors eager to make a
quick buck fail to do the proper due diligence. Like previous bubbles,
the rising tide of capital seeking a return in China has been raising all
the entrepreneurial boats. But in the meantime, the real engine for
eradicating poverty has been China's entrepreneurial citizens, who
work 24/7 creating wealth around the world.

As mentioned in chapter 1, a full 50 percent of the profits from production in China go straight to U.S. companies. If the United States
is serious about addressing its inequality issues at home and around
the world, U.S. companies have the choice and the leverage to redistribute its profits to its workers, as opposed to giving them mostly to

their shareholders or granting exorbitant pay packages to the CEOs. By spreading the wealth in a more equal way, the United States can serve as a role model for giving back to the people who produced the wealth rather than the people who are merely rent seeking, which in economic terms means to extract fees and other privileges not associated with adding value.

U.S. human rights activists have often complained that China isn't responsive enough to catastrophes like Darfur where they have leverage. They believe China should be pushing for freedom and democracy at home and abroad. However, many rights activists also underestimate the extent of poverty in Africa, Asia, and other parts of the world where supplying basic needs and infrastructure make a bigger difference to the population than free speech and elections. Stories of Westerners donating microwaves to the poor who don't even have electrical outlets underscore a profound lack of understanding. The poor have to fetch clean water from a pond and would rejoice at having even one meal of porridge a day. Without that, it will be extremely difficult to get them to want much else in life, let alone free speech. If they speak, they will say they want food and water, which is what the Chinese are providing them anyway. The right to live is probably the most fundamental human right, and China has done more helping the poor by alleviating life-threatening poverty than the United States has. As we have seen, China is always very quick to respond and make changes once it's convinced an issue is important and it is confident of a solution. If it seems that they are not acting, the Chinese are either not sufficiently convinced that the strategy presented is the best or they are actually acting behind the scenes without the knowledge of the Western public. But the Chinese, like the Japanese, take their time in deliberating, often conducting innumerable studies before an important decision is reached. When Zhou Enlai was asked in 1971 about the impact of student riots in 1968, he was famous for replying, "It is too early to say."

Sure, China could do more to end tragedies such as Darfur. But

China respects sovereignty and understands that making exceptions the way the United States has done can take a nation down a slippery slope in which the ends may not justify the means. When the Chinese have to choose between providing economic/humanitarian assistance and using military intervention in Sudan, they will choose the former because they believe it will go a longer way in benefiting the impoverished. So before rights activists pass judgments too quickly, they ought to be sure they have the relevant facts. Acquiring those facts often requires going out to the field and speaking to the locals, free from the agendas and opinions of certain stakeholders in developed nations.

## Environmental Sustainability

Our fragile planet that has finite resources may one day finally go on strike swiftly and without warning. Already, floating piles of trash the size of the United States occupy the Pacific, the Atlantic, and the Indian Oceans, killing marine life in untold numbers. In 1900, countries like Brazil had almost all of their land canopied in jungles; now most of the trees are gone. With the rise of developing nations, the demand on our dwindling resources will grow, and the situation will only get worse.

Already, researchers expect that the increasing concentration of human-produced greenhouse gases will cause "more frequent, persistent, and intense heat waves" throughout Europe, like the one in Russia during the summer of 2010 that killed 55,000 people, caused crop failures, and sparked wild fires. The probability of crippling heat waves that break 500-year-old records and cause extensive damage to life on earth will increase by a factor of 5 to 10 over the next 40 years, according to a study published by *Science* magazine.[10]

Whether you accept the reality of climate change or not, the rate at which the world population is devouring natural resources is not sustainable in the long run. The amount of pollution that has been emitted into the air and that has contaminated the world's water supply has also reached levels that are becoming life threatening. Scientists around the world have warned that once part of the ecosystem has been irretrievably destroyed, we will quickly approach the tipping point at which pollution causes a death spiral in the food supply. Already many species have gone extinct or are endangered. It will only be a matter of time before humankind destroys Earth as we know it if we don't drastically change our lifestyles and technology to accommodate the needs of a growing population.

It is widely known that China's pollution had reached alarming levels. In 2009, China consumed 46 percent of the world's coal, and one third of its water was affected by acid rain.[11] The famous Yellow River has been running dry downstream, and its fish are fast going extinct.

Fortunately, the CCP has repeatedly demonstrated its ability to make dramatic changes within short periods of time. During the summer of 2010, Premier Wen promised to wield an "iron hand" to improve China's energy efficiency. By fall, the government had forced the closure of over 2,000 cement plants, steel mills, and other energy-intensive factories.[12]

Beijing has also used its money and muscle to push the green revolution in other ways, such as offering financial incentives to corporations and consumers to buy electric cars.[13] The United States can also start taking steps in this regard. General Electric actually showcased an electric car that was hands-free and run by GPS at the 2010 Shanghai Expo. According to its designer, it is only a few years away from being completely functional as a commercial product. But adoption of such vehicles may require U.S. government mandates or financial incentives to level the playing field since there are many subsidies to the oil companies to deliver artificially cheaper gasoline to the American public.

China also understands that global markets are approaching saturation, so to maintain growth, differentiation is required. Innovation can spontaneously sprout under the right conditions, but those conditions include a supportive institutional infrastructure and talent to take advantage of those structures. As I mentioned earlier, the CCP responded quickly by beginning multiple programs to recruit talent from around the world and simultaneously develop talent internally. Although China often has been dismissed as a cheap imitator, predicting China's future by looking at its past will cause the United States and the world to underestimate China, especially when Chinese engineers have learned a great deal from international R&D firms operating on China's soil. Microsoft's most cutting-edge telephone research and development in speech recognition software for Mandarin is but one of hundreds of examples of high-level research being conducted in China by foreign firms.[14]

China's domestic firms are also starting to compete in innovative industries. BYD, a Chinese company that makes an electric car, has already received a large investment from Warren Buffett.[15] Even American real estate developers are learning from the Chinese. Bruce Ratner, who has plans to develop the world's tallest prefabricated steel structure, has been investigating modular construction after being inspired by a YouTube video depicting the Ark Hotel in China erected in just a matter of days.[16]

Finally, its ability to build sophisticated space technology has finally come of age. Recently China announced that it was the third country in the world to develop its own global satellite navigation system which they call Beidou.[17] Over the next decade, China's innovative capabilities will become more widespread since innovation can only occur where insight springs from the point of contact, and the point of contact for manufacturing and R&D is now increasingly in China.

To keep up, the United States needs to refocus its priorities in developing the right kind of human capital because it will rue the day when most of the top scientists will be moving elsewhere. One immediate problem the United States can rectify is to increase funding to national research and development programs like the National Institutes of Health (NIH). According to Dr. Lawrence Shapiro, associate professor of biochemistry at Columbia University, scientists competing for grants at the NIH, as well as the amount of money available, has been steadily shrinking, which is a distressing trend. Another disturbing truth about the program is that it has become increasingly politicized. Directors who have been appointed to the NIH in recent years often prioritize certain research over others according to the government's agenda, as opposed to freely giving grants for a broad spectrum of research. This process may delay or deter the pure research that can often lead to accidental, breakthrough discoveries. By attaching certain priorities to certain categories, the politicians are in effect telling scientists that they know more about science than the scientists. Thus they dictate the terms of research. But innovations by definition are unexpected. If all the dollars are funding only specific methods of curing cancer, for instance, it is like looking for a lost earring by the light from a lamppost at night.

Furthermore, the NIH is only funding singles and doubles as opposed to home runs. The NIH views potential home runs as too risky when Congressional guidelines dictate that funds should only be granted to research that is perceived to have a higher threshold for success, according to Stephanie Fernandez, a neuroscientist at Yale University. She also states that sometimes great research proposals don't even get read or get passed up because a previous researcher received multi-year funding from the NIH that squeezes out the development of future great ideas. Today, talented scientific researchers spend 80 to 90 percent of their time devoted to grant writing rather than more productive research activities such as cross-pollination of ideas between researchers.

Finally, since accessing the research funding is so competitive, American researchers have become very territorial and are reluctant to openly share ideas and credit. Dr. Fernandez reports that many of her colleagues, especially the older ones, tend to rest on their laurels and act as if the molecules that they have discovered are proprietary. They are reluctant to engage in further research to see how their molecules interact with other molecules in the system, which could lead to breakthrough treatments for debilitating diseases like Alzheimers. Dr. Fernandez conveyed to me that, like many of her contemporary colleagues, she believes that the research system that the NIH has created is totally broken.

Assistant Professor Kristin Baldwin summed up the difference between the United States and China with the following phrase: "The Billion-Dollar Paper." The Scripps Research team published in the journal called *Nature* that they had successfully bred live mice from mouse skin cells. A week earlier, two teams of Chinese researchers published the same results online for the same journal. But while the U.S. Federal government has yet to offer Professor Baldwin a single dime in research grants, the Chinese government rewarded the Chinese researchers with $1 billion to expand their research activities upon hearing the groundbreaking news.

The U.S. government's shortsightedness has clearly upset the scientific community. The good news is that many U.S. companies are not waiting around for American politicians to get their acts together. Nonprofit design firm Terreform, for instance, has already embarked on cutting-edge work in reimagining what a sustainable city in the future can look like. Although its ideas border on the bizarre—homes made out of beef jerky and Goodyear blimps that replace city buses— the principals led by Mitch Joachim have already secured meetings with Chinese officials who are responsible for building new cities from scratch. These kinds of collaborations show great promise in changing our unsustainable lifestyles and breaking political strangleholds on technology.

The United States also should not shy away from using nuclear power plants to meet future energy needs. According to Dr. Patrick Albert Moore, founder of Greenpeace and author of *Confessions of a Greenpeace Dropout*, nuclear energy is the safest energy technology ever invented. He claims that the fear factor of radiation causing cancer promoted by the antinuclear movement is completely irrational based on over 25 years of scientific evidence following victims of Chernobyl. He puts it in stark terms: 1.3 million people die from vehicle accidents every year, 1–2 million people die every year prematurely from coal-polluted air, 3,000–5,000 coal miners die every year from mining accidents, and only 1.2 persons die per year from nuclear radiation. Three nuclear accidents are on record. No one died of radiation from either Three-Mile Island or Fukushima. Of those exposed to radiation at Chernobyl, 7,000 people were cured and only 56 died, 34 of whom were fighting the fire from the explosion. The difference in cancer rates amounted to 1–2 percent higher compared to the control group.

Given the safety record, Dr. Moore believes that nuclear energy is the only realistic way to reach the stated carbon emissions reduction goals of 20 percent by 2022. Solar and wind technology will have to account for 42 percent of energy generation in order to meet those targets, which he calls "pure fantasy."

But the bigger challenge remains—changing belief and incentive systems—because as long as people use the wrong models, the wrong measurements, and the wrong incentives, changing human behavior will prove impossible. Currently our economic and political system is based on growth economics, which is highly correlated with growing populations. But the world population should not, and probably will not, grow as it has for the last 70 years. Extrapolating that human growth will continue indefinitely into the future is not realistic, especially when educated women in most societies are not reproducing at the same rate as prior generations. To rely on such assumptions is to act like the rating agencies who rated subprime housing securities based on only three years of data, which was ridiculous on Wall Street's part. But today's financial economists do this for a living. So when the population growth rate slows or starts going into reverse, we can expect problems to arise. Already it has created problems, such as extreme debt when populations are not keeping up with growth expectations, but it could create even worse problems for the environment if we expect consumption to rise faster and faster to off-set slowing population growth rates without finding ways to renew and replace the resources at similar rates. We are already in danger of not being sufficiently organized or sufficiently creative to avoid these calamities.

Benoit Mandelbrot wrote that everything depends on what you're measuring. For instance, the eastern coastline of the United States is 2,000 miles, if one were to measure it in a straight line from top to bottom; but it's 40,000 miles if one includes all the indentations. Today's economic models measure only things that can be readily priced with money, such as the cost of a ticket to a professional base-ball game, but not the joy of taking your kids to the local park to play baseball with them.

We have a ticking time bomb on our hands, and new economic models must replace the ones that policymakers now rely upon. Pyramid schemes like social security could fall apart if we alter our economic models, but perhaps better models for human civiliza-tion and sustainable living will supplant them once human ingenu-ity can overcome untenable ideas. Perhaps in the interim model, we must de-materialize growth by simply including and increasing the value of certain assets in GDP calculations. After all, a painting worth $100 can just as easily be worth $10,000 to produce the miracle of "growth" without directly impacting the environment. But eventu-ally we must incorporate non-material growth in economic calcula-tions. If we can measure and value the output of clean air, happiness, and other critical elements for life on earth, then re-prioritizing what we create and how we spend our time will become much easier and more straightforward. To reach this stage, we may need to invent a new language in economics the same way Isaac Newton invented the language of calculus to enable modern science to flourish.

The United States can work with China more closely to come up with alternative economic models and theories. Even though George

Soros funded a new think tank called the Institute of New Economic Thinking (INET) with $50 million to re-conceive the field of economics, the problem is that the group is composed of all the same economists, such as Kenneth Rogoff and Lawrence Summers, who comprise the vanguard of the old economic thinking. New economic thinking will necessarily require more input from economists whose ideas are now considered on the fringe, as opposed to mainstream or those co-opted by the establishment. New ideas can also come from people who may not be trained in economics but can add insight from other disciplines or real-world experiences that current career economists simply lack. After all, China's economic growth model was conceived by engineers, not economists. But the real test is whether the United States and China can come up with pragmatic solutions that do not absolve either side from simply kicking the can down the road. The Chinese believe that Americans are not capable of austerity or of "eating bitterness," as they might say. The United States is good at expounding what others should do as they have demonstrated through the Washington Consensus and numerous other ways. But in recent years the United States has lacked the willingness to commit to what it will do when it comes to cocreating a more sustainable and cooperative future with the entire world. But to achieve a real breakthrough, the Americans will have to prove the Chinese wrong.

## A Single Global Currency or Three Regional Ones?

China has been calling for a global currency since the 2008 global financial crisis because its leaders realized they were getting a raw deal in the current foreign exchange system with the dollar as the dominant international reserve currency. Just like the Former French Finance Minister Valéry Giscard d'Estaing who first referred to the "exorbitant privilege" of the United States back in the 1960s, China and most of the world have realized that relying on the U.S. dollar for global trade is dangerous because as the issuer of the currency of the world, the United States can create wealth at the expense of everyone else. An economist by the name of Robert Triffin argued that seigniorage of using the U.S. dollar as the world's reserve currency would lead to America having an artificially high standard of living because it can get all the resources it needs by spending little green pieces of paper that cost it nothing to print. This monopoly power to print money at will is no different than the colonialist extracting resources from the colonies for practically nothing. These free resources then enable further colonial expansion through military means. This asymmetrical ability to control money is one important reason that motivated the European nations to create the euro in order to protect themselves against the dangerous consequences of relying on the U.S. dollar.

Predictably, over the last forty years, the abundance of U.S. dollars has caused the value of the currency to decline, defrauding creditors such as China and the Middle East of the value owed them for the real goods and services they already delivered. While this reserve currency arrangement hurts everyone else in the world, it benefits the United States by funding its unrestricted spending in military and other consumption.

China's leaders understand that they face the same dilemma as the Europeans did a few decades earlier. When hundreds of millions of Chinese have slaved for years and polluted their country in order to sell goods to the United States, they need to know that the compensation they will receive will be worth something in the future. Money must have a lasting store of value; otherwise, no one would agree to accept it in exchange for real goods and services. People need food to live, but no one can eat money.

Unfortunately, the United States has not given the Chinese any assurances on that front. The U.S. Federal Government continues to run deficits into the multi-trillions, and the Federal Reserve has shown no appetite to hike interest rates. By showing no restraint in both fiscal and monetary policies, the United States is abusing its uniquely powerful position as the issuer of international reserve currency and ignoring its fiduciary responsibilities to the world as the world's banker. The U.S. government continues to issue a record number of IOUs on programs such as the military with no limit in sight.

Meanwhile, the Federal Reserve continues to give U.S. bankers free money to buy whatever they want in the world. They have been borrowing money at zero interest rates and buying the world's assets and commodities for quick profits. Chairman Ben Bernanke has claimed that his policy is necessary to "stimulate" the U.S. economy, but it has done nothing of the sort. Structural unemployment in the United States remains in the double digits while the fires of stagflation are being stoked. (*Structural* here refers to the kind of unemployment that arises from major long-term changes in the economy. Stagflation is occurring because, as of July 2011, the U.S. producer price index recorded an annualized inflation rate of 7.2 percent without commensurate growth.) Poor people around the world, who are most affected by rising food prices, are discovering they can no longer afford to eat. The food riots and violent protests erupting around the world are people crying out, not for the right to freedom, but the right to live. Like in colonial times, the poor are robbed to support the rich; only today, the rich are the bankers who claim they need to rebuild their balance sheets to stay solvent.

One might wonder why the United States even has the reserve currency status when its record has shown it to be reckless. One reason is that when the United States unilaterally decoupled its peg to gold in 1971—a move known as the Nixon Shock—it also propped up the dollar by making Saudi Arabia agree to conduct all oil transactions in U.S. dollars. In return, the United States provided military security for the royal Saudi family to keep them in power. Being the largest oil-producing country in the region, Saudi Arabia gave the United States the ability to enforce the continued use of the dollar as the currency for global commodity exchange. There were a number of times when countries tried to move away from this arrangement but without success. When Saddam Hussein of Iraq made the political move to accept only euros instead of dollars for oil in the fall of 2000, many believe that contributed to the U.S. decision to overthrow his regime. Although reasons cited for his overthrow include fighting terrorism, searching for weapons of mass destruction (WMD), and bringing democracy to Iraqis, one motivation may have been gaining strategic control over Iraq's vast petro reserves in order to maintain the dollar's monopoly over oil pricing. With Iran threatening to do the same by creating an Iranian oil bourse, it comes as no surprise that the U.S. military has been eyeing it as the next victim. Even if those who argue that oil transactions no longer account for a major percentage of capital transactions in the world, oil is still the underpinning that gives the dollar value. Without that relationship, the trillion-dollar transactions that exist today in the form of speculative derivative trades could simply be reduced to monopoly money. Without oil priced in dollars, the United States would likely have difficulty securing enough energy resources to sustain its current standard of living. Who would exchange anything of value for dollars if they believed them to be worthless? Countries like China and Russia have already dropped the dollar in bilateral trade.[18] Thus, the world has been using the dollar as the reserve currency, not because it necessarily wants to or thinks it attractive, but because no one wants to challenge the United States, the sole military superpower.

China, France, Brazil, and others have pushed for currency reforms at the G-20 meetings, while the United States has stubbornly resisted such moves.[19] This stalemate between the United States and the rest of the world has not gone far beyond a discussion of possibly using Special Drawing Rights (SDR), which is a reserve asset created by the IMF based on multiple currencies, as an interim solution. As a result, China, Russia, and many other nations started diversifying their reserve assets away from U.S. dollars.[20] China has also been actively cultivating the use of its own currency, the yuan or renminbi, in transactions with its largest trading partners to avoid the foreign exchange costs of using the dollar.[21] Even corporations such as

McDonald's have started issuing bonds dominated in yuan.[22] While these diversification efforts are still in the embryonic stage, a number of people like Professor Barry Eichengreen are already calling for an end to the U.S. dollar hegemony.

What will happen to the United States if the world were to use three major reserve currencies instead of just two? This is a growing possibility since countries in Europe and China are slowly moving away from their reliance on oil and fulfilling their needs with alternative energy. In such a scenario, the United States could potentially suffer a severe adjustment in its standard of living, possibly worse than the Great Depression. Consumer prices could shoot up as a result of a free-falling dollar against the other currencies since the United States currently imports close to 90 percent of its manufactured products in addition to 60 percent of its oil needs. Products in Walmart may no longer be cheap if the U.S. dollar depreciates too much against the yuan and other currencies. The silver lining is that the United States can survive this adjustment. Because U.S. farmers are heavily subsidized, America is self-sufficient with its own food and water supplies and has an abundance of other natural resources within its own borders. An economically wounded United States could be painful, but not insurmountable.

Over the longer term, U.S. entrepreneurs may decide to outsource their manufacturing needs to U.S. manufacturers instead of those in China if they feel that domestic costs to produce will be cheaper. This reallocation of resources could then recreate jobs that once left our country in search of cheaper labor.

But this happy outcome, which many Americans advocate, may also not happen, because restarting an economy will depend on a variety of factors, including the availability of a pliant, skilled, hardworking labor force and appropriate government fiscal and monetary policies. For instance, if the U.S. government can't control its deficits and continues to issue IOUs in the form of Treasuries, then the Federal Reserve will be forced to buy them because other countries will no longer want to. But when the Federal Reserve purchases Treasuries, it has the same effect as printing money, which can eventually lead to high inflation in a closed economy. High inflation, as many countries can attest to, can derail economies when businesses have no price stability. If this scenario materializes, which can happen if real economic activity cannot keep up with inflation, then the United States will suffer fates similar to those of Argentina in the 1970s and 80s, Weimar Germany after World War I, and Zimbabwe at the turn of the third millennium.

As of February 28, 2011, the Total Public Debt Outstanding of the United States of America was $14.19 trillion and was 96.8 percent of 2010's annual GDP of $14.66 trillion, a debt overhang that is similar to Greece's.[23] The ratio of debt growth to GDP growth is even more disturbing at 7.8x, meaning that it takes $7.80 of debt in order to produce $1 of value in the U.S. economy, an incredibly inefficient enterprise if the nation was subject to the same metrics as a company. Finally, the Federal Reserve's balance sheet has tripled from roughly $800 billion to almost $3 trillion in just three years.[24]

For this reason, the United States has often used military force against nations that have threatened to stop using the dollar because this move would directly threaten "U.S. interests." However, China is too large for the United States to win against in the event of war. The two other times the United States went into the Far East to fight— Vietnam and Korea—did not end well for the United States. Even the Middle East wars in Iraq and Afghanistan against terrorist insurgents do not bode well for U.S. victory.

A nonmilitary solution is much more complex, requiring the U.S. government to exercise more self-discipline and self-restraint in both its monetary and fiscal policies while making hard political choices of where to invest and who to tax. For the United States to maintain a strong currency that can be relied upon for trade, for business, and for a store of value, the U.S. government must create the conditions for a stable economic environment. Private citizens need to feel comfortable initiating and engaging in innovative activities that power an economy forward. That is obviously much easier said than done. Choosing this route would inevitably upset the wealthy and powerful who now control American politics. A transition can also extend the current economic stagnation in the United States since people will require time to adjust to new rules and conditions. But the cost of living in denial of current realities and relying only on the military and the ability to print more money to solve all problems is a much worse outcome for everyone.

## Mirror, Mirror on the Wall, Which Type of Government Is Fairest of All?

The United States has openly questioned whether China will be a responsible stakeholder as it becomes more prominent on the world stage. It is true that China needs to do a better job of protecting intellectual property rights, cracking down harder on corruption scandals that involve health risks, and broadening protections of human freedoms. But because of China's historical ideology around Communism, Western democracies and China have not shed their mutual suspicions of each other. Perhaps at some point, all parties can relax in the coexistence of power centers sharing differences of opinion without forcing a resolution. Until then, let me address some common concerns to help raise the level of understanding in the West about China's government.

Westerners often point to China's growing military budget as something ominous. While its military budget is growing, China knows that its military capabilities are nowhere close to America's and therefore would never consider initiating a war. Countries initiate wars only when they think they can win, not when they know they will lose. The accusations of China being a threat don't sound credible when the United States has such an outsized lead in its military spending and capabilities. If anything, from the perspectives of

China and other nations, the United States is the real threat. They could point to aggressive American military action in recent history with Iraq, Afghanistan, and Libya from administrations in both parties. The high unemployment rate and soaring debt levels also look eerily similar to Germany just prior to World War II. If Americans have any reason to fear for their own safety, perhaps they should direct those concerns at our own militant government whose belligerent rhetoric and sanctioned use of torture could presage even greater use of violence in the not-too-distant future.

Another Western argument is that China has a poor track record when it comes to human rights and therefore should not be trusted. Human rights are definitely not its strong suit. Tiananmen Square remains a sore spot for its government. But China learned its lesson and has become far more restrained in dealing with threats to its power. When the public responded to calls for a Jasmine Revolution shortly after protests broke out throughout the Middle East, the Chinese government used street-cleaning trucks to spray water on the crowds instead of dispersing them with military tanks. Granted, mostly journalists and tourists showed up to witness the anticipated demonstrations, which hardly took place. The vast majority who appeared took pictures of each other.

The truth is that hundreds, perhaps thousands, of protests have taken place in China since Tiananmen, but the overwhelming majority of them were not about demanding democracy. These protests were usually from poor farmers who felt that land developers had taken advantage of them and hadn't given them a fair price for their land. Protester demands are usually handled by local Party officials; but if the offense is of a larger nature, such as the inept reporting of the SARS outbreak, the top leaders intervene by replacing key personnel in response to the public outcry.

Some Westerners have also been critical of China's leadership clashes with the Tibetans. They argue that China should have left Tibet independent. Arguably, the logic is similar to saying the United

States should not have absorbed Hawaii as the 50th state. True, China and Tibet have had a long, complicated history over disputed territory. I am not defending their claim but only want to point out that, aside from border disputes, Western reporting of the Tibetan situation is incomplete. Material facts are often omitted that would make the Chinese perspective less offensive. The Tibetans were a feudal serfdom[25] before the Chinese takeover. The PRC wanted to dissolve slavery, so it dealt with the situation by offering generous compromises, in which it paid the religious leaders their full salaries while also granting them the freedom to pray and conduct their religious rituals. In exchange, the Tibetans had to dismantle their institution of serfdom and promise not to secede from the nation. The riots covered by Western media just before the Beijing Olympics were instigated by the Tibetans who burned the homes and stores of innocent civilians, even killing them in a few cases. China sent in its army to stabilize the situation, as any government would when unruly behavior gets out of control. The full context, however, was never explained by Western media at the time these events occurred, creating unnecessary hostility and misunderstanding between the Chinese and the West.

The Falun Gong, another sensitive area for China, was opposed by the government for different reasons. According to officials from the State Council Appeal Office, a bureau that handles public complaints, some of the Falun Gong demonstrators were former government officers who were unhappy with the new direction the PRC was heading. They were against China embracing capitalism and thus used a newly invented religion as the basis of protest. Given the political nature of their religious practice, the Chinese government viewed their organized silent protests as a cult group threatening authority and potentially causing another violent overthrow. From the outset, Jiang Zemin believed that the sect's slogan of "truthfulness, benevolence, and forbearance" was deceiving because it was trying to usurp the Party's moral authority. The Ministry of Public Security issued an edict in July 1999 stating that the Falun Gong was an unlawful organization that has been outlawed. In addition, Jiang warned in his speech to the Conference on Religious Affairs that no one would be allowed to abuse religion to sabotage the socialism, national security, or the Party, which was a reference to Falun Gong. He also admonished "infiltration of foreign forces cloaked in the mantle of religion."

Although the Chinese government's handling of certain situations may be viewed as heavy handed, the Chinese government has acted in such ways only in limited circumstances. In each of those instances, the government acted predictably because it wanted to maintain peace and stability for the broader interests of society. Their fear of chaos is real, given the psychological stress the nation has undergone from the Cultural Revolution and the wars that preceded it. Only by keeping order can the country continue to lift itself out of poverty and enjoy greater freedoms down the road.

When China is understood in this light, it is not as threatening to the United States as some Americans assert. China is simply a nation making progress according to the rules and values of an international order that has largely been designed by Western powers. It has developed by embracing capitalism as the means to access resources, as opposed to invading and plundering nations by force. Most importantly, because China has been run by responsible, levelheaded leaders with plans to groom future talent, the nation can be regarded as not only stable, but also thoughtful in its planning for the future. Considering that its younger generation adores America, China is unlikely to pose a threat to us and indeed should provide huge relief as a source of new leadership where others have failed and a true blessing in disguise to Americans and the whole world.

Still others have argued that democracy is preferable to autocracy because data starting from 1960 onward shows that democratic nations have not spectacularly failed or succeeded, but that autocracies have done both. However, such an argument is problematic for several reasons. The arbitrary use of select time periods means it excludes the evidence that contradicts the theory. Obviously, prior to 1960, democracy failed spectacularly when Hitler came to power in an advanced democratic society that nearly destroyed all other democracies. This theory also doesn't account for the destruction of human lives from democracies outside their own borders. Nobel Laureate Harold Pinter has highlighted the double standards of democratic nations such as the United States, who has a long list of secret wars. Moreover, the very essence of democracy is to let the citizens of a nation decide what they want and how they want to be governed. If a nation imposes democracy on another nation, the very act of doing so is undemocratic. To date, no comprehensive study takes such considerations into account, which renders this debate still inconclusive.

Democracy has many definitions, but in the United States, we have constitutional democracy, in which the governed are supposed to have power over their government, as opposed to the other way around. The U.S. Constitution also guarantees rights so that the majority or privileged should not exercise tyranny over the minority or common people. Abraham Lincoln once said, "As I will not be a slave, I will also not be a slave holder." As Americans, we must remember that even our democracy is a work in progress. The disaster of Hurricane Katrina reminds us that America still suffers from racism even after more than a century of Emancipation. Ideally, democracy would be based on the Golden Rule, the reciprocity principle that encourages compassionate behavior. That China's leaders choose to rule with Confucian principles consistent with this version of democracy further blurs the ideological distinctions.

The United States should avoid using democracy as an excuse for military interventions. Democracies can take different forms—such as those in Pakistan and Iraq—and do not necessarily benefit those who are governed. But when U.S. politicians use *democracy* as justification to topple governments, then the liberal democracy that the United States stands for gets undermined.

If the United States wants to sell democracy abroad, then it must do a better job at home. Could Guantanamo Bay exist in a true democracy? There are dozens of cases ignored by the more mainstream media that expose the dark underbelly of a democratic government. The truth is that power politics, rather than democracy, will continue to dominate world affairs. In a growing multipolar world, the United States should refrain from demonizing and instead begin a dialogue with China about democracy, without assuming that it is the best system for every nation. Robert Zoellick, president of the World Bank, stated, "America's biggest enemy is America itself," meaning it doesn't really matter to the United States if China becomes democratic. Saudi Arabia is not a democracy, and yet it is a close U.S. friend and ally. Using democracy as a condition for friendship with China is a convenient excuse and destructive to the bilateral relationship.

A more constructive approach would be for both sides to work harder at reaching consensus about difficult concrete issues, such as carbon reduction, while maintaining a long-term dialogue about common values. Historically cherished Western values, such as individualism and liberalism, may not necessarily be embraced equally by China, but the United States should also delve deeply into its collective consciousness to question whether these values that have shaped our normative lifestyles are still serving us well in the 21st century. Perhaps China's priorities of sustainability, community, and humanity deserve a second look by the United States as well?

We know that we need to live differently in the coming decades, which will require incorporating new perspectives into our thinking. We need to develop the courage to change what no longer works for the broader interests of the world. Given all the growing contemporary problems, if the world is going to successfully get along, we must first beware of politicians whose solutions capitalize on latent prejudices. To solve 21st-century problems will require extensive cooperation so we must conscientiously stop ourselves from making snap judgments and instead put ourselves in others' shoes. Bluntly speaking, everyone needs to rethink their interactions with others in the world. Thus the debate over whether democracy or benevolent autocracy is a better form of government may only have value as an intellectual exercise. In practical terms, the debate may be irrelevant since the old cliché that the devil is in the details still carries weight. All bets are also off if we have a Malthusian crisis.

The need to reach agreements that prioritize the long-term needs of the entire planet ahead of short-term national concerns is now more important than ever. But the road to robust global cooperation is far from certain. Fostering compassion and learning to work across disciplines may prove more crucial than installing democracy as a way to achieve world peace and long-term survival. Our preconceived notions of democracy and benevolent autocracy may be no more than differences in semantics after all. We will continue to face dilemmas and differences of opinions, but at least if our leaders have empathy and a better sense of the big picture, they may be more willing to acknowledge, listen, and compromise on decisions that offer no easy solutions.

Maximizing human happiness ought to be the ultimate goal for everyone. But Western democracies have assumed that technological progress and economic growth increases human happiness, when there has been a growing body of evidence that neither assumption is true.[26] More countries, including China, are developing Gross National Happiness (GNH) indices as a move away from relying on Gross National Product (GNP) as a better, more holistic measure of well-being.

Furthermore, if we are to put the general good (as defined by the hundreds of factors that serve to increase happiness) as a primary goal in the 21st century, then we must also start thinking about redesigning our existing institutions with that goal in mind. Milton Friedman said that corporations exist only for the profit motive, and only greed and self-interest have ever propelled societies forward. But to what end? Isn't the drive for more profits merely a means to an end, the end being happiness? Isn't the drive for money and power in our current system just a cry for help to feel valued, important, safe, and loved? Aren't some of the most powerful dictators and megalomaniacs also the most unhappy people who ever lived? Can we design a system that better incorporates the general good into our market economies so that corporations do not just exist for the profit motive?

As we can see from the Greek debt crisis, the logic of financial market capitalism has already hit an internal contradiction that may cause it to unravel and eventually implode. When investors and speculators buy credit default swaps (CDSs) as insurance for holding Greek sovereign bonds, they expect to be paid for any event that would qualify as a technical default of those bonds. They expect the rule of law to honor the contracts of this insurance. Yet when the European leaders announced that they would let Greece have a "soft" default but would not recognize it as a default, the officials are in essence denying the holders of CDSs the right to be paid, thus flaunting the rule of law and market capitalism in the interest of maintaining market stability. These two goals are in direct contradiction of each other. Either the governments honor the contracts and experience market mayhem from market selloffs or they overrule the legal contracts in the "interest of market stability," thereby causing a lack of confidence by investors in the rule of law as practiced by Western governments, which would instigate a market selloff nonetheless. What is clear is that the current market capitalist system cannot serve its own needs while maintaining its existing logic. How this internal contradiction gets resolved remains to be seen at the time of this writing, but it does make an eventual convergence with the Chinese form of governance an even more likely outcome down the road. The marriage of the best practices from both the East and the West could kick-start a whole new chapter in human history.

Finally, in order to cocreate a better world with China and all the other nations, we must find it within ourselves to challenge our own assumed attitudes and ideas about freedom, justice, and progress. To reach a higher state of enlightenment, yogis and other spiritualists have always maintained that we must let go of myths, abstractions, and other inadequate ideas with which we've been indoctrinated. Alternatively, we can have an honest conversation about the kind of world we want to leave our children and how we need to act to achieve that goal. For instance, in *Les Miserables,* Jean Valjean steals a loaf of bread during an economic depression and spends the next 19 years trying to avoid capture by the policeman Javert, who prides himself on getting crime off the streets and hunts Jean Valjean with a vengeance. Is the persecution of Jean really serving justice or would society be better off granting forgiveness? Inevitably, how a society functions and the laws that are created reflect the society's normative values. We can't expect society to change collectively for the better unless we also accept responsibility to change ourselves individually for the better.

Unfortunately, social conventions and economic circumstances do exert a disproportionate effect on the life we end up living rather than the one we would choose for ourselves. It therefore takes self-enlightened awareness to recognize the limits that we have imposed on ourselves and an immense of amount of courage, willpower, and imagination to experiment and rewrite the rules of engagement to extend our boundaries of what is achievable. With the world under-going tremendous changes, we may have a historic opportunity to cast off conventional straitjackets that keep us from reaching across the aisle to forgive past wrongs and befriend former enemies. If we don't let the past have any power over us, we can make the impossible possible and forge a new future free from fear and hatred. It can be a future in which productive global cooperation can lead us to a new renaissance that will finally actualize the common desires for the common benefit of all people.

EPILOGUE

# What China Can Learn from America

Human history becomes more and more a race between education and catastrophe. —H. G. WELLS

SETTING ASIDE PROGNOSTICATIONS of the decline of the United States and the rise of China, everyone must not forget the enormous contributions the United States has offered the world, namely its model for liberalized thinking that has led to innovations in many areas. The United States is still among the most free of societies and has generated a lot of unconventional thinking that has propelled the world forward.

## Respecting Uniqueness

Singapore stands in stark contrast to the United States. Although Singaporeans have enjoyed strong economic growth and live in a fairly wealthy society by most standards, Singapore has never generated a single Nobel Prize winner or has ever been the source of disruptive innovations. More tellingly, their society has become too conditioned to obey authority and lacks most vestiges of individualism. As an example, despite over 90-degree humid weather, Singaporeans dare not jaywalk across a street that has no cars. Instead, they wait patiently for the light to turn green at the crosswalk because they fear being punished for even small infractions. Most people walk with their heads down, another telling sign that depression has overrun a population whose freedom of expression has been suppressed for too long.

If China isn't careful with its governance, Singapore may be a glimpse of the future face of China, one that is materially successful, safe, and boring. China must exercise vigilance not to suppress individual thought and expression. In order for humanity and creativity to thrive, the temptation to mold individuals to conform like bricks must be avoided at all costs. China should learn how the United States has made room for the infinite variety of stones to coexist—even the critical ones such as Ralph Nader and Noam Chomsky—without feeling insecure about its power and legitimacy.

Simply putting people in close contact with each other also doesn't guarantee breakthroughs in innovation. Cross-fertilization of ideas from people who think differently, however, increases the odds dramatically. Because the United States remains the melting pot of the world, it still has an advantage in generating creative and innovative ideas. By being more accepting of people dyeing their hair purple, painting their houses pink, and other non-conformist behavior, it allows for extraordinary breakthroughs; American society still tolerates relatively free expression and free experimentation.

I've explained this phenomenon to my students as the volatility rule. A society such as Singapore that restricts volatility or deviation from the norms of society will produce a society that is highly predictable and in some ways robotic. The United States permits much greater volatility, comparatively speaking. When there is greater volatility introduced, then there is greater opportunity for genius to surface. Of course, the society as a whole may also have to tolerate more disruptive behavior as a downside consequence of introducing more individual volatility into society, but that could be a price worth paying.

## Okay to Fail

Many developed nations in both Asia and Europe suffer from the stigma of failure. For instance, entrepreneurism is not respected in Japan. NYU Professor Edward Lincoln recalls being surprised to see three men from Japan at a Young Presidents' Organization (YPO) meeting, given that YPO members are 50 or younger, and most Japanese CEOs are older than 50. He later learned that these men were all sons who replaced their fathers at these companies. He added that these Japanese men were the least cosmopolitan among the YPO members.

In contrast, many of the YPO members from the United States had started their own businesses, a sign that risk-taking is more acceptable here. This phenomenon is further supported by Silicon Valley venture capitalists who indicated in conversations that they almost unanimously preferred to invest in entrepreneurs who had experienced failure at least once with a previous start-up, an attitude that many Japanese and Koreans find strange because they go out of their way to avoid failure. But because U.S. culture is more forgiving of failure and has bankruptcy law to protect failed businesses, people here have been able to bounce back from economic setbacks more easily than in many other places in the world.

China should recognize this strength and choose to embrace it as its own, especially when it reaches a point where its economic growth no longer allows it to depend on modifying foreign technology to suit its own needs. If China is to continue being a strong economic engine for the world, it needs a culture that does not penalize failure in research or in entrepreneurial activity. Breakthrough innovations almost always happen by accident after years or even decades of repeated failures. Marketing new innovations can likewise require much experience, expertise, and even past failure in order to gain the necessary insights to make something a huge success. So for China to replicate this phenomenon, it needs to implement similar bankruptcy laws, ensure that the largest companies do not stifle new ideas from springing to the foreground, and remove any cultural stigmas attached to failures.

Aside from developing a culture that embraces entrepreneurial-ism, the PRC must be prepared to slow growth in the short term by investing more in people doing pure research, which is riskier than applied research from the standpoint of return on investments. Pure research can be far from certain in yielding anything immediately useful or commercial, but it can lead to quantum leaps in innovation. Most private companies do not have the financial resources to make such investments, so governments must lead the way on this front.

## Girl Power

China should also continue emulating America's and Europe's more progressive attitudes toward women holding positions of power. Women are discriminated against in most of the world, and to under-utilize talent in half the world's population is a terrible waste of human resources. Although Japan passed the Employment Act and thus raised the number of Japanese women in management roles from 1.4 percent of the population to 3.1 percent, the number is still far less than the 40 percent figure in the United States. China has shown that it has overcome a lot of gender inequality since the PRC came into power, but the bias to prefer sons over daughters still exists, par-ticularly in poorer rural areas. China must continue working against deeply entrenched sexual prejudice so that more Chinese women can live up to their potential of running corporations and taking seats at the pinnacle of government.

One result from this policy of gender equality is the dramati-cally declining birth rates among women with education, which has affected developed countries, including China. Part of the reason is that women postpone marriage and pregnancy when they have careers to pursue, but the phenomenon also stems partly from the lack of compatibility between men and women in China's modern age. They also won't tolerate male chauvinist behavior to the same degree that their mothers did. Additionally, some men do not value women's education and are more comfortable with a spouse less educated than themselves. A way to help the transition into new gender realities is to provide more educational and support resources for Chinese males who need help adjusting their behavior and values.

## Brand Awareness

Another thing China can learn from the United States is sales, public relations, and branding. The U.S. culture has a worldwide reach. Its fast food restaurants, movies, celebrities, consumer products, and even politics have attained global recognition through mass marketing. The effectiveness of the United States to sell the world everything it has to offer is a skill, the importance of which cannot be underestimated. While a couple of Chinese brands, such as Huawei and Haier, are gaining recognition in overseas markets, China has a great deal to learn in this regard.

The Chinese have historically been biased against salespeople and sales as a profession since they have always believed that actions speak louder than words. The Chinese, due to their Confucius upbringing, abhor boasting about their accomplishments, while Americans rattle them off at every opportunity they get.

But in order to compete in a globalized world, where everyone is faced with innumerable choices and everything can eventually become commoditized, the ability to stand apart from the crowd is a necessary survival tactic. If China wants to go global with its own brands, rather than just accept outsourcing orders, it must learn not only how to break into new sales channels, it must also learn how to create brands that can compete against American brands, such as Apple and Nike, which have won widespread customer loyalty.

Taken to a national level, China can learn a thing or two from the

United States about improving its public relations. The United States maintains the strongest media presence throughout the world, and its messages often penetrate the most homes and thus influence the most people. Becoming media savvy and understanding how to craft and manage public messages is crucial to becoming a world leader because effective communications will affect the world's opinions and politics.

The fact that the Nobel Committee awarded the 2010 Peace Prize to a locked-up dissident, Liu Xiaobo, instead of Hu Jintao for leading a billion people to prosperity in a peaceful way is testament to the huge failure of public relations on the part of the Chinese to communicate their position and present their image to the world. Even if the award was politically motivated, China still should not have responded the way it did by pressuring other nations to boycott it. By doing so, it gave Western critics even more firepower to accuse it of bullying. Instead of shying away from the media, China needs to learn how to manage a hostile media. China can learn from the art of framing the conversation—or more colloquially, the American art of spin—if it disagrees with the West's version of the issues. China is still being perceived as undemocratic and antiliberal by the West, but the problem can be easily corrected with more astute public relations training.

Similarly, when Western analysts comment that Obama is far more charismatic than Hu Jintao during a state visit, the Chinese should respond by finding ways to present their leaders with more appeal on the world stage. While it is natural of the Chinese to dismiss these observations as shallow and disregard them when other issues seem more pressing, China must realize that perceptions can heavily influence reality. Granted, integrity and accomplishments should carry more weight than mere showmanship, but when humans are easily swayed by powerful orators, as we have seen with Hitler and others, the power of image often reaches further than it first appears.

## And Justice for All

China should also continue to reform its judicial system to emulate the standards of fairness found in the United States. While the jury system exists on paper and has been tried in China, its use is still not widespread for reasons unclear without further research. However, the time will come when the Party cannot deliver the same extraordinary growth that China has enjoyed in the last few decades. When that happens, China's citizens will not sit idly by as injustices mount. They will want satisfactory retribution for wrongs they have suffered, and unless they can trust the majority of Chinese judges, they will want a different judicial system.

Last, China cannot give up its fight on corruption, especially among local officials in the lower rungs of government. Despite the high incidence of corruption among economic and political elites in the United States, it is still perceived to be much less corrupt than China in many circles. China needs to tackle provincial corruption much more thoroughly if it plans to avoid more serious societal unrest down the road. Premier Wen acknowledged that corruption in China is a serious problem, but the fact that the top leader in China cannot put an end to it indicates how difficult it is even in China to drive constructive political changes.

While this book is about China's best practices that the United States could try on for size, the fact remains that the United States still does a lot of things right. Americans must remember not to lose confidence in their own government and engage in too much self-defeating talk. Like the Tunisians who inspired democratic movements throughout the Middle East, Americans should also rise to the occasion and demand the best solutions in our own government, not just on Election Day, but every day.

# NOTES

## Introduction: A New Year's Resolution

1. David Pendery, press release, February 27, 2009, "Three Top Economists Agree 2009 Worst Financial Crisis Since Great Depression; Risks Increase if Right Steps Are Not Taken," http://www.reuters.com/article/2009/02/27/idUS193520+27-Feb-2009+BW20090227.

2. Nikki Schwab, "A National Crisis of Confidence," *U.S. News & World Report*, November 12, 2007.

3. Ellen Kelleher, "Americans Forfeit Citizenship to Avoid Tax," *Financial Times*, July 17, 2010.

4. Lydia Saad, "More Americans Say U.S. a Nation of Haves and Have-nots," Gallup Poll, July 11, 2008; Jodie T. Allen and Michael Dimock, "A Nation of 'Haves' and 'Have Nots'?: Far More Americans Now See Their Country as Sharply Divided along Economic Lines," Pew Research Center, September 13, 2007.

5. "Is U.S. Losing Its Competitive Edge?" IBD Editorial, *Investor's Business Daily*, September 9, 2010; Karen Kerrigan, "U.S. Losing Its Competitive Edge," Fox News, October 5, 2006; Timothy O'Brien, "Are U.S. Innovators Losing Their Competitive Edge?" *New York Times*, November 13, 2005.

6. Bob Willis, "Recession Worst Since Great Depression, Revised Data Show," *Bloomberg*, August 1, 2009.

7. Sarah Burgard, Jennie Brand, and James House, "Perceived Job Insecurity and Worker Health in the United States Research Report," Populations Studies Center, University of Michigan, July 2008; Declan McCullagh, "Anti-China Hypocrisy in Congress?" CNET, February 1, 2006; Shaun Rein, "Anti-China Rhetoric Can Cost America $2T," CNBC, May 9, 2011; Renata Rodriguez, "Florida Anti-Immigration Legislation Moving Quickly through House and Senate," *Voto Latino*, April 22, 2011.

8. Michael Lewis, "All You Need to Know About Why Things Fell Apart," *Bloomberg News*, February 15, 2011.

9. Lexington, "China in the Mind of America," the *Economist*, January 20, 2011.

10. Robert X. Cringley, "Inflection Point: This Week Changed the World of High Tech Forever, Though Most of Us Still Don't Know It," *I, Cringely,* May 12, 2005, http://www.pbs.org/cringely/pulpit/2005/pulpit_20050512_000852.html.

## Chapter 1. The China Miracle

1. Xin Dingding, *China Daily*, March 30, 2008.

2. Tony Jin, *China Perspective*, October 30, 2009.

3. China Internet Network Information Center (CNNIC), http://www.cnnic.net.cn/en/index/0O/index.htm.

4. *Xinhua*, July 20, 2010, http://news.xinhuanet.com/english2010/sci/2010-07/20/c_13406639.htm.

5. Hurun Rich List, *Hurun Report*, September 9, 2011, http://www.hurun.net/user//newsshow.spx?.nid=151.

6. National Science Board, Science and Engineering Indicators 2010, January 15, 2010, http://www.nsf.gov/statistics/seind10/c0/cos11.htm.

7. Chris Isidore, *CNN Money*, January 12, 2011, http://money.cnn.com/2011/01/12/news/companies/china_auto_bubble_risk/index.htm?iid=MPM.

8. *Trading Report*, December 16, 2010, http://www.thetradingreport.com/2010/12/16/chinese-ipos-making-waves-in-the-market-but-beware-of-bubbles/.

9. "China to Raise Minimum Wage Levels," *China Briefing*, January 29, 2010; Tingsong Jiang, "Government Transfer Payments and Regional Developments in China," Centre for International Economics, Canberra and Zhiyun Zhao, Institute of Finance and Trade, Chinese Academy of Social Sciences, Beijing, 2003.

10. Derek Chen and Carl Dahlman, "The Knowledge Economy, the KAM Methodology, and World Bank Operations," The World Bank, October 19, 2005.

11. Jamil Anderlini, "China: The Wild West with Razor Thin Margins," *Financial Times*, April 20, 2010.

12. Sebastian Briozzo, "The Growing Importance of China-Brazil Trade," *Finance Asia*, November 23, 2010.

13. Tao Wang, "Ten Big Questions on China's Property Sector," UBS Investment Research, May 12, 2010.

14. Ibid.

15. Chinese State Council, 2009.

16. Akbar Noman, "Scoring Millennium Goals: Economic Growth Versus the Washington Consensus," Initiative for Policy Dialogue, March 2005; William Finnegan, "The Economics of Empire: Notes on the Washington Consensus," *Harper's*, May 2003.

17. Celia Dugger, "Ending Famine, Simply by Ignoring the Experts," *New York Times*, December 2, 2007; Dani Rodrik, "Goodbye Washington Consensus, Hello Washington Confusion?" Harvard University, January 2006.

18. "Prime Minister Gordon Brown: G20 Will Pump Trillion Dollars into World Economy," April 2, 2009; "Seoul Development Consensus for Shared Growth," G20 Seoul Summit, November 12, 2010.

19. Anthony Painter, "Washington Consensus Is Dead," *Guardian*, April 10, 2009.

20. Luca Di Leo and Jeffrey Sparshott, "Corporate Profits Rise to Record Annual Rate," *Wall Street Journal*, November 24, 2010; "The Emerging Global Labor Market," McKinsey Global Institute, 2003.

21. Top Foreign Holders of U.S. Treasuries, U.S. Treasury, December 2010.

## Chapter 2. Confucian Philosophy

1. Giving USA Foundation, June 9, 2010, http://www.givingusa.org/press_releases/gusa/gusa060910.pdf; Giving USA, 2009, http://www.philanthropy.iupui.edu/News/2009/docs/GivingReaches300billion_06102009.pdf.

2. Su Xiaohuan, *Education in China: Reforms and Innovations* (Shanghai: China Intercontinental Press, 2002).

3. "International Students Rose Modestly in 2009/2010, Led by Strong

Increase in Students from China," Institute of International Education, November 15, 2010, http://www.iie.org/en/Who-We-Are/News -and-Events/Press-Center/Press-Releases/2010/2010-11-15-Open-Doors -International-Students-In-The-US.aspx.

4. "Income Limits for Each Fifth and Top 5 Percent of Families, 1947– 2007," Current Population Survey, Annual Social and Economic Supplements, United States Census Bureau, April 12, 2009.

5. Ben Tracy, "More American Families Slip into Poverty," CBS News, September 13, 2010; Ajay Kapur, "The Plutonomy Symposium Rising Tides Lifting Yachts," Citigroup, October 16, 2005.

6. David Cay Johnston, "Income Gap Is Widening, Data Shows," *New York Times*, March 29, 2007.

7. Robert Frank, "Income Inequality: Too Big to Ignore," *New York Times,* October 16, 2010.

8. Udaya Wagle, "Economic Inequality in Kathmandu: A Multi-indicator Perspective," *Himalayan Journal of Development and Democracy* Vol. 1, No. 1, 2006.

9. D'vera Cohn and Paul Taylor, "Baby Boomers Approach 65— Glumly: Survey Findings about America's Largest Generation," Pew Research Center, December 20, 2010.

10. Brian Riedl, "How Farm Subsidies Became America's Largest Corporate Welfare Program," The Heritage Foundation, February 25, 2002; Testimony of Ralph Nader before the Committee on the Budget, U.S. House of Representatives, June 30, 1999.

11. "One in 100: Behind Bars in America 2008," Pew Center, 2008.

12. Bill Gorman, "Thursday Cable Ratings: 'Jersey Shore Keeps Rising'; 'Royal Pains,' 'Fairly Legal' Premiers, 'Real Housewives' Finale & More," *TV by the Numbers*, January 21, 2011.

13. Richard Rushfield, "Secret Rituals of American Idol Auditions Exposed," *Daily Beast,* January 19, 2010.

14. Occupational Employment Statistics Survey Program, Bureau of Labor Statistics.

15. Christine Lagorio, "U.S. Education Slips in Rankings," CBS News, September 13, 2005; Ben Feller and Angela Charlton, "Dropping Out, Falling Behind," Associated Press, September 13, 2006; Maria Glod, "U.S. Teens Trail Peers around World on Math-Science Test," *Washington Post*, December 5, 2007; Sam Dillon, "Many Nations Passing U.S. in Education, Experts Say," *New York Times*, March 10, 2010.

16. Editorial Projects in Education, "Diplomas Count 2008: Can Prate P-16 Councils Ease the Transition?" Special Issue, *Education Week*, No. 40, 2008; Stacy Khadaroo, "Graduation Rate for U.S. High Schoolers Falls for Second Straight Year," *Christian Science Monitor*, June 10, 2010.

17. U.S. Census Bureau and Bureau of Labor Statistics, Population surveys 2010.

18. Marcos Chamon, Kai Liu, and Eswar Prasad, "Income Uncertainty and Household Savings in China," IMF Working Paper WP/10/289, December 2010; Robert Shiller, "The Difference in Savings Rates Between China and the U.S.," *Economist's View*, August 25, 2006; Guonan Ma and Wang Yi, "China's High Saving Rate: Myth and Reality," Working Paper 312, Bank of International Settlements, June 2010.

19. MP Dunleavy, "How Teens Get Sucked into Credit Card Debt," MSN Money Central, May 31, 2006; "Many Teens Carrying Credit and Debit Cards," Associated Press, April 14, 2005.

20. John Taylor, Donald A. Lloyd, and George J. Warheit, "Self-Derogation, Peer Factors, and Drug Dependence among a Multiethnic Sample of Young Adults," *Journal of Child and Adolescent Substance Abuse* 2006: 15 (2) 39–51.

21. Dan Pink, TED Global, July 2009.

22. Jane Krieger, "What Price Fame—to Dr. Salk; The Man Who Developed the Polio Vaccine and Became Almost a Folk Hero Overnight Is a Public Figure against His Will. His One Thought Is to Get Back to His Laboratory," *New York Times*, July 17, 1955.

23. Stephan Chapman, "New Bill Gates Interview: 'Legacy Is a Stupid Thing! I Don't Want a Legacy,'" ZDNet, June 12, 2011; Steve Jobs, 2005 Commencement address at Stanford University.

24. Gordy Slack, "Source of Human Empathy Found in Brain," *New Scientific Magazine* Issue 2629, November 12, 2007; J. Decety, J. K. Michalska, and Y. Akitsuki, "Who Caused the Pain: A Functional MRI 2008 Investigation of Empathy and Intentionality in Children," *Neuropsychologia,* 46, 2607–2614.

25. National Human Genome Research Institute, Genetic Variation Program, June 29, 2010, www.genome.gov/110081551#1; National Human Genome Research Institute, International HapMap Project, October 31, 2010, http://www.genome.gov/10001688.

26. *First Individual Diploid Human Genome,* J. Craig Venter Institute, September 3, 2007.

## Chapter 3. Meritocracy

1. National Crime Records, India January 16, 2010.

2. Surya Prasai, *People's Review*, February 19, 2011.

3. UNICEF 2009.

4. "The Cry of Blood," Report on Extra-Judicial Killings and Disappearances, Kenya National Commission on Human Rights, September 2008.

5. Clifford J. Levy, "Russia's Leaders See China as Template for Ruling," *New York Times*, October 17, 2009.

6. "Corruption Breeds Poverty," *Nation*, April 4, 2011; "Acute Causes of Poverty," MSU Women and International Development; *Causes of Poverty in the Philippines*, Chapter 6, Asian Development Bank; George Abed and Sanjeev Gupta, "Governance, Corruption, and Economic Performance," International Monetary Fund, September 23, 2002.

7. Mark Jacobson, "The Singapore Solution," *National Geographic,* December 2009.

8. Andrew Mango, *Atatürk: The Biography of the Founder of Modern Turkey* (New York: Overlook Press, 2002).

9. Amet Bakir, "Atatürk's View on Education," Republic of Turkey, Ministry of National Education, 2002. http://www.meb.gov.tr/Stats/apk2001ing/Section_0/AtaturksViewon.htm.

10. The World Bank: The World Development Indicators Database—Gross Domestic Product 2009, September 2010; IMF World Economic Outlook Database April 2011, GDP per capita and GDP-PPP per capita estimates for Turkey.

11. Fareed Zakaria, *The Future of Freedom: Illiberal Democracy at Home and Abroad* (New York: W.W. Norton and Company, 2003), 92.

12. Mark N. Franklin, "Electoral Participation," in *Controversies in Voting Behavior*, 4th ed., eds. Richard Niemi and Herbert Weisberg (Washington, DC: CQ Press, 2001).

13. Lawrence Lessig, "Citizens United at One: The Change American Democracy Does (and Does Not) Need," speech given at All Souls Unitarian Church, New York City, April 29, 2011.

14. Kristi Oloffson, "A Brief History of Filibusters," *Time*, November 2, 2009.

15. China Vitae 2011.

16. "Communist Party Chief of Chongqing," *Xinhua*, August 31, 2007; Kent Ewing, "Bo Xilai, China's Brash Populist," *Asia Times*, March 19, 2010.

17. Daniel Kaufman, Director of Global Governance, World Bank, http://allafrica.com/stories/200412140044.html.

18. Kenneth Schortgen Jr., "George Soros Uses Empire to Purchase and Influence Mainstream Media," *Examiner.com*, May 13, 2011; Alexander Lynch, "US: The Media Lobby," *Alternet*, March 2005; Sebastian Jones, "The Media Lobbying Complex," *Nation*, March 1, 2010.

19. Sarah Philips, "Politburo Profiles," *Guardian*, October 27, 2007.

20. Tim Reid, "SEC's Revolving Door to Wall Street Gets Fresh Scrutiny," *Reuters* May 13, 2011; OpenSecrets.org.

21. Hardball, MSNBC, http://hotair.com/archives/2007/10/25/video-bushies-committed-treason-by-outing-me-says-plame/.

22. "Halliburton's Iraq Role Expands," BBC News, May 7, 2003, http://news.bbc.co.uk/2/hi/business/3006149.stm.

23. Daniel Gross, "The Captain of the Street," *Newsweek*, September 20, 2008.

24. "No Line Responsibilities," *Wall Street Journal*, December 3, 2008; Michael Fonte, "Robert Rubin Angling for Big China Fish," *Taipei Times*, November 7, 1999.

25. Philip Rucker and Joe Stephens, "White House Releases Financial Disclosure Forms," *Washington Post*, April 3, 2009.

26. "Peter Orzag to Join Citi as Vice Chairman in Global Banking," Citi, December 9, 2010.

27. Dan Freed, "Goldman Sachs' Favorite Lapdog," *Street*, May 26, 2011; Peter Truell, "A Fed Official's Romance Raises Issue of Conflict," *New York Times*, April 9, 1997.

28. Robert Pear, "Health Industry to Hire Medicare Chief," *New York Times*, December 3, 2003.

29. National Corruption Index, May 19, 2008.

30. Sourcewatch, http://sourcewatch.org/index.php?title=Bennett_Raley; "The Ungreening of America: Behind the Curtain," *Mother Jones*, September/October 2003, http://motherjones.com/politics/2003/09/ungreening-america-behind-curtain.

31. "Americans Mistrust Politicians on Economy," Angus Reid Public Opinion Poll, November 29, 2008.

32. Aaron Task, "Americans' Mistrust of Government Is Rational and Warranted, but also Dangerous," *Yahoo! Finance,* March 16, 2010.

33. Jack Spencer, "The Gulf Coast Oil Spill: Does the Federal Govern-

ment Share Responsibility?" The Heritage Foundation, May 12, 2010, http://security.nationaljournal.com/contributors/michael-brown.php.

34. "Regulatory Failure Contributes to Eco-Disaster in the Gulf," Center for Progressive Reform, http://www.progressivereform.org/BPOilSpill.cfm.

35. Dan Froomkin, "Regulatory Capture of Oil Drilling Agency Exposed in Report," *Huffington Post*, September 8, 2010.

36. *Face to Face*, January 18, 2011.

37. CNN Poll: Majority Says Government a Threat to Citizens' Rights. February 26, 2010; "Poll Cites Rising Distrust of Government in America," CNN Politics, April 19, 2010.

38. Dane Smith, "Leaving through the Lobby," *Star Tribune*, December 29, 2003; Bob Collins, "Should There Be a Restriction on Lobbying by Ex-Lawmakers?" *Newscut*, December 8, 2009.

39. Publishersglobal.com and China International Publishing Group; Robert Lawrence Kuhn, *How China's Leaders Think: The Inside Story of China's Reform and What This Means for the Future* (Hoboken, NJ: Wiley, 2009), 317.

40. Peter Francia and Paul Herrnson, "Begging for Bucks," *Campaigns and Elections*, April 1, 2001.

41. Eric Appleman, "Presidential Campaign Finance," George Washington University, 2009.

42. Paritosh Bansal, "TARP Loss Revised Down to $89B," *Reuters*, April 12, 2010.

43. United States Department of Justice, http://www.justice.gov/pardon/statistics.htm.

44. Fareed Zakaria, *The Future of Freedom: Illiberal Democracy at Home and Abroad* (New York: W.W. Norton and Company, 2003), 180.

45. Ibid., 181.

46. Ibid., 198.

47. "How to Fight a Crisis," *Socialism Today,* March 9, http://www.socialismtoday.org/126/fight.html.

## Chapter 4. Five-Year Plans

1. Nassim Taleb, *The Black Swan: The Impact of the Highly Improbable* (New York: Random House, 2007), 1.

2. Barry Schwartz, *The Paradox of Choice: Why More Is Less* (New York: Harper Perennial, 2004), 75.

3. "China Develops New Maglev Train," *China Daily*, May 15, 2006.

4. Michael Cooper, "U.S. Infrastructure Is in Dire Straits, Report Says," *New York Times*, January 27, 2009.

5. Charles Philips, Laura Tyson, and Robert Wolf, "The U.S. Needs an Infrastructure Bank," *Wall Street Journal*, January 15, 2010.

6. Winnie Hu, "A School District with Officials but No Schools? New Jersey Has Them," *New York Times*, November 15, 2006.

7. "'Disabled' Cop's New Payday," *New York Post*, August 17, 2010, http://www.nypost.com/p/news/opinion/editorials/disabled _cop_new _payday_iktMomCWumOl65iGz1JWQJ.

8. Molly Petersen, "Google Growth May Depend on Lobby Outflanked by Foes," *Bloomberg*, June 6, 2007; Naomi Klein, "The Summit That Couldn't Save Itself," *Guardian*, September 4, 2002; "State of Entrepreneurship Address," Kauffman Foundation, January 19, 2010.

9. Science Park and Innovation Center.

10. Editor, *China Tech News*, July, 8, 2010.

11. "Innovation Tops Hu Jintao's Economic Agenda," *Xinhua News*, October 15, 2007, http://news.xinhuanet.com/english/2007-10/15/content _6883390.htm; Marguerite Gong Hancock and George Krompacky, "The Rise of China: Changing Patterns of Global Innovation and Entrepreneurship," Stanford Program on Regions of Innovation and Entrepreneurship, January 1, 2007.

12. "Wolters Kluwer CEO Says 'Explosive' China Lawyer Growth Will Fuel Sales," *Bloomberg News*, August 30, 2010, http://www.bloomberg .com/news/2010-08-31/wolters-kluwer-says-explosive-china-growth -fuels-sales-for-law-firms.html.

13. Jonathan Watts, "China Puts Its Faith in Solar Power with Huge Renewable Energy Investment," guardian.co.uk, May 26, 2009.

14. Lori Ann LaRocco, "China: A Country of Imitation or Innovation?" *Wall St. Cheat Sheet*, January 25, 2011.

15. Center for China and Globalization, www.ccg.org.cn/en/center .asp.

16. Hannah Seligson, "American Graduates Finding Jobs in China," *New York Times*, August 10, 2009; Chen Jia and Lu Chang, "American Students Chase China Dream," *China Daily*, January 21, 2011; Katherine Dorsett, "Should You Look for Work in China?" CNN, January 17, 2011.

## Chapter 5. Special Economic Zones

1. World Trade Organization, Press Release, April 7, 2011, http://www
.wto.org/english/news_e/pres11_e/pr628_e.htm#atable3.

2. "Cal Poly Engineering Students Win First Shell Eco-Marathon,"
April 17, 2007.

3. Jennifer Manning, "Membership of the 111th Congress: A Profile,"
Congressional Research Service, November 19, 2010; Doug Trapp, "The
Newest Doctors in the House: Physicians Become Legislators," *American
Medical News*, February 23, 2009.

4. Jack Ewing and Liz Alderman, "Deutche Bank's Chief Casts Long
Shadow on Europe," *New York Times*, June 22, 2011; Dawn Kopecki,
"Dimon Challenges Bernanke in Wall Street Bid to Tame Regulators,"
*Bloomberg News*, June 9, 2011.

5. Pew Research Center, "Economy, Jobs Top Public's Policy Agenda,"
January 20, 2011, http://pewresearch.org/pubs/1865/poll-public-top
-policy-priorities-2011-health-care-reform-repeal-expand.

6. CBO monthly budget review, September 2009.

7. "Bird Rescue Experts Kept on Sideline After Gulf Oil Spill," *St. Peters-
burg Times*, September 6, 2010.

## Chapter 6. Real Economy First

1. Kevin Phillips, *American Theocracy: The Peril and Politics of Radical
Religion, Oil, and Borrowed Money in the 21st Century* (Farmington Hills,
Michigan: Thorndike Press, 2006), 268.

2. Robert Shroeder, "Goldman, Morgan to Become Holding Companies," *MarketWatch*, September 21, 2008.

3. David Cho, "Banks 'Too Big to Fail' Have Grown Even Bigger," *Washington Post*, August 28, 2009; Karen Weise, "Banks 'Too Big to Fail' Could
Get Bigger," *Businessweek*, April 7, 2011.

4. Robert Gavin, "As Bain Slashed Jobs, Romney Stayed to Side," *Boston
Globe*, January 27, 2008; Robert Dallos, "Sky High Airline Debt Feeds Air
Safety Debate: Transportation: Leverage Buyouts and Takeovers Have Left
U.S. Air Carriers More Heavily in Debt Than Ever, Raising Concerns That
Cost Cutting Could Lead to Inadequate Staffing, Poor Aircraft Mainte-
nance, and Endanger Passengers," *Los Angeles Times*, October 22, 1989.

5. William Dudley, "The Economic Outlook and the Fed's Balance
Sheet: The Issue of 'How' versus 'When,'" Federal Reserve of New York,

July 29, 2009; Federal Reserve Statistical Release H.4.1, "Factors Affecting Reserve Balances," Federal Reserve, June 9, 2011.

6. Deborah Levine, "Corporate Bond Yields Touch Record Low: BofA," *MarketWatch*, July 23, 2010.

7. Saijel Kishan, "Hedge Fund Manager O'Shea Says Fed Risks Losing Credibility with Asset Purchases," *Bloomberg*, September 8, 2010; "Federal Reserve's Bernanke's Credibility on Line with New Move," *Washington Post*, November 1, 2010.

8. Michael Snyder, "19 Reasons Why the Federal Reserve Is at the Heart of Our Economic Problems," *Daily Markets*, March 31, 2011.

9. Jason Simpkins, "Emerging Markets Consider Capital Controls to Combat 'Hot Money' Inflows," *Money Morning*, November 20, 2009; "Cheap Money Driving Commodity Boom: BOJ," *Business Spectator*, February 2011.

10. "CNBC Poll: Is Commodities Speculation Driving up Food Prices?" April 26, 2011; Rachel Beck, "Institutional Money Drives up Commodities," Associated Press, May 31, 2008.

11. *Reuters*, February 23, 2011, http://uk.reuters.com/article/2011/02/23/wallstreet-bonuses-idUKN2317972120110223?feedType=RSS&feedName=rbssFinancialServicesAndRealEstateNews.

12. "Goldman Sachs 2009 Pay up as Profit Soars," MSNBC, January 21, 2010; Jill Treanor, "Goldman Sachs Bankers to Receive $15.3B in Pay and Bonuses," *Guardian*, January 19, 2011.

13. G. William Domoff, "Wealth, Income, and Power," *Who Rules America?* September 2005 (updated July 2011), http://sociology.ucsc.edu/whorulesamerica/power/wealth.html.

14. Lex Team, "China Hedge Funds," *Financial Times*, September 1, 2010.

15. Triennial and Semiannual Surveys, Bank of International Settlements, November 2010.

16. News Release, Bureau of Economic Analysis, January 28, 2011, http://www.bea.gov/newsreleases/national/gdp/2011/pdf/gdp4q10_adv.pdf.

17. Vincent Bevins, "Just How Dependent Is Brazil on Chinese Demand?" *Financial Times*, August 16, 2010; Sarah Childress, "IMF Lifts Africa Growth View," *Wall Street Journal*, October 26, 2010.

18. Nouriel Roubini, "Beijing's Empty Bullet Trains," *Slate*, April 14, 2011; Vivian Giang and Robert Johnson, "108 Giant Chinese Infrastructure Projects That Are Reshaping the World," *BusinessInsider*, June 8, 2011.

19. Bill Gertz, "Financial Terrorism Suspected in 2008 Economic Crash," *Washington Times*, February 28, 2011.

20. Megan Barnett, "An Einhorn in Her Side," *Portfolio*, May 23, 2008.

21. Alice Gomstyn, "High Flying Hedge Funds See Dark Days," ABC News, September 26, 2008; Alistair Barr, "Naked Short Selling Is Center of Looming Legal Battle," *MarketWatch*, June 14, 2006.

22. David Barboza, "New Investment Tools Approved by Regulator in China," *New York Times*, January 8, 2010.

23. Victor Mallet, "China Promises to Buy Spanish Bonds," *Financial Times*, January 3, 2011; Ingrid Melander and Harry Papachristou, "China's Wen Offers to Buy Greek Debt," *Reuters*, October 2, 2010; Victor Mallet and Peter Graham, "Traders Make $8B Bet Against the Euro," *Financial Times*, February 8, 2010.

24. John Makin, "Emerging Markets Are Importing Fed Monetary Policy," *Economist*, November 12, 2010.

25. James Neuger, "Euro Breakup Increases as Germany Loses Proxy," *Businessweek*, May 14, 2010.

26. Forex Basics: Leverage, *Trader Choice FX*, http://www.traderschoice fx.com/forex-trading-basics/leverage.html.

27. Tetsushi Kajimoto and Yuko Yoshikawa, "Japan Vice Finmin: G7 Ready to Act Again to Curb Speculation," *Reuters*, March 18, 2011.

28. Statement from G7 and Central Bank Governors, March 18, 2011.

29. Ewen MacAskill, "Isaeli-US Cyber Attack on Iran's Nuclear Facilities Heads Off US Strike," *IrishTimes*, January 17, 2011.

30. Catherine Rampell, "U.S. Corporate Profits Were the Highest on Record Last Quarter," *New York Times*, November 23, 2010; Annie Lowrey, "More Profits, Fewer Jobs," *Slate*, March 28, 2011.

31. Jonathan Huebner, "A Possible Declining Trend for Worldwide Innovation," *Technological Forecasting and Social Change*, vol. 72, issue 8, October 2005.

32. Mancur Olson, *The Rise and Decline of Nations: Economic Growth, Stagnation, and Social Rigidities* (New Haven, CT: Yale University Press, 1984).

33. James Kanter, "European Solar Power from African Deserts?" *New York Times*, June 18, 2009; Kate Connolly, "German Blue Chip Firms Throw Weight Behind North African Solar Project," *Guardian*, June 16, 2009.

34. Statistics about Business Size (including Small Business) from the

U.S. Census Bureau, Employment Size of Firms, Table 2a, http://www.census.gov/econ/smallbus.htm.

35. Laurie Bernett, "Bass Brothers and Other Millionaires Take Advantage of SBA Loan Programs," January 12, 2009; John J. Sanko and David Milstead, "CAPCOs Draw More Heat," *Rocky Mountain News,* October 29, 2003; "CAPCO, a Trojan Horse Scammed at Least 10 States," *Prowling Owl,* 2010, http://www.prowlingowl.com/Scams/CAPCO/CAPCO.cfm.

36. "Cost to Bring Drug to Market: $802M," *Healthcare Economist,* April 29, 2006, http://healthcare-economist.com/2006/04/29/802m/.

## Chapter 7. Soft Power

1. Sharyl Attkisson, "Following the Aid Money to Haiti," CBS News, July 12, 2010; "Haiti Tops World Corruption Table," BBC News, November 6, 2006; Mojave Mike, "Why the U.S. Owns Haiti's Hardship," *Daily Kos,* January 14, 2010.

2. Carol Lancaster, *Foreign Aid,* 2007.

3. Carrie Kahn, "Haiti Aid Groups Criticized as Money Sits Unspent," National Public Radio, January 11, 2011; Surendra Gangan, "Government Eye on NGO Money Laundering," *Daily News and Analysis,* June 5, 2011; Anup Shah, "Non-Governmental Organizations on Development Issues," *Globalissues.org,* June 1, 2005.

4. "Afghanistan: Report Says Foreign Aid Being Wasted, Billions Still Not Delivered," Radio Free Europe, March 25, 2008; "How Haiti's Aid Money Is Being Spent," National Public Radio, January 8, 2011.

5. Linda Polman, "Easy Money: The Great Aid Scam," *Times,* April 25, 2010; Barry Mason, "Africa Reports Expose Fraud of G-8 Pledges of Aid and Debt Relief," August 15, 2006, wsws.org; David Kaufman, "Aid Effectiveness and Governance: The Good, the Bad, and the Ugly," Brookings Institute, May 17, 2009; Aleksander Dardeli, "International Development Aid, Distrust, and Lesser Impact: An Overview on Civil Society Perspectives"; James Bovard, "Bush's Foreign Aid Fraud, The Future of Freedom," October 24, 2005; George Russell, "U.S. Ignored U.N. Aid Agency's Fraud and Mismanagement," FoxNews.com, January 1, 2010.

6. David Dollar, "Supply Meets Demand: Chinese Infrastructure Financing in Africa," World Bank, July 10, 2008; "China Promises Billions in Aid, Loans to Africa," Associated Press, November 8, 2009.

7. Wing-Gar Cheng and Xiao Yu, "China's Hu Pledges More Investment, Loans in Africa," *Bloomberg News,* November 4, 2006.

8. "U.S. Embassy Cables: African Countries Prefer Chinese Aid to US-China Cooperation," *Guardian.co.uk*, December 4, 2010.

9. "Chinese Scholarships for Africans Set to Double," *China Daily*, November 3, 2006, http://www.china.org.cn/english/education/187542 .htm; Dr. Martyn Davies, "How China Delivers Development Assistance to Africa," Centre for Chinese Studies, University of Stellenbosch, February 2008.

10. "Chinese Premier Pledges Funds, Aid to Africa," Associated Press, November 8, 2009.

11. Comision Economica para America Latina (CEPAL); Nathan Gill, "China to Loan Ecuador $1B for Public Works, Expreso Says," *Bloomberg*, June 14, 2011; "China Surpasses US as Brazil's Biggest Investor," Greenwood Management Growth Investments, April 4, 2011.

12. CNN wire staff, Bolivia's President Says He Remains Afraid of U.S. Plot, CNN July 28, 2011, http://edition.cnn.com/2011/WORLD/americas/ 07/27/bolivia.morales.interview/index.html.

13. "Argentina, Brazil Condemn U.S. Bombing over Iraq," March 22, 2003; "Brazil: Iraq, U.S. Guilty of Disrespect," *Newsmax*, March 20, 2003.

14. "Chile: Chinese Vehicle Import Surge," *Just Auto*, March 8, 2008.

15. Alan Cowell, "19 Countries to Skip Nobel Ceremony, While China Offers Its Own Prize," *New York Times*, December 7, 2010.

16. Juan Forero, "China's Oil Diplomacy in Latin America," *New York Times*, March 1, 2005.

17. Martin Nkolomba and Zangose Chambwa, "Chinese Create 15,000 Jobs in Zambia," The Lusaka Paper, December 27, 2009; "Chinese Businesses Create Jobs and Boost Trade in South Africa," *Brunei Times*, September 20, 2010; "Angola and Mozambique to Create Jobs Through Chinese Scheme," Ranstad, August 23, 2010.

18. "China's Medical Aid to Africa," CRI English, July 5, 2009; "China's Barefoot Doctors an Inspiration to Africa: WHO," *People's Daily*, July 28, 2010.

19. Domenico Montanaro, "Patronage Pick Ambassador Quits; Derided as 'Disaster,' 'Abysmal,'" MSNBC, February 4, 2011; Jeanne Cummings, "Obama Rewards Donors with Plum Jobs," *Politico*, November 19, 2009.

20. Budget of the United States Government: Historical Tables, www .gpoaccess.gov/usbudget/fy10/hist.html; Fred Kaplan, "President Obama has Proposed the Largest Military Defense Budget Since World War II," *Slate*, February 1, 2010.

21. President's FY 2010 budget.

22. Robert Higgs, "The Trillion Dollar Defense Budget Is Already Here," March, 15, 2007.

23. Li Jiao, "China Sets Huge R&D Boost," *Science Insider,* July 7, 2009.

24. Gideon Rose, *How Wars End* (New York: Simon & Schuster, 2010), 3.

25. Gideon Rose, "Think Again: America Decline—This Time It's for Real," *Foreign Policy,* January/February 2011.

26. Fergus Hanson, The 2010 Lowy Institute Poll, Lowy Institute for International Policy.

27. Lesley Wroughton and Simon Rabinovitch, "G20 Parts Ways in Search of Lasting Recovery," *Reuters,* June 27, 2010.

28. "Wikileaks Founder has Support of Icelandic MP Despite Sweden Rape Case," *IceNews,* September 10, 2010.

29. Deutsche Welle, "German Foreign Minister Seeks Improved Relations with Russia," November 20, 2009.

30. "Spain Signs Business Accords with China," MENAFN-Arab News, January 7, 2011; "China Vows to Boost Cooperation with Greece," *Euronews,* February 10, 2010.

31. Dave Wang, "How China Helped Shape American Culture: The Founding Fathers and Chinese Civilization," *Virginia Review of Asian Studies,* 2010.

32. Bryony Jones, "What Is the Muslim Brotherhood?" CNN, January 28, 2011; "Profile: Egypt's Muslim Brotherhood," BBC, February 9, 2011.

33. Abayomi Azikiwe, "African Union Calls for End of NATO Bombing of Libya," Pan-African Newswire, June 6, 2011; Henry Meyer, "Putin Stokes Libya Crusade Spat on NATO Bombing Anniversary," *Bloomberg,* March 23, 2011.

34. Ammar Abdulhamid, "Defending America's 'Freedom Agenda,'" *Project Syndicate,* January 8, 2008.

35. Ray Tsuchiyama, "China Turns Its Focus to Africa," *Forbes,* June 10, 2010.

36. Mary Beth Marklein, "A Culture Clash over Confucius Institutes," *USA Today,* December 7, 2009.

37. Kelly Chung Dawson, "Confucius Institutes Enhance China's International Image," *China Daily,* April 4, 2010.

38. "316 Confucius Institutes Established Worldwide," *Xinhua,* July 1, 2010, http://news.xinhuanet.com/english2010/culture/2010-07/13/c_13398209.htm.

39. Kelly Chung Dawson, "Confucius Institutes Enhance China's International Image," *China Daily*, April 23, 2010, http://www.chinadaily.com.cn/china/2010-04/23/content_9766116.htm.

40. "Alabama Signs Tougher Immigration Laws," *U.S. Election News*, June 10, 2011, http://uselectionnews.org/alabama-signs-tougher-immigration-laws/853971/; Wang Jun, "More Chinese Flock to US Schools but at Steep Price," *China Daily*, June 13, 2011.

41. Deborah Brautigam, "Is China Sending Prisoners to Work Overseas?" *China in Africa: The Real Story*, August 13, 2010; Lucy Ash, "China in Africa: Developing Ties," BBC News, December 4, 2007.

42. Editorial Staff, "American Brain Drain: U.S.-Born PhDs Are Hard to Come by," *Wall Street Journal*, November 27, 2007.

43. Madhavi, *The Trajectory*, http://thetrajectory.com/blogs/index.php/2009/12/shashi-tharoors-impressive-take-on-indias-soft-power/.

44. Samir Amin, *Conversations with Harold Hudson Channer*, April 21, 1991, http://www.channer.tv/wednesday.htm,%2006-30-10.htm.

45. "Department of Energy to Invest $366M in Energy Innovation Hubs," December 22, 2009, http://energy.gov/articles/department-energy-invest-366m-energy-innovation-hubs; "MIT Partners in DOE-Funded Nuclear Energy Innovation Hub," *MIT News*, June 4, 2010; Yael Borofsky, "Tracking a Rising Tiger," speech given at Breakthrough Institute, November 11, 2005, and October 19, 2010.

46. Suresh Kumar, "The National Export Initiative and the Role of the Commercial Service," February 23, 2011, speech given at NYU Kimmel Center.

47. "Europe Grapples with Youth Unemployment," *Financial Times*, February 16, 2011; "Employment and Unemployment Among Youth Summary," Bureau of Labor Statistics, August 27, 2010.

## Chapter 8. Cocreating a Better World

1. World Bank report, April 8, 2009.

2. Kui Kuiyanjui, "Chinese Firm to Invest 9 Billion in Solar Power Plant," Nairobi *Business Daily*, August 17, 2007; Princeton Lyman, "China's Rising Role in Africa," Presentation to the U.S. China Commission, July 21, 2005; Peter Bosshard, "China's Role in Financing African Infrastructure," International Rivers, May 14, 2007; Grace Augustine, "Chinese Activity in Africa, Part 2: The Path of Least Resistance," *Stanford Social Innovation Review*, August 27, 2008; Tom Phillips, "Brazil's Huge New Port

Highlights China's Drive into South America," *Guardian*, September 15, 2010; Thomas Lum, Hannah Fischer, Julissa Gomez-Granger, and Anne Leland, "China's Foreign Aid Activities in Africa, Latin America, and Southeast Asia," Congressional Research Service, February 25, 2009.

3. Elizabeth Rosenthal, "African Huts Far from the Grid Glow with Renewable Power," *New York Times*, December 24, 2010.

4. Michelle Faul, "China Solar Bids for African Business," Associated Press, March 3, 2011; "China to Supply Solar Panels Countrywide," *Tanzania Daily News*, April 15, 2010.

5. Sarah Boseley, "World Bank Poverty Drive a Failure, Says a Report," *Guardian*, July 3, 2003; Mark Weisbrot, "Protests Keep Spotlight on IMF and World Bank Failures," CommonDreams.org, September 25, 2000; Bryan Johnson, "The World Bank and Economic Growth: 50 Years of Failure," The Heritage Foundation, May 16, 1996.

6. Shu-Ching Jean Chen, "Chinese Wage Increases Outpacing Economic Growth," *Forbes*, July 2, 2007; Ying Diao, "China Provinces Raise Minimum Wages to Curb Disputes," *Bloomberg Businessweek*, July 1, 2010.

7. "China to Boost Consumption, Domestic Demand," *Reuters*, November 11, 2010, http://www.reuters.com/article/2010/11/12/g20-china-idUSA SN0000502010111112; "China Eases Tariffs to Boost Domestic Consumption," *People's Daily*, February 21, 2011.

8. "20 Facts about U.S. Inequality that Everyone Should Know," The Stanford Center for the Study of Poverty and Inequality, June 2, 2011.

9. Natalie Erlich, "Chinese IPOs Top Nasdaq's Foreign Market," CNBC, October 29, 2010; Richard McCormack, "Growing Number of IPOs Bypassing U.S. Equity Markets," *Manufacturing and Technology News*, September 1, 2005; Sue Chang, "Chinese IPOs Poised for Top Billing in U.S. Market," *MarketWatch*, October 12, 2010; Soo Ai Peng, "China IPOs Seen Hitting Record High in 2010," *Reuters*, July 5, 2010.

10. David Barriopedro, University of Lisbon, 2011.

11. Michael Lelyveld, "Coal Use Set to Soar," Radio Free Asia, February 7, 2011.

12. *China Daily*, May 6, 2010, and September 20, 2010, http://new .gbgm-umc.org/media/newsletters/100921dlchinanewssummary.pdf.

13. Keith Bradsher, "China Outlines Plans for Making Electric Cars," *New York Times*, April 10, 2009.

14. Yanli Zheng, Richard Sproat, Liang Gu, Izhak Shafran, Haolang Zhou, Yi Su, Dan Jurafsky, Rebecca Starr, Su-Youn Yoon, Accent Detection

and Speech Recognition for Shanghai-Accented Mandarin, www.stan-ford.edu/~jurafsky/p1304.pdf.

15. Marc Gunther, "Warren Takes Charge," *CNN Money*, April 13, 2009.

16. Charles Bagli, "Prefabricated Tower May Rise at Brooklyn's Atlantic Yards," *New York Times*, March 16, 2011.

17. "Beidou 1 Experimental Satellite Navigational System," http://www.sinodefence.com/space/satellite/beidou1.asp.

18. Chris Oliver, "China, Russia to Drop Dollar in Bilateral Trade," *MarketWatch*, November 23, 2010; Emma O'Brien and Artyom Danielyan, "Yuan-Ruble Trade Starts as Russia, China Shun Dollar," *Bloomberg Businessweek*, December 15, 2010.

19. "Sarkozy Visits Obama in Campaign to Blunt Dollar's Dominance," *Bloomberg Businessweek*, January 7, 2011; "Reserve Accumulation and International Monetary Stability Report," International Monetary Fund, April 13, 2010; Alex Newman, "BRICs Leaders Attack the United States Dollar," *New American*, April 21, 2011.

20. Peter Goodman, "China Set to Reduce Exposure to the Dollar," *Washington Post*, January 10, 2006; Brad Setser, "China Reduced Its Dollar Holdings in February," Council of Foreign Relations, April 15, 2009.

21. "Turkey, China to Use Lira/Yuan in Bilateral Trade," *Reuters*, October 8, 2010; "Brazil-China Bilateral Trade in Real and Yuan Instead of U.S. Dollar," *MercoPress*, June 30, 2009; "China Starts Trading Malaysian Ringgit Against Yuan," *China News Asia*, August 19, 2010.

22. Patricia Kuo and Shelley Smith, "McDonald's Sets Benchmark for China with Yuan Bond Sale," *Bloomberg Businessweek*, August 20, 2010.

23. United States Department of the Treasury, Bureau of the Public Debt, December 2010.

24. Credit and Liquidity Programs and the Balance Sheet, Federal Reserve, June 3, 2011.

25. Melvyn Goldstein, *Journal of Asian Studies*, May 1971.

26. "Facebook May Lead to Unhappiness," ABC News, January 30, 2011.

# SELECTED BIBLIOGRAPHY

Allen, Robert. *The British Industrial Revolution in Global Perspective*. New York: Cambridge University Press, 2009.

Alterman, Eric. *Kabuki Democracy: The System vs. Barack Obama*. New York: Nation Books, 2011.

Behrman, Greg. *The Most Noble Adventure: The Marshall Plan and the Time When America Helped Save Europe*. New York: Free Press, 2007.

Berger, Peter, and Thomas Luckmann. *The Social Construction of Reality: A Treatise in the Sociology of Knowledge*. New York: Anchor Books, 1966.

Bremmer, Ian. *The End of the Free Market: Who Wins the War Between States and Corporations?* New York: Portfolio, 2010.

Buderi, Robert, and Gregory Huang. *Guanxi (The Art of Relationships): Microsoft, China, and Bill Gate's Plan to Win the Road Ahead*. New York: Simon & Schuster, 2006.

Cerny, Philip. *Rethinking World Politics: A Theory of Transnational Neo-pluralism*. New York: Oxford University Press, Inc., 2010.

Chandler, Marc. *Making Sense of the Dollar: Exposing Dangerous Myths about Trade and Foreign Exchange*. New York: Bloomberg Press, 2009.

Chang, Leslie. *Factory Girls: Voices from the Heart of Modern China*. London: Picador, 2008.

Endlich, Lisa. *Goldman Sachs: The Culture of Success*. New York: Touch-stone, 2000.

Fischer, David Hackett. *The Great Wave: Price Revolutions and the Rhythm of History*. New York: Oxford University Press, 1996.

Frank, Robert, and Philip Cook. *The Winner-Take-All Society: Why the Few at the Top Get So Much More Than the Rest of Us*. New York: Penguin Books, 1996.

Friedman, George. *The Next 100 Years: A Forecast for the 21ˢᵗ Century*. New York: Doubleday, 2009.

Friedman, Thomas. *Hot, Flat, and Crowded: Why We Need a Green Revolution and How It Can Renew America*. New York: Farrar, Straus, & Giroux, 2008.

Fukuyama, Francis. *The End of History and the Last Man*. New York: Free Press, 1992.

Galbraith, John Kenneth. *The Good Society: The Humane Agenda*. New York: Houghton Mifflin, 1996.

Gray, John. *Men Are from Mars, Women Are from Venus: The Classic Guide to Understanding the Opposite Sex*. New York: HarperCollins Publishers, 1992.

Greene, Jay. *Education Myths: What Special-Interest Groups Want You to Believe about Our Schools and Why It Isn't So*. Lanham: Rowman and Littlefield Publishers, 2006.

Gup, Ted. *Nation of Secrets: The Threat to Democracy and the American Way of Life*. New York: Doubleday, 2007.

Guthrie, David. *China and Globalization: The Social, Economic, and Political Transformation of Chinese Society*. Revised Edition. New York: Routledge, 2009.

Halper, Stefan. *The Beijing Consensus: How China's Authoritarian Model Will Dominate the Twenty-First Century*. New York: Basic Books, 2010.

Hamilton, Rebecca. *Fighting for Darfur: Public Action and the Struggle to Stop Genocide*. New York: Palgrave Macmillan, 2011.

Heather, Peter. *The Fall of the Roman Empire: A New History of Rome and the Barbarians*. New York: Oxford University Press, 2006.

Henry, James. *The Blood Bankers: Tales from the Global Underground Economy*. New York: Four Walls Eight Windows, 2003.

Hexter, Jimmy, and Jonathan Woetzel. *Operation China: From Strategy to Execution*. Boston: Harvard Business School Press, 2007.

Jacques, Martin. *When China Rules the World*. New York: The Penguin Press, 2009.

Karabell, Zachary. *SuperFusion: How China and America Became One Economy and Why the World's Prosperity Depends on It*. New York: Simon & Schuster, 2009.

Khanna, Tarun. *Billions of Entrepreneurs: How China and India Are Reshaping Their Futures and Yours*. Boston: Harvard Business School Press, 2007.

Kristof, Nicholas, and Sheryl Wudunn. *Half the Sky: Turning Oppression into Opportunity for Women Worldwide*. New York: Alfred A. Knopf, 2009.

Krueger, Alan. *What Makes a Terrorist: Economics and the Roots of Terrorism*. Princeton: Princeton University Press, 2007.

Krupp, Fred, and Miriam Horn. *Earth: The Sequel, the Race to Reinvent Energy and Stop Global Warming*. New York: W.W. Norton & Co., 2008.

Kuhn, Robert Lawrence. *How China's Leaders Think: The Inside Story of China's Reform and What This Means for the Future*. Singapore: John Wiley & Sons, 2010.

Kupchan, Charles. *When Enemies Become Friends: The Sources of Stable Peace*. Princeton: Princeton University Press, 2010.

North, Douglas. *Institutions, Institutional Change and Economic Performance*. Cambridge: Cambridge University Press, 1990.

Olson, Mancur. *The Rise and Decline of Nations: Economic Growth, Stagnation, and Social Rigidities*. New Haven: Yale University Press, 1982.

Peerenboom, Randall. *China Modernizes: Threat to the West or Model for the Rest?* New York: Oxford University Press Inc., 2007.

Pettis, Michael. *The Volatility Machine: Emerging Economics and the Threat of Financial Collapse*. New York: Oxford University Press, Inc., 2001.

Pierson, Paul, and Jacob Hacker. *Winner-Take-All-Politics: How Washington Made the Rich Richer—and Turned Its Back on the Middle Class*. New York: Simon & Schuster, 2010.

Pojman, Louis, and Lewis Vaughn. *Classics of Philosophy*. New York: Oxford University Press, Inc., 2011.

Ridley, Matt. *The Rational Optimist: How Prosperity Evolves*. New York: HarperCollins Publishers, 2010.

Rose, Gideon. *How Wars End: Why We Always Fight the Last Battle*. New York: Simon Schuster, 2010.

Schumacher, E.F. *Small Is Beautiful: Economics as if People Mattered*. New York: Harper & Row Publishers, 1989.

Schwartz, Barry. *The Paradox of Choice: Why More Is Less*. New York: HarperCollins Publishers, Inc., 2004.

Schwartz, Timothy. *Travesty in Haiti: A True Account of Christian Missions, Orphanages, Food, Fraud, Food Aid, and Drug Trafficking*. Charleston: BookSurge Publishing, 2008.

Shirk, Susan. *China: Fragile Superpower: How China's Internal Politics Could Derail Its Peaceful Rise*. New York: Oxford University Press, Inc., 2007.

Steil, Benn, and Robert Litan. *Financial Statecraft: The Role of Financial Markets in American Foreign Policy*. New Haven: Yale University Press, 2006.

Stewart, Rory. *The Prince of the Marshes and Other Occupational Hazards of a Year in Iraq*. Orlando: Harcourt, Inc., 2006.

Strauss, William, and Neil Howe. *The Fourth Turning: What the Cycles of History Tell Us about America's Next Rendezvous with Destiny*. New York: Broadway Books, 1997.

Surowiecki, John. *The Wisdom of Crowds*. New York: Anchor Books, 2005.

Taleb, Nassim. *The Black Swan*. New York: Random House, 2007.

Wasserstrom, Jeffrey. *China in the 21ˢᵗ Century: What Everyone Needs to Know*. New York: Oxford University Press, Inc., 2010.

Wedel, Janine. *Shadow Elite: How the World's New Power Brokers Undermine Democracy, Government, and the Free Market*. New York: Basic Books, 2009.

Weston, Mark. *Prophets and Princes: Saudi Arabia from Muhammad to the Present*. Hoboken: John Wiley & Sons, 2008.

Winchester, Simon. *The Man Who Loved China: The Fantastic Story of the Eccentric Scientist Who Unlocked the Mysteries of the Middle Kingdom*. New York: HarperCollins Publishers, 2008.

Zakaria, Fareed. *The Future of Freedom: Illiberal Democracy at Home and Abroad*. New York: W.W. Norton and Company, 2003.

# ACKNOWLEDGMENTS

Though I enjoy reading current affairs books, it had not occurred to me that I should write one myself. But after the suggestion came up multiple times from different friends and colleagues, I was finally convinced to embark on the journey. Thank you to everyone who encouraged me to put my ideas in writing.

The book wouldn't have been possible without the countless hours of conversations I had with friends, acquaintances, students, and colleagues during my time in China. I particularly want to thank Gareth Chang, Erh-Cheng Hwa, Michael Pettis, Shi Zulin, Gerard Debenedetto, Joanna Wang, Min Shao, Hu Xuehao, Xinqiao Ping, Li Jing, Simon Zhang, Wu Peng, Jimmy Hexter, and Joyce Man for all their insights, time, and generous hospitality.

On the U.S. side, Ian Bremmer, Charles Kolb, Alan Krueger, Frank Wisner, and Arthur Levitt have been wonderful mentors over the years. Their insider perspectives of Washington helped crystallize many of my views about America's political economy.

I truly appreciate the support of Lew Daly and David Callahan at

Demos who believed in the project from the beginning. The rest of the Demos staff has also been wonderfully supportive.

I owe deep gratitude to Jill Marsal and my editor Neal Maillet for their constructive feedback and support in making this book a reality. They kept going to bat for me even when success seemed out of reach. Thank you, Deanna Zandt, for connecting me to Neal. Jeevan Sivasubramaniam, thanks for enduring my endless anxieties as a first-time author. And thanks to the entire Berrett-Koehler team for their warm welcome and enthusiastic response to my book.

Similarly, I must acknowledge my friends Michele Wucker, Lawrence McDonald, Marc Chandler, Po Bronson, and Nassim Taleb for their help and advice on getting a book published. Thank you so much for sharing your experiences and providing assistance.

Certain individuals unrelated to the writing of this book but who played a positive role in opening doors in the policy world include: Patricia Huntington, Mallory Factor, Steve Sokol, Gerry Ohrstrom, and Vera Jelinek.

My heartfelt thanks goes to my great friends Alex Castaldo, Bill Hunt, George Wozencraft, Russ Meneve, and Whitney Armstrong, and my super wonderful parents who took the time to read through my drafts and provide invaluable comments. My brother John also devoted time to review my initial book proposal. I don't know how to thank all of you enough.

# INDEX

## ABOUT THE AUTHOR

**ANN LEE** is a Senior Fellow at Demos, a non-partisan think tank. She has written for the *Financial Times,* the *Wall Street Journal, Newsweek, Businessweek, Forbes, Worth,* and the *Hong Kong Economic Journal* and other trade publications. She has provided political and economic commentary on ABC, CBS, CNBC, CNN, Fox Business, Bloomberg TV and radio, NPR, and many foreign news channels. A former investment banker and fixed income trader, she now teaches at New York University. Currently a resident of New York City, Lee is a Woodrow Wilson National Fellow and a graduate of Harvard Business School.

# Dēmos
## IDEAS & ACTION

220 FIFTH AVENUE, 2ND FLOOR | NEW YORK, NEW YORK 10001
PHONE: (212) 633-1405 | FAX: (212) 633-2015

**Dēmos is a non-partisan public policy research and advocacy organization founded in 2000. Headquartered in New York City, Dēmos works with advocates and policymakers around the country in pursuit of four overarching goals:**

» *a more equitable economy with widely shared prosperity and opportunity*
» *a vibrant and inclusive democracy with high levels of voting and civic engagement*
» *an empowered public sector that works for the common good*
» *responsible U.S. engagement in an interdependent world*

### THE AMERICAN PROSPECT

Dēmos has recently established a new strategic partnership with *The American Prospect*, a leading DC-based magazine that provides insightful and timely policy analysis on the political issues affecting our nation. The partnership brings together our 10-year history of collaboration, shared values, and complementary strengths and allows both organizations to increase our reach and impact toward the shared goal of bringing about progressive change.

### DĒMOS FELLOWS PROGRAM

Dēmos is proud to be part of a progressive movement that is reshaping the way new ideas inform the public and policy debates, operating on a basis of shared responsibility and shared progress. We are working to incubate and execute new and diverse solutions to shared problems, and to offer long-range goals that can create stability and prosperity for Americans and people around the world. Through the work of the Fellows Program, Dēmos supports scholars and writers whose innovative work influences the public debate about crucial national and global issues. The program an intellectual home and public engagement platform for more than 20 fellows from diverse backgrounds: emerging public intellectuals, journalists, distinguished public figures, and academics whose research can be used to inform the policy world."

### POLICYSHOP.NET

CHECK DEMOS' BLOG FOR THE LATEST ANALYSIS AND COMMENTARY
FROM DĒMOS EXPERTS & FELLOWS.

VISIT **DEMOS.ORG** OR FOLLOW US ON TWITTER: **@DEMOS_ORG**
FACEBOOK.COM/**DEMOSIDEASACTION**

# Berrett–Koehler
## Publishers

**Berrett-Koehler** is an independent publisher dedicated to an ambitious mission: *Creating a World That Works for All*.

We believe that to truly create a better world, action is needed at all levels—individual, organizational, and societal. At the individual level, our publications help people align their lives with their values and with their aspirations for a better world. At the organizational level, our publications promote progressive leadership and management practices, socially responsible approaches to business, and humane and effective organizations. At the societal level, our publications advance social and economic justice, shared prosperity, sustainability, and new solutions to national and global issues.

A major theme of our publications is "Opening Up New Space." Berrett-Koehler titles challenge conventional thinking, introduce new ideas, and foster positive change. Their common quest is changing the underlying beliefs, mindsets, institutions, and structures that keep generating the same cycles of problems, no matter who our leaders are or what improvement programs we adopt.

We strive to practice what we preach—to operate our publishing company in line with the ideas in our books. At the core of our approach is stewardship, which we define as a deep sense of responsibility to administer the company for the benefit of all of our "stakeholder" groups: authors, customers, employees, investors, service providers, and the communities and environment around us.

We are grateful to the thousands of readers, authors, and other friends of the company who consider themselves to be part of the "BK Community." We hope that you, too, will join us in our mission.

### A BK Currents Book

This book is part of our BK Currents series. BK Currents books advance social and economic justice by exploring the critical intersections between business and society. Offering a unique combination of thoughtful analysis and progressive alternatives, BK Currents books promote positive change at the national and global levels. To find out more, visit **www.bkconnection .com**.

# Berrett–Koehler
# Publishers

A community dedicated to creating
a world that works for all

**Visit Our Website: www.bkconnection.com**

Read book excerpts, see author videos and Internet movies, read our
authors' blogs, join discussion groups, download book apps, find out about
the BK Affiliate Network, browse subject-area libraries of books, get special
discounts, and more!

**Subscribe to Our Free E-Newsletter, the *BK Communiqué***

Be the first to hear about new publications, special discount offers, exclusive articles, news about bestsellers, and more! Get on the list for our free
e-newsletter by going to **www.bkconnection.com**.

**Get Quantity Discounts**

Berrett-Koehler books are available at quantity discounts for orders of ten or
more copies. Please call us toll-free at (800) 929-2929 or email us at **bkp
.orders@aidcvt.com**.

**Join the BK Community**

BKcommunity.com is a virtual meeting place where people from around
the world can engage with kindred spirits to create a world that works for
all. **BKcommunity.com** members may create their own profiles, blog, start
and participate in forums and discussion groups, post photos and videos,
answer surveys, announce and register for upcoming events, and chat with
others online in real time. Please join the conversation!

**MIX**
**Paper from**
**responsible sources**
**FSC®** **C012752**
www.fsc.org